Amnesty After Atrocity?

Also by Helena Cobban

The Palestinian Liberation Organisation: People, Power, and Politics (Cambridge: Cambridge University Press, 1984)

The Making of Modern Lebanon (Boulder, CO: Westview Press, 1985)

The Superpowers and the Syrian-Israeli Conflict (New York: Praeger, 1991)

The Israeli-Syrian Peace Talks: 1991–1996 and Beyond (Washington, DC: U.S. Institute of Peace, 2000)

The Moral Architecture of World Peace: Nobel Laureates Discuss Our Global Future (Charlottesville: University Press of Virginia, 2000)

AMNESTY AFTER ATROCITY?

Healing Nations After
Genocide and War Crimes

HELENA COBBAN

Routledge
Taylor & Francis Group

LONDON AND NEW YORK

For Bill, with love and huge appreciation for all your gifts

First published 2007 by Paradigm Publishers

Published 2016 by Routledge
2 Park Square, Milton Park, Abingdon, Oxon OX14 4RN
711 Third Avenue, New York, NY 10017, USA

Routledge is an imprint of the Taylor & Francis Group, an informa business

Library of Congress Cataloging-in-Publication Data

Cobban, Helena.
    Amnesty after atrocity? : healing nations after genocide and war crimes / Helena Cobban.
      p. cm.
    ISBN: 978-1-59451-317-6 (paperback : alk. paper)
    1. War crimes.   2. Crimes against humanity.   3. War crimes trials.   4. Victims of crimes.   I. Title.
    K5301.C63 2007
    341.6'9—dc22

                                                                        2006012144

Designed and Typeset by Straight Creek Bookmakers.

ISBN 13: 978-1-59451-316-9 (hbk)
ISBN 13: 978-1-59451-317-6 (pbk)

Contents

Contents

Acronyms

ADL	Association for the Defense of Human Rights and Public Liberties
ANC	African National Congress
CAVR	Commission for Reception, Truth, and Reconciliation
CCM	Christian Council of Mozambique
CNE	National Elections Commission
Codesa	Conference for a Democratic South Africa
COSAG	Concerned South Africans Group
DDR	disarming, demobilizing, and reintegrating
DRC	Democratic Republic of Congo
FADM	Mozambican Armed Defense Force
FAM	Mozambique Armed Forces
FH	Freedom House
GPA	General Peace Agreement
HDI	Human Development Index
HRVC	Human Rights Violations Committee
ICC	International Criminal Court
ICTR	International Criminal Tribunal for Rwanda
ICTY	International Criminal Tribunal for Yugoslavia
IDPs	internally displaced persons
IEC	Independent Electoral Commission
IFP	Inkatha Freedom Party
IJR	Institute for Justice and Reconciliation
MHRL	Mozambican Human Rights League
MK	Umkhonto we Sizwe ("Spear of the Nation")
MPNP	Multi-Party Negotiating Process
NECC	National Education Coordinating Committee
NP	National Party
NSGJ	National Service for Gacaca Jurisdictions
NURC	National Unity and Reconciliation Commission
OIOS	Office of Internal Oversight Services
OTP	Office of the Prosecutor
PAC	Pan-African Congress
PDR	Party for Democracy and Renewal
PRI	Penal Reform International
R&R	Reparation and Rehabilitation

Acronyms

RPF	Rwandan Patriotic Front
RTLM	Radio et Télévision Libre des Milles Collines
SABC	South African Broadcasting Corporation
SANDF	South African National Defense Force
SAP	South African Police
SE	Sant' Egidio Community
TEC	Transitional Executive Council
TRC	Truth and Reconciliation Commission
UDF	United Democratic Front
UNAMIR	United Nations Assistance Mission for Rwanda
UNDP	UN Development Program

Preface to the March 2012 reprint

I started weaving the fabric of this book in 2000–2001, when several threads of my intellectual and ethical concerns about the world started coming together in new ways. Like millions of others around the world, I had been deeply inspired by the fact that South Africa's people were able to escape the structural violence of apartheid and build a new democratic and inclusive political order without plunging their country into a widely feared bloodbath. In 1998 I had the privilege of meeting and listening to Archbishop Desmond Tutu here in Virginia; then I learned much more about him and about South Africa's political transformation as I wrote my 2000 book *The Moral Architecture of World Peace.* I have a long-standing interest in the human and political dimensions of peacemaking, though previously I studied these topics mainly in Middle Eastern contexts. In the late 1990s, in addition, I became concerned about several aspects of the criminal justice system, both locally and globally, and I started to study the various theories used to justify punishment in Western thinking.

These concerns and others came together at one moment in late 2000. I was speaking at the annual conference organized by the Hilton Humanitarian Foundation and was stunned when one of my fellow panelists casually mentioned that six years after the end of Rwanda's genocide, that country of 7.5 million people had 135,000 suspected genocide participants in its prison system—and had no foreseeable way of trying them all within fewer than 150 or 200 years. I concluded almost immediately that it could be fruitful to compare the very different ways in which Rwanda and South Africa had tried since 1994 to escape from their legacies of atrocious violence. A few months later, I decided to add Mozambique to the inquiry. I certainly understood that I would need to study the societies, politics, and histories of these countries a lot more deeply if I were ever to have anything worthwhile to write about them.

Many people have helped me along the way. Three who engaged in key early consultations were Francis Deng, then the UN Secretary General's Representative on Internally Displaced Persons; Harold Saunders, director of international programs at the Kettering Foundation; and my spouse, William B. Quandt, professor at the University of Virginia. Another timely supporter was Jeanette Mansour of the C. S. Mott Foundation, which provided funding for my early work on the project. Later, a grant from the U.S. Institute of Peace helped me complete the field research; at the Institute, Neil J. Kritz and Judy Barsalou helped sharpen my thinking considerably.

In 2001 I conducted some preliminary interviews in the Hague and elsewhere in Europe. Lorna Quandt came with me and helped with the note taking. That year I also conducted some interviews in South Africa and Mozambique. Harold Annegarn and Shirley Pendlebury (both then of Witwatersrand University) and Peter Maseloa helped a lot during that trip. They all continued to keep in touch with me, providing further insights; and when I returned to Johannesburg in 2003, they once again gave generous help. (Peter even helped organize an interview with Khoisan X—only later did I realize what a big scoop that was!) In Maputo, the Justapaz organization and its program officer Francisco Assis provided vital help during the short preliminary trip I made there in 2001.

In 2002, I conducted interviews and visited some sites in Rwanda. David Bucura and his colleagues at Friends Peace House in Kigali, Michel Kayetaba of Moucecore, Klaas de Jonge of Penal Reform International, and Oswald Rutimburana of the National Unity and Reconciliation Commission all gave invaluable help.

In 2003 I made a research trip to Arusha (Tanzania), Maputo, Johannesburg, and Cape Town. In Arusha, judges, staff members, and attorneys at the International Criminal Tribunal for Rwanda were unfailingly courteous and helpful. Gabriel Gabiro, then the Arusha bureau chief for Hirondelle News Agency, gave me his own insights and provided other substantial help to the project. (Later, back in Rwanda, he conducted the key interview with which the book opens.) In Maputo, Salamão Mungoi of Pro Paz was a talented associate in the research. He organized numerous individual interviews, two short field trips, and three very productive discussion circles for the project, and provided invaluable cultural negotiation services. Afiado Zunguza of Justapaz also provided good help. Leila Rached joined me in Maputo: she did the note taking there and in Johannesburg and Cape Town, and added her own insights to the project.

Numerous other colleagues, friends, and colleagues who became friends helped the inquiry along. In Charlottesville, Ruth Gaare Bernheim and Michael Smith provided an institutional niche for me at the University of Virginia Institute for Practical Ethics. In

Washington, D.C., Princeton Lyman and Marina Ottaway both made constructive comments on early drafts of some chapters. Robert Gerald Livingston helped explain the role the Nuremberg Trials played in modern German history, and put me in touch with German historians of the postwar years. (Sarah McKim helped with that part of the project, including conducting interviews in Germany in the summer of 2002.)

Joshua Cohen and Deborah Chasman at *Boston Review* published some of my early writings about Rwanda (and about the whole challenge of transitional justice). Andrea Bartoli, at Columbia, taught me about Mozambique's history and culture and helped me reflect on the conceptual and policy issues with which I was wrestling. Ramesh Thakur of the United Nations University and Michael MccGwire of Dorset, UK both gave welcome intellectual support to the project. So did Jonathan Edelstein, the breadth of whose knowledge about political transitions in Africa is matched only by the wisdom with which he thinks through the difficult justice issues involved. My editors at the *Christian Science Monitor* gave me many opportunities to share my interview material and my preliminary findings along the way. Moisés Naím and the staff of *Foreign Policy* let me introduce in their pages the broad public debate on this topic that I hope this book will further stimulate. Deborah (Misty) Gerner and others of my fellow Quakers gave vital moral and spiritual support as I worked on the project. Misty also put me in touch with Paradigm Publishers, and I have been delighted with the relationship with Jennifer Knerr and others at Paradigm thereby initiated. Misty Gerner passed away in June 2006. Her passing leaves a great void.

Others in the United States, Europe, and Africa who are too numerous to name here have made generous gifts of time and wisdom without which this book would never have come to fruition. Most of all, though, I want to acknowledge the many individuals in Rwanda, Mozambique, and South Africa who gave time from their often hard-pressed lives to answer questions that they may sometimes have found ill-considered, strange, or hard to answer. I hope I have done justice to the voices, life stories, opinions, concerns, and wisdom of the scores of Rwandans, Mozambicans, and South Africans whom I was able to interview: you will find their names and their affiliations signaled throughout the text.

At the end of the day, though, I had to draw and present my own conclusions from all I had heard. (I never had the resources to take the further step of bringing together people from all three countries, or inviting them to reflect together on their broadly vary-ing experiences and to formulate some broad conclusions together. Maybe in the future?) Therefore, while I thank everyone who helped this project along in so many ways, all the mistakes and errors of judgment in the final work are my own.

One last point: Though the societies that I write about here are all in sub-Saharan Africa, I strongly maintain that the book's themes have relevance far beyond that glorious continent. For example, the tensions I write about here between the needs of "peace" and of "justice"—as represented, for many Westerners, in the satisfac-tory conduct of a war-crimes trial—have been on very public view in recent years in all the countries of the Middle East (including North Africa) and Central Asia that have seen rapid and radical political transitions. They were evident in Iraq every time there was a new session of Saddam Hussein's trial, and they were certainly evident at the time of the shocking spectacle of his rushed-through and highly politicized hanging in December 2006. These tensions have been evident in Afghanistan, Tunisia, Egypt, Libya, Bahrain, and Yemen. They have formed a potent sub-theme in all attempts at Palestinian-Israeli peacemaking, and they are emerging as a key issue to be dealt with in all the Middle Eastern countries under-going deep political change. In these countries, as in the three African countries studied in this book, there are no easy answers. In these countries, as in the three African countries, the question of *who* makes the big decisions in these matters is a key ingredient in a potentially explosive political mix. There are, indeed, many non-African countries in which the questions raised in this book also have great relevance.

One big conclusion in this book is the need, as societies emerge from the horrors of political violence, to give the goal of building a democratic and hope-filled political order going forward some pri-ority over the desire to look back and tease apart the ever-complex and contentious matter of precisely who did what to whom in the past and then deciding what to do about that. After an intellectual (and geographical) odyssey of several years, I finish this project deeply enriched but also in one way still close to where I started: filled with admiration for the wisdom displayed in these matters by so many community leaders in the countries I studied.

1
Atrocities, Conflicts, and Peacemaking

In a bland, Scandinavian-style courtroom in a conference center in the middle of Africa, a scared farm-woman from Rwanda answers questions put to her by a black-robed attorney. It is 1997. The attorney works for Clément Kayishema, the man accused of having orchestrated the killing of many members of her family. Kayishema also sits in the courtroom, off to the left from where Agnès sits answering the attorney's questions. The whole space is a bustle of black attorneys' robes and strange languages.

Agnès had come to this courtroom in Arusha, Tanzania, just a few days before, traveling by plane for the first time in her life. "I was so anxious to see the powerful Kayishema in handcuffs! You would never understand how much power this man used to have in our community," she recalled much later. Back in 1994, Kayishema had been the prefect (governor) of the western Rwanda province of Kibuye. Agnès and many other survivors of the genocide that occurred in Rwanda that year held him responsible for what had befallen them and their families.

One sunny morning in 1997, Agnès was awakened by the sound of an SUV coming up the hilly path to her home. She guessed rightly that the people in it were members of the prosecution team at the Arusha-based International Criminal Tribunal for Rwanda (ICTR). But she was surprised to learn that this would be the very day on which these court officials would whisk her off to the Rwandan capital and put her on a plane to go to Arusha to testify. She had only a few minutes to prepare for the trip. She recalled:[1]

> I didn't have time to gather any clothes or other personal items. I only had time to take a quick shower. In Arusha, the other witnesses I came with and I all spent two days without clean clothes. I didn't even have clean underwear! The officials there appeared not to care at all. It was not until the third day that they brought us some clothing.
>
> It wasn't only the clothing. We were generally given the kind of reception that tells you something like "Thanks for coming here, we need your testimony and now you can quickly leave." Two of the men I had traveled with, who had also come to testify, started crying and cursing. I knew both of them, especially Karoli whose wife was killed at the church where I had taken refuge. "Let's be calm and focus on the fight against Kayishema," we finally agreed.
>
> We spent several days in Arusha before going to court to testify. The moment I entered the court, I couldn't believe that the moment I had waited for was finally only a few minutes away. But I quickly noticed something that I hadn't thought about: *there wasn't going to be anyone from Kibuye other than Kayishema in the courtroom,* listening to what I was saying—they were all strangers.
>
> I started answering questions from the prosecutor. He was nice to me. But I couldn't stop thinking that the man questioning me and the judges listening most likely didn't understand what genocide is. They would never understand it since they were not there. No matter how much, and how, I explained it to them.
>
> Once it came to Kayishema's lawyer's turn to question me, he was deliberately working on humiliating me and injuring my feelings. He asked me questions like "How come you survived if Tutsis were being killed?"—as if the fact that I was alive meant that my testimony on the massacres of Tutsis was false.

Agnès comes from a country that uses the civil-law system. There, the questioning of witnesses is generally done by the judges and is much less adversarial than in the Anglo-American (common-law) system, so the experience of hostile cross-examination she had at the Arusha court came as a shock to her.[2]

Other aspects of her experience at the court upset her considerably, too:

> Kayishema was sitting about ten meters away from me on the left side of the courtroom, in the row behind his attorney. There he was, smartly dressed in an expensive suit. He also appeared very healthy. It

never occurred to me that a detainee would look like that. He looked the same! Nothing had changed from when I had last seen him.

Then came one of my worst experiences of the entire trip. As I answered questions from his defense lawyer, Kayishema tapped his mouth with his hand exactly the same way the *interahamwe* [the militias who carried out the genocide] did while making a special clicking noise that they made whenever they flushed Tutsis out from a hiding place.

My blood suddenly ran cold. I could see the militias again. I could see blood.

Although this event had occurred some years ago, in recalling it Agnès covered her face with her hand as though blocking from sight the scary part of a horror movie. She said that Kayishema continued to do the same thing each time she looked in the direction of where he was sitting.

After the morning break, I told the prosecutor about it but *it seemed he didn't understand what I told him.*

It appeared to me that Kayishema and his defense team ruled that courtroom. The defense asked me all kinds of irrelevant questions with rare intervention from the judges. When Kayishema wasn't tapping his mouth with his hand, he looked at me as if he was wondering how come I had survived him and his henchmen.

Still, I was contented to be finally telling what he did. But I kept imagining, "How I wish this trial was taking place in Kibuye!" How I wish I had testified in front of the people of Kibuye whom he wronged, and not an audience made up of only foreigners. I felt like walking up to his chair, grabbing him, and bringing him with me to Rwanda.

Dealing with the Aftermath of Atrocity

The court in which this survivor of Rwanda's early 1994 genocide appeared was established in November 1994 at a meeting of the UN Security Council in midtown Manhattan. Thirteen of the Council's fourteen members, including all five of the veto-wielding "Permanent Members," supported the resolution that created ICTR. Outside the Security Council's famous circular chamber, leaders and activists in the worldwide human rights movement were delighted. They saw the court's establishment as helping to mitigate the "guilt" of the United Nations for having failed to do anything effective to stop

3

the Rwandan genocide while it was still under way.[3] Rights activists from around the world also saw ICTR's creation as one more hopeful step toward building a world in which many of the pious, rights-related resolutions adopted by the United Nations over preceding decades could finally start to be *enforced*. ICTR was created just eighteen months after the United Nations had established its first ad hoc criminal tribunal, "ICTY," the court dealing with atrocities in former Yugoslavia. In the years after 1994, the work of these two tribunals added great momentum to the worldwide campaign for the creation of a permanent International Criminal Court (ICC), which came into existence in June 2002.[4]

At the same time that ICTR was starting its work in late 1994, two other African nations were also struggling to deal with the legacies of recent, atrocious political violence; and the approaches they used as they faced this task were very different from the prosecutorial, criminal-justice approach that the United Nations used in response to the genocide in Rwanda. Most crucially, these two other countries—South Africa and Mozambique—were each offering a version of *amnesty* to those who had committed acts of politically motivated violence against their fellow citizens. In South Africa, this amnesty was offered through the country's much-hailed Truth and Reconciliation Commission (TRC), which gave it to all those perpetrators of past, politically motivated violence who could convince the TRC that they had provided a full and truthful record of all the political violence in which they had participated, or of which they had knowledge. What were on offer in South Africa, therefore, were individual and very conditional amnesties: *amnesty in return for truth-telling*.

In Mozambique, the type of amnesty the government gave to all who had committed inhumane acts during the atrocious civil war that ended in 1992 was very different. It was a blanket amnesty that covered all the numerous misdeeds committed by Mozambicans against their compatriots during the fifteen-year civil war. Those misdeeds included many of the worst kinds of violations associated with civil wars around the world: mass killings, mutilations, the impressment of children as soldiers and sex-slaves, the use of mass starvation as a political weapon, large-scale forced relocations of persons, and so on and on. But in 1992, in a single sweeping act that was unanimously supported by the country's parliament and endorsed by nearly all of its people, a veil of silence and intentional forgetting was formally laid over all those deeds.

Mozambicans, who live in one of the world's very poorest countries, then turned their attentions to trying to build a new future for
their nation. The era of violence, they firmly told each other and
interested outsiders, was now definitely past. And the UN position
on this? The Mozambique peace agreement had been concluded in
October 1992, just four months *before* the United Nations established
its first ad hoc court (the one for former Yugoslavia), so there was
still no precedent for the world body to oppose, or even express
disapproval of, the country's amnesty. Indeed, the United Nations
provided essential financial and logistic support for the Mozambique
amnesty by funding stipends and retraining programs to help 90,000
former combatants there to reintegrate into civilian life. Many of
those who received these UN stipends were undoubtedly *the very
same people who had committed the war-time atrocities.* But no one ever
made any attempt to screen former perpetrators out of the UN-run
demobilization programs.

International rights organizations based in rich Western countries had worked hard and effectively in the years preceding the
South African and Mozambican settlements to uncover, document,
and publicize all they could of the atrocities committed in those
countries. And when each of these countries adopted a political
settlement that involved widespread amnesties for perpetrators of
past misdeeds, the rights organizations expressed their displeasure
very vocally. Allowing amnesties for people who had perpetrated
such atrocities would, they argued, merely perpetuate the climate
of "impunity" that in too many parts of the world allowed malefactors to get off scot-free and thus prepared the ground for further
commission of atrocities.

These are issues of deadly seriousness. Over the past century,
scores of millions of people in different places around the world
have been killed, maimed, or scarred for life in acts of atrocious
political violence. Very often, that violence has been spearheaded,
organized, or at least condoned by the very national leaders that
should—under one increasingly widespread understanding of the
term "national sovereignty"—bear the primary responsibility for
protecting their citizens' well-being. Too often throughout centuries
past, these abusive leaders did indeed enjoy a seeming impunity
from any meaningful reckoning: This impunity was upheld, on the
one hand, by a version of *realpolitik* that often cowed critics from

inside and outside the countries in question, discouraging them from confronting the malefactors openly about their misdeeds, and, on the other hand—at the international level—by adherence to a long-held interpretation of the concept of sovereignty that left every national-level ruler quite free to treat his own "subjects" exactly as he pleased.

Throughout the latter decades of the twentieth century, international rights activists—many of them inspired by, and seeking to replicate, the achievements of the 1945–1946 Nuremberg Tribunal in Europe—urged that the first order of business in postatrocity situations should be to *launch criminal prosecutions* against as many as possible of at least the higher-level suspects accused of responsibility for those acts—and also, to disallow any provision of amnesties to such persons. But now, a dozen years after the settlements in Mozambique, Rwanda, and South Africa, it is possible to re-examine that approach to the challenge of dealing with the legacies of past atrocities. Specifically, it is possible to compare the effectiveness of the prosecutions-based approach, as used in the case of postgenocide Rwanda, with that of the very different approaches used in South Africa and Mozambique. This book represents a first attempt at doing this. It also explores a number of key subquestions:

- Has the prosecutorial approach, as used in Rwanda,[5] actually contributed to healing the wounds of the past—especially, and crucially, by preventing the re-eruption of iterations of the earlier forms of violence? Or has it instead perpetuated and exacerbated past differences among human groups?
- How, indeed, should we start to list the broader social and political goals at which criminal prosecutions *or any other approach to dealing with the legacies of atrocious political violence* should aim?
- How should we weigh the differing values of these goals, if it becomes clear that trade-offs are necessary among them?
- How may we start to compare the effectiveness of these different approaches in meeting the listed goals?
- *Who* should it be that makes these judgments regarding the expected effectiveness of the different kinds of policy approach, and the resulting decisions regarding which particular policy or mix of policies to adopt? Most important, should these decisions be taken at the national, the international, or some other level?

It is very important to emphasize here that the kinds of atroci-

6

ties with which this book—as well as the entire emerging body of "international atrocities law"—is concerned are acts that are committed in conditions of deep-seated political conflict, and not in circumstances of broad political agreement and social peace. It is true that individual psychopaths, or small groups of psychopaths, can exist and perpetrate grisly acts of torture or mass murder in any kind of society, even the most settled ones. But a situation in which such psychopathic or sociopathic behavior becomes widespread and deeply ingrained is always one of serious political conflict, whether the atrocities in question are committed by an entrenched dictatorial regime facing (or merely fearing) political challenges to its power, or by government operatives, poorly trained militiamen, or insurgent forces in a situation of outright civil war. If, therefore, the members of the affected communities are to gain assurance that the atrocities will be definitively stopped, then the political dissonances underlying their perpetration will always also need to be understood, addressed, and rectified.

The "who decides?" question mentioned above also needs underlining. It was particularly salient in the case of Rwanda. I noted earlier that when the UN Security Council voted on the resolution that established ICTR, only thirteen of the Council's fourteen members voted "aye." *The fourteenth member was Rwanda itself,* whose postgenocide government happened to be one of the nine UN members holding a rotating seat and a full vote in the Council that year. Rwanda's ambassador at the United Nations, Manzi Bakuramutsa, did not merely abstain from voting on the resolution in question; he voted *against* it. In the discussion that preceded the voting he gave several reasons for his opposition. They included the facts that the resolution mandated that ICTR be established *outside* Rwanda, that it not be empowered to impose capital punishment, and that in addition to trying cases of alleged genocide it should try cases of alleged war crimes and crimes against humanity. (These latter kinds of charges—unlike that of genocide—were ones that could credibly also be brought against individuals allied with the postgenocide Rwandan government itself.)

But the rest of the Council's members were determined to go ahead. So they simply overruled the Rwandan government's reservations and went ahead and established the court, regardless.

7

South Africa

In late April 1994—just as the thirteen-week-long frenzy of genocidal killing inside Rwanda was reaching its height—South Africa's
40 million people were joyfully taking part in the first one-person-
one-vote election ever held in their country.

The violence inflicted prior to that historic occasion on the 88
percent of South Africa's citizens who were not "White" had been
different in many respects to that suffered by Rwanda's Tutsis during
the genocide. South Africa's Blacks, Coloureds, Indians, and other
non-Whites had suffered for four centuries from intense colonial
violence that involved mass killings, dispossession, enslavement,
ethnic cleansing, and many other forms of serious, "classic" colonial
rights abuse.[6] More recently, they had been oppressed by more than
four decades of the more "modern," systematized form of structural
violence known as apartheid. But at the heart of apartheid's brutal
system of control there were also many instances of individuals or
small groups of people using against other humans direct physical
violence of a ferocity that bore many resemblances to the acts of
hands-on killing, mutilation, and sexual defilement undertaken during the Rwandan genocide.[7]

In South Africa, apartheid and its many associated atrocities were
brought to a clear end by the democratic election of April 1994. But
even as representatives of the outgoing apartheid regime and of the
antiapartheid forces were reaching final agreement on the details of
administering that election they were also, simultaneously, negotiating the tricky issue of what to do about the many people who had
committed atrocities during the now-waning apartheid era. Given
that South Africa already had a fairly well-established criminal-justice
system, many of those who had been the most severely victimized by
apartheid-era violence argued loudly that their persecutors should be
prosecuted. But in negotiations that continued right into the four-
day span of the historic 1994 polls, Nelson Mandela and the other
antiapartheid leaders ended up promising their interlocutors from
the old regime that some form of amnesty would be available to the
torturers and hit-men who had worked for the apartheid government,
as well as to the government officials who had supervised and knowingly funded their activities. Indeed, many South African historians
have noted that it was *only* this promise of amnesty that persuaded
the country's powerful military bosses to continue cooperating in the
vast job of ensuring security for the elections. Had no amnesty been

available, these historians say, the elections and the broad transformation of power relations within the country that they represented could never have been so peacefully concluded.

The elections were held April 26–29, 1994. On April 27, the negotiators drafting the country's new Interim Constitution reached agreement on one final short chapter that stated, "In order to advance ... reconciliation and reconstruction, amnesty shall be granted in respect of acts, omissions and offences associated with political objectives and committed in the course of the conflicts of the past."[8]

In 1995, the country's newly democratic parliament passed a law prescribing how applications for this amnesty would be handled. The law established a Truth and Reconciliation Commission (TRC) as the mechanism through which individuals who had committed politically motivated acts of violence during the apartheid years could apply for amnesty for them. The TRC would grant these amnesties—*provided* it was satisfied both that the acts in question had had a clear political motivation and that the applicants had told the entire truth about what they had done. The TRC's architects explained that establishing (and gaining public acknowledgment of) the truth about the violence of the apartheid era was in itself a valuable social goal that would serve a number of purposes. It could help provide details to family members about what had happened to loved ones who had simply "disappeared" from public sight in the apartheid years; more concretely, it might help family members locate the mortal remains of loved ones whose bodies had been dumped or hastily buried in remote areas.[9] It could give important public acknowledgment of the multiple kinds of pain suffered by apartheid's survivors. And it could produce a public historical record of the deeds of the apartheid era as incontestable as that provided by Germany's Nuremberg Tribunal. This record, it was hoped, would make the job of future deniers or whitewashers of the apartheid era much more difficult, while also providing to all of humanity an account as to how a supposedly "civilized" society like that of the White South Africans could sink to the use of such mind-numbing levels of ferocity.

Such were some of the hopes invested in the TRC's innovative, victim-centered process. As we have seen, the amnesties that were a crucial part of that process had been imposed on South Africa's new democratic rulers through the sheer political necessity of being able to persuade the apartheid-era security forces to provide security for the 1994 elections. But the man appointed to head the TRC, former Anglican Archbishop Desmond Tutu, worked hard to reinterpret the "necessity" of that act of political deal-making, transforming it into a solid (and quintessentially "African") act of political virtue, instead. At the heart of the TRC's work, as Tutu tirelessly explained, was an approach to dealing with antihumane violence that was very different from the prosecutorial, punishment-centered approach favored in most Western societies. Instead of aiming merely at the punishment of offenders, the TRC was determined to effect at all levels in society the *repair of relationships* that had been ripped apart by the segregation, exploitation, and naked violence of the past. The form of justice that the TRC would deliver, Tutu explained, was "restorative justice," a type of justice that is just as valuable as—indeed, he argued, much more valuable than—the essentially retributive form of justice embodied in Western-style court systems. He explained that the TRC's approach was based both on traditional Christian concepts of forgiveness and on the traditionally African worldview of *ubuntu,* a theory that holds that humans are human by virtue of their recognition of the equal humanity of others and, therefore, that building and maintaining respectful relations with others is central to the well-being of all humans.[10]

The process of the ICTR or any other standard criminal proceeding focuses centrally on the alleged perpetrator: *his* guilt or innocence, *his* state of mind when he acted, the severity with which *he* should be punished, and so on. If the interests of victims are considered at all—and all too frequently, they are not—then this concern is added on to the central "drama" enacted in the courtroom as only an untidy afterthought. The victim/survivor of a crime may be brought in by the prosecutors as a "witness" just like any other witness; and under the Anglo-American system she may be subjected to hostile cross-examination. She may, in some jurisdictions, be brought in to provide a "victim impact statement" in the sentencing phase. Or, she may have no formal part in the proceedings at all. The South African TRC, in contrast, was designed from the beginning to place much more emphasis on the presence and needs of victims and survivors of apartheid-era violence. To this end, as one of its first acts, victims and survivors were invited to submit to the TRC written testimonies of the violations committed against them and their loved ones. Then, some of these individuals were invited to come to open hearings of the Commission and tell their stories in public. Over the fifteen months between April 1996 and July 1997 the Commission held 160 days of "victim hearings" in more than sixty different parts of the country. On each hearing day, between eight and twelve survivors of the violence told their stories. They included victims of violence committed by the African National Congress (ANC) and other Black organizations as well as violence committed by the apartheid regime.[11]

The first of the TRC's victim hearings opened in April 1996 in the ornate, British-designed Town Hall in the Eastern Cape town of East London. Tutu presided in his purple archbishop's robes, and he opened the proceedings with a prayer. One of the first to testify was Nomonde Calata. Her husband, Fort Calata, had been one of four pro-ANC activists assassinated by regime undercover agents in 1985. Listening respectfully and sympathetically to Nomonde Calata's words that day were two of the other women whose husbands had also been killed that day; Tutu and other TRC Commissioners; some victim-support counselors provided by the TRC, who sat directly behind Calata and her fellow widows during the hearing, often reaching forward to express their support with the grip of a friendly hand on their shoulders; and representatives of the public including print and broadcast journalists from around the world. Calata's experience at the Commission, while perhaps a bit unnerving for her, was thus very different from that undergone by survivors of the Rwandan atrocities who, like Agnès, were brave enough to face the international travel, the cold formality, foreign legal practices, and the very real possibility of hostile cross-examination at the UN court in Arusha.

Calata told the TRC hearing about the long hours that passed after Fort and his friends failed to come home from a day-trip they had made together by car. By the evening, after the time of their expected return home, they had *still* not come back. Then, very early on the third morning after Fort's departure she received the bundle of newspapers that she delivered every day to homes in her neighborhood. As she told the hearing, "I looked at the headlines and one of the children said that he could see that his father's car was shown in the paper as being burned. At that moment I was trembling because I was afraid of what might have happened to my husband, because I wondered, if his car was burned like this, what might have happened to him?"

Calata was twenty years old at the time, with two children already and a third on the way. Still paralyzed by fear—and perhaps, too, understandably reluctant to draw the authorities' attention to herself—she started taking the newspapers around to the other homes as usual. The dry words of the official TRC transcript continued the tale thus:

> Mrs. Calata: I started distributing the papers as usual, but I was very unhappy. After a few hours some friends came in and took me and said I must go to Nyami [Nyameka Goniwe], who was always supportive. I was still 20 at the time and couldn't handle this. When I got to Nyami's place Nyami was crying terribly and this affected me also. (sobbing)
>
> Mr. Smith [her questioner]: Mr. Chairman, may I request the Commission to adjourn maybe for a minute, I don't think the witness is in a condition to continue at the present moment.
>
> Chairperson [Tutu]: Can we adjourn for 10 minutes please?
>
> Observers singing: What have we done? What have we really done? What have we done?[12]

Video footage aired at the time certainly shows more drama than this written record suggests.[13] It shows Calata not merely "sobbing" but swaying back and forth in her red-orange dress, wailing her grief in a long-drawn-out way more eloquent and soul-searing than any words. The White South African journalist Antjie Krog was one of the media people at the hearing. She wrote later, "For me, this crying is the beginning of the Truth Commission—the signature tune, the definitive moment, the ultimate sound of what the process is about."[14] Krog also spelled out that it was *after* the short break suggested by Tutu that the singing started, that what was sung was well-known antiapartheid hymn—and that it was *Tutu himself who started the singing*. It was evident, from that day on, that the TRC's hearings would be very different from any standard criminal-court proceeding.

Mozambique

It is not easy, at the outset, to find a story to tell that would parallel, for Mozambique, the stories of the encounters that Nomonde Calata and Agnès each had with their respective forms of postatrocity justice. In Mozambique, there was no formal process sponsored by either the national government or the international community through which survivors of the country's atrocity-laden civil war could tell their version of the story of that violence in public.

The standpoint of victims is not, I realize, the only one from which a search for justice and a keener understanding of the phenomenon of atrocities should stem. Society—whether at the level of local communities, the national community, or the global community—also has its own compelling interest in pursuing the identification of wrongdoers, the incapacitation of their ability to wreak further harm, the healing of intergroup relations, and the (re)construction of a healthy, productive community dedicated to strong norms of decent, nonviolent behavior. Nevertheless, the viewpoint of victims/ survivors of atrocities is an extremely important one. They form a sizeable proportion of the population in any postatrocity society, and if their needs are not adequately met then there is no chance that those of the broader society can be met either.

In post–civil war Mozambique, no official public forum was provided in which victims/survivors of civil war atrocities could *tell their stories*—and indeed, many or most Mozambicans seem strongly guided by a set of deeply held norms that act *against* the discussion of painful events in public. But this is not to say that in the postwar era the needs of the very large number of Mozambican victims/ survivors of wartime atrocities went unmet. Indeed, a number of different, intentional steps were taken by the national government, the United Nations, and community leaders at all levels of Mozambican society that had a definite and positive effect on the lives of the war's millions of deeply traumatized survivors.

At the national level, the government implemented a peace plan in which the former insurgents from the "Renamo" organization were incorporated into the political system as a peaceful opposition party; and it launched a broad array of postwar development projects aimed at rebuilding the lives and livelihoods of all the war's survivors. At the international level, the United Nations gave funding and other forms of support to those reconstruction efforts. It also helped to organize (and largely financed) the programs that aimed at demobilizing former fighters from both sides and reintegrating them into civilian society. A vast majority of those combatants had been pressed into service through either the government's formal conscription process or the less formal (but often very violent) impressment undertaken by Renamo. All of those involuntary combatants can, at one level, be considered victims/survivors of the war's violence—as well as, perhaps, in many cases, enactors of it. In addition, all the combatants—regardless of whether they had "volunteered" for service or been conscripted—had noncombatant family members whose fates were directly intertwined with their own. The UN support for demobilization programs can therefore be seen as having brought benefits to many victims/survivors of the war's violence, and not just to its perpetrators. (Indeed, as the foregoing discussion already suggests, in the Mozambique civil war as in other instances of prolonged, widespread violence, it is extremely hard to maintain the sharp, dyadic distinction between "perpetrators" and "victims" that is usually a bedrock of any criminal-justice system.)[15]

One of the most distinctive and effective projects aiding survivors of Mozambique's civil war was not, however, a formal, officially recognized "program" at all. This was the series of healing projects carried out informally throughout the country and over a prolonged period, both during and after the war, by leaders in Mozambique's broad array of churches, mosques, and "traditional" and other faith communities. These healing projects were carried out at the individual or small-group level; and they built on an entire series of beliefs about the nature of the world, the nature of humankind's presence in it, and the nature of violence among humans that are very deeply held by members of all or nearly all of Mozambique's two dozen different language groups.

In 2001, I met one of the country's leading traditional healers, Dr. Fernando Manuel Dos Santos Zimba. He explained his view of violence, and how to deal with its after-effects on those who have perpetrated acts of violence, in the following terms:

> If someone is violent, then that is not a normal state of affairs. It must be a spiritual problem he's suffering from, and this must be dealt with through traditional medicine. Someone who kills another person lacks love for that person. That is a huge problem. That is a *spiritual* problem. He must have some kind of a wrong spirit with him. ...
>
> We talk to the bad spirits and tell them to go away. And then, we talk to the person, the former combatant, and say he must come back to a peaceful life. We help him come back with medicines and rituals. We talk to the former combatants and say they shouldn't fight, they must come back to civilian life.[16]

The anthropologist Carolyn Nordstrom spent considerable amounts of time in Mozambique both during and after the war. She has written about the nationwide nature of Mozambicans' commitment to extracting the "wrong spirits" from those who have been affected by earlier violence: "From the south of Maputo to the north of Niassa, from urban centers to rural outposts, from refugee camps to burned-out villages, every place I visited hosted people who shared similar views about dealing with violence. These views were encoded in medical and healing traditions, religious traditions, and community values about power and sustenance. They were set into play through local dispute-resolution councils and coded in precepts of justice and human rights. And ... they spawned entire social movements."[17]

It should be noted that after the conclusion of the 1992 peace accord, the Mozambicans were remarkably *successful* in bringing to an end the deadly, widespread violence that had held the country in its thrall for more than fifteen years by then; and the peace agreement has "stuck" very successfully since then. After 1992, Renamo became an opposition party. Mozambicans struggled through many of the same processes of economic hardship and economic "reform" that other very low-income countries were going through in the 1990s. In 2000 and again in 2001, they had to deal with extremely serious floods—the kind of national disaster that puts huge strains on fragile political systems. There were some continued rights abuses, charges of graft and corruption, and occasional reports of low-level acts of violence that seemed related to politics. But nothing like a re-eruption of the violence of the civil war era ever threatened the country again in the thirteen years after 1992. In 1994, 1999, and 2004, the country held national elections that were recognized by international observers as generally (though not totally) "free and fair." And by the end of 2005 its broad political calm seemed set to continue.

This is a notable record. But precisely because Mozambique is *not* now a conflict-ridden society, it rarely makes it to the front pages of global media that still seem obsessively attracted to that old saw of "yellow" journalism: "If it bleeds, it leads." And perhaps as a result of that, Mozambique's rich and successful experience of dealing with postatrocity challenges is seldom taken into account in most of the public discussions that short-memoried Westerners conduct on what kinds of policies societies should adopt to deal with these challenges. One of my aims in this book is to resurrect and reexamine Mozambique's record—both because it was so successful and because the approach that Mozambicans adopted to deal with these issues poses such a strong and potentially productive challenge to the ideas that many people in Western nations hold about what needs to be done in the aftermath of atrocities.

The Mozambican approach directly challenges common Western notions on two main scores:

- First, it challenges Western ideas about the need to hold as many people as possible "accountable" on an individual basis, and preferably through a court of law, for the atrocities committed during earlier periods of intense intergroup conflict.
- Second, it challenges Western ideas about the many virtues—both for society and for the individual—of undergoing extensive public processes of truth-establishment and truth-telling.

I have written a little already about how Mozambique's embrace of blanket amnesties as part of its peace agreement ran counter to the notions most Westerners have about the need for a criminal-justice form of "accountability." During discussions I held with scores of Mozambicans between 2001 and 2003, I found that support for the 1992 amnesties still ran very high—indeed, it seemed just about unanimous. Many Mozambicans I talked to said something along the lines of "In war-time, everyone does bad things. But that was during the time of violence. Now we are in a time of peace. Our main concern now is to prevent any return to a time of war.... Besides, if you started prosecuting people for what they did during war there would be no end to it. In war-time, everyone does bad things."[18]

On the issue of truth-establishment, too, the ideas of most Mozambicans run counter to those of Westerners who maintain that it is important both for survivors of violent acts and for society as a whole that the survivors be encouraged to talk with others about those experiences—preferably, within both an intimate, "therapeutic" setting and a more public, "truth-establishing" setting.[19]

Mozambican anthropologist Alcinda Honwana has conducted extensive studies of how people in war-ravaged communities in Mozambique (and Angola) have dealt with the sequelae of the political violence they have suffered in recent decades. Honwana has an intimate understanding of the processes of postviolence healing undertaken by the traditional healers in these two southern African countries. "These healing and protective rituals do not involve verbal exteriorization of the experience," she writes:

Healing is achieved through nonverbal symbolic procedures, which are understood by those participating in them.... [R]ecounting and remembering the traumatic experience would be like opening a door for the harmful spirits to penetrate the communities. Viewed from this perspective, the well-meaning attempts of psychotherapists to help local people deal with war trauma may in fact cause more harm than help.[20]

Thus, a person who was a survivor of atrocious violence in Mozambique was not offered the kind of venue for public truth-telling that has been a strong feature of the postatrocity court system in Rwanda, and of the TRC in South Africa. What kinds of mechanisms, therefore, have been available through which such a survivor could deal with the potential for mental trauma that her experiences have most likely left her with? Carolyn Nordstrom has given us a lovely description of the "nonverbal symbolic procedures" she saw enacted with regard to one such woman; and this description can stand as a Mozambican counterpart-story to the stories of Nomonde Calato and the Rwandan testifier "Agnès."

During the civil war the young woman Nordstrom wrote about had been held at a military base—and, most likely, used as a sex slave—for several months. After escaping from her abusers, she returned to her village, in Nordstrom's words, "physically sick and emotionally traumatized." Given the views about female purity that are widespread in Mozambican society, the prospects for such a woman might be grim: no possibility of a husband, continuing to live as an unwanted burden on her father's family, social shunning, and so on. But for this woman—as, it seems, for many others like her—the local culture had already developed a special purification ceremony. The people of her home village undertook several days of preparations for the ceremony, in an atmosphere expressing considerable community support for the woman. Nordstrom wrote that on the main, final day of the process,

> food was prepared, musicians called in, and a dirt compound shaded by pleasant trees and plants swept and decorated with lanterns and cloth. The ceremony itself continued throughout the night, a mosaic of support and healing practices. Several high points included the ritual bath the woman received at dusk. Numerous women picked up the patient, and carefully gave her a complete bath—a cleansing of the soul as well as the body. The bathing was accompanied with songs and stories about healing, about dealing with trauma, about

reclaiming a new life and being welcomed into the community. The patient was then dressed in her new clothing, and fed a nutritious meal. Shortly thereafter, the musicians began a new rhythm of music, and all the women gathered about the patient to carry her inside the hut.... Throughout the ceremony, the woman was continually reassured with stories of ongoing support; of her need to place responsibility for her plight with war and not her own actions; and of *her own responsibility to heal war's wounds so she does not inflict the violence that she was subjected to on others.*[21]

Rwanda

The operations of ICTR, the UN court in Arusha, have been fairly well reported in the global media (even if nowhere near as thoroughly reported as those of its sister court for former Yugoslavia). But ICTR's work is by no means the only—or even the main—step that has been taken to deal with the after-effects on Rwanda's 8 million people of their country's 1994 genocide. I noted above that the postgenocide government in Rwanda used the seat it had in the Security Council that year to vote *against* the establishment of ICTR. That opposition, however, was not based on any broad philosophical resistance (such as Archbishop Tutu, or many Mozambicans, would have expressed) to the idea of using prosecutions to deal with the after-effects of atrocity. On the contrary. Many of the Rwandan government's objections to ICTR's statute expressed its opposition to the perceived *leniency* with which ICTR would treat the accused. Back home in Rwanda, meanwhile, the government started out extremely eager to pursue its own, very broad program of prosecutions in response to the genocide. It started off by undertaking a broad campaign to detain all those accused of having participated in the genocide, with the aim that as soon as possible these detainees would be tried and punished within the national legal system.

Almost immediately, however, that approach encountered very sizeable problems. The biggest was the scale of the task. The Rwandan genocide had not been the highly "technicalized" form of mass killing carried out by the Nazis against their Jewish, Roma, and other victims in Europe. Instead, it was often carried out in public streets or public squares, with considerable (if often coerced) public participation. Many of the killers used inefficient, "primitive" means of killing like machetes or nail-studded clubs in their attacks against members of the country's million-strong Tutsi community or against Hutus judged to be "too tolerant" of their Tutsi neighbors. Yet their daily rate of killing was many times higher than that during the Nazis' Holocaust. That meant that a high proportion of Rwanda's Hutu population were involved or directly implicated in the killing.

It is true that many courageous Hutus managed to resist the strong public pressures placed on all members of their community to participate in the genocide; and some even ran considerable risks by trying to save the lives of Tutsi neighbors or relatives.[22] The undoubted existence and brave actions of these "righteous Hutus" should not, however, blind us to the very wide participation of other members of their community in the grisly, largely public activities of the genocide. By the time the genocide had ended, there were indeed many hundreds of thousands of Hutus who could justifiably be accused of having participated in it in some way.

The number of those whom the postgenocide government detained and held in overcrowded lockups around the country rapidly rose above 100,000. The Catholic writer and human rights activist André Sibomana visited Gitarama Prison for the first time in 1995. "What I saw defied imagination," he recalled in 1996:

> There were three layers of prisoners: at the bottom, lying on the ground, there were the dead, rotting on the muddy floor of the prison. Just above them, crouched down, there were the sick, the wounded, those whose strength had drained away. They were waiting to die. Their bodies had begun to rot and their hope of survival was reduced to a matter of days or even hours. Finally, at the top, standing up, there were those who were still healthy. They were standing straight and moving from one foot to the other, half asleep. Why? Simply because that's where they happened to be living. Whenever a man fell over, it was a gift to the survivors: a few extra centimeters of space. I remember a man who was standing on his shins: his feet had rotted away.[23]

He added that within nine months, almost 1,000 of Gitarama's 7,000 detainees had died as a result of this treatment.

By late 1998, the number of detainees countrywide reportedly topped 140,000. By then, the detention program was keeping a nontrivial proportion of the national population—the vast majority of them men of working age with a number of family members highly dependent on them—out of productive employment. For a low-income country like Rwanda, the burden this placed on the national economy was enormous. A further problem the Rwandan government faced was that for many years after 1994 it had not even the most rudimentary investigative mechanism capable of sorting unsubstantiated accusations against various suspects, or even cases of simple mistaken identity, from those accusations that might indeed have some basis in fact.

During and immediately after the genocide, a large proportion of the country's judges and lawyers were killed or fled the violence to seek refuge elsewhere. Sibomana reported that after 1994, fewer than 250 of Rwanda's prewar roster of 719 magistrates were left in the country. Because of the devastation of the justice system, only a tiny number of the detainees ever had concrete charges brought against them—and fewer still saw the inside of a courtroom. By 2001, and even after international donors had poured large amounts of money into the Rwandan justice system, the courts were still only able to process cases at a rate of 1,500 to 2,000 per year. At this rate it would take the courts around 150 years to hear all the genocide-related cases—even if they did nothing else at all meanwhile.

The continued detention without trial of so many alleged *géno-cidaires* was problematic for another reason, too. These detainees were all members of the country's Hutu majority. The government detaining them was dominated by previously exiled Tutsis who returned to the country with the armed units of the Rwandan Patriotic Front (RPF), which, in July 1994, had toppled the country's earlier, progenocide government forcibly from power.[24] These uncomfortable facts further fueled accusations that the government was using the detention program to try to impose a form of collective punishment on the entire Hutu community.

At some point in the late 1990s, the RPF-dominated government started reconsidering its reliance on regular-style prosecutions and looking for an alternative. The one it turned to, *gacaca* ("ga-CHA-cha"), was a hearing mechanism used by earlier generations in Rwanda to resolve minor disputes at the local community level. In early 2001 the government established a special new mechanism called "*gacaca* courts" that, within each of the country's 9,000–plus small neighborhood groupings (*cellules*), would hear the vast majority of the genocide-related cases alleged to have occurred within that neighborhood. Only the most serious genocide-related cases would stay in the regular courts.[25] For the vast majority of cases heard in the *gacaca* courts the punishment would consist of some form of community service that would provide restitution or compensation to the genocide's survivors. It was planned, in connection with the holding of the *gacaca* court hearings, that a large proportion of the less serious suspects would be released back into their communities.

Given the broad scale of this project it was not surprising that the government fell seriously behind with its timetable for implementing it. At one point, the opening of the main phase of their work was scheduled for June 2002. But it was rescheduled many times and finally took place in March 2005.

The *gacaca* court system bore a number of apparent similarities to South Africa's TRC. Where the TRC offered individual amnesties in return for truth-telling, the *gacaca* courts offered potentially large reductions in sentences in return for truth-telling. In both these countries (unlike Mozambique), the establishment of a strong historical record of the period in which the atrocities were committed was a central goal of the process.

When I visited Rwanda in 2002 I heard a variety of views expressed by genocide survivors on the value of using criminal prosecutions to deal with their former persecutors. Nearly all of the more than two dozen Rwandans with whom I had serious discussions of the *gacaca* courts project expressed strong support for it. (So, too, did most of the Rwandans with whom I talked during my 2003 research visit to ICTR's headquarters, in Arusha.) Many members of both groups of Rwandans expressed strong support for the government's decision to keep the most serious cases in the regular courts. A small number of the Rwandans with whom I spoke inside the country—including at least one direct survivor of the genocide—said they felt that traditional-style court proceedings were *not* the way to deal with the aftermath of a disaster as vast and complex as their country's genocide. However, all the survivors I spoke with expressed strong support for the idea that establishing as complete a record as possible of what happened during the genocide was an important goal.

On this last issue, one young man I spoke with in 2002 at the headquarters of the large survivors' organization "Ibuka" expressed his own, very deeply felt view. This young man, Robert Niwagaba Rusitega, said he had not himself been in the country during the genocide but in August 1994, immediately after the genocide, he traveled around the country to find out what had happened to his various family members. He found that seventeen of them, including his parents and nearly all his siblings, had been killed in different places, and most of their bodies had never been found. Ever since then, Rusitega said, he had been extremely fearful of Hutu people in general. "I don't know, for any Hutu person I come across—especially, people from my home village—whether he was one of the ones who participated. For me, therefore, it's very important to establish the record of who did what. In that way, I will know who to steer clear of and who it's all right to be with. And I shan't have to continue to live in such a climate of fear."

What Are the Policy Meta-Tasks?

From the short sketches of the situations of Rwanda, Mozambique, and South Africa given above, it emerges clearly that societies coming out of periods of atrocious mass violence face a number of searingly difficult policy choices, and that inevitably complicated trade-offs have to be made among them. In such a situation, people and their political leaders need to evaluate very carefully *what their main goals are,* since it is only by reference to these goals that the effectiveness of apparently competing policy options can be compared and contrasted.

Harvard University law professor Martha Minow is one of those rare Westerners who has written very thoughtfully about the policy choices that societies and governments face in the aftermath of atrocities, and about the broader social and political goals they are working for as they make these choices. In 2000, she noted:

After mass violence, a nation or society needs to address at least eight goals:

1. Overcome communal and official denial of the atrocity; gain public acknowledgment.
2. Obtain the facts in an account as full as possible in order to meet victims' need to know, to build a record for history, and to ensure minimal accountability and visibility of perpetrators.
3. Forge the basis for a domestic democratic order that respects and enforces human rights.
4. Promote reconciliation across social divisions; reconstruct the moral and social systems devastated by violence.
5. Promote psychological healing for individuals, groups, victims, bystanders, and offenders.

6. Restore dignity to victims.
7. Punish, exclude, shame, and diminish offenders for their offenses.
8. Accomplish these goals in ways that render them compatible rather than antagonistic with the other goals.[26]

This list provides a useful starting point. In discussing it with survivors of atrocities and members of the policy elites in all three of the countries I studied, I found that these people tended to identify some of the items from this list as clearly more important to them than others; to dismiss others as virtually irrelevant to their own situation; and, often, to suggest other goals not listed by Minow as more important than some of those she had listed. It was evident from these discussions, too, that in each of the three countries the general balance of what the people and their leaders seemed to prefer regarding this (or a similar) list of policy goals came down in favor of a distinctly different—and, in Rwanda, apparently shifting—ranking of their society's meta-tasks than in the other two countries. Nor was the public and elite opinion in any of these countries totally monolithic, though it was in South Africa that the range of differences on these issues seemed the widest.

The idea that there is a "one size fits all" approach to such a goal-prioritizing exercise therefore seems not only misplaced but also possibly very dangerous for the members of these vulnerable postatrocity societies; and any attempt to impose such a solution from outside would seem very damaging to the (hopefully, reemerging) sense of agency experienced by communities exiting from periods of atrocious political violence. The strong stress that many members of the Western-based rights movement have placed on criminal prosecutions as constituting an essential part of any mix of postatrocity policies runs a clear risk of acting like such an externally imposed "solution," especially when it is advocated in a context that does not include a serious attempt at respectful dialogue with members and leaders of the society concerned.

On many or perhaps most occasions, respected community leaders in societies that have been seriously damaged by an ongoing or recent record of atrocities will say that attaining social peace, the ending of the atrocities, and the rebuilding of the kinds of links inside society that can prevent the future commission of atrocities are their highest priorities. Throughout most of history down into the most recent age, the need to craft a sustainable peace before any achievements in other spheres can be ensured has been recognized by nearly all the world's governments as they sought to regulate and resolve their disagreements with each other. Therefore, where an amnesty for former malefactors was seen as necessary in order for peacemaking diplomacy to succeed, government leaders were usually prepared to offer it. The UN's establishment of the two ad hoc tribunals in the early 1990s changed that picture. And now, the existence of the new, permanent ICC raises the possibility that it may be much, much harder to offer amnesties as part of peace agreements in the future than it generally has been in the past. Indeed, we have already seen something of this sort taking place regarding the ICC's late-2005 issuance of indictments and arrest warrants for leaders of the still quite unresolved insurgency in northern Uganda. Moreover, in a world in which the ICC exists, would the United Nations still be able to run programs like those in Mozambique in which the perpetrators of very recent atrocities were given stipends and other help to reintegrate into civilian society?

All members of the global community (and not just the vocal groups of rights advocates based in rich, secure Western countries) need to work together to engage with these very serious issues. I hope that this book provides pointers for such a discussion. In later chapters, I will attempt to analyze some of the tricky issues having to do with how the often-competing interests of "justice," "truth," and "peace" may be disentangled, compared, and ranked, and what other factors societies—including "global society"—need to take into account as they attempt to accomplish these objectives.[27] In the bulk of the book, however, I want as much as possible to present the views of people who are the real experts on trying to deal with the legacies of recent atrocities—the Rwandans, South Africans, and Mozambicans who have already grappled directly with these issues over the past dozen years within their own societies.

2
Rwanda
Court Processes After Mass Violence

Atrocities, War, and War Termination

Two Testimonies

In 1994, Agnès and her family lived in a modest house in a small farming community in Kibuye, in western Rwanda.[1] On the evening of April 6, the presidents of Rwanda and neighboring Burundi, both of them Hutus, were killed instantaneously when the plane in which they were traveling was brought down by a mysterious missile attack near the Rwandan capital, Kigali. A few days later Hutu militiamen armed with machetes, garden hoes, nail-studded clubs, and spears began combing the hills around Agnès's home, seeking out people of presumed Tutsi "ethnicity" like Agnès and her family, in order to kill them.[2] Agnès, her husband, and their three children fled to the nearby church, where they joined about 8,000 other local people who also sought refuge there from the killers.

"On the fourteenth of April, three days after we arrived at the church, there were minor attacks by militias on the church complex," Agnès said. "Women and children collected stones while the men repulsed the militias with the stones."

Kibuye's Catholic church complex is built on a raised area overlooking Lake Kivu and Kibuye town center, so Agnès and the other refugees could see something of what was going on in those areas. "The following day, we began to see bodies floating below us in Lake

Kivu," she said. "We started realizing that things were now becoming difficult. Then, on the sixteenth, a veterinary doctor was burned to death at the town's main roundabout. The mayor and other authorities applauded as the man got incinerated. The seventeenth was a Sunday. Even though we filled up every space in the church, the convent and the compound, we began to prepare for the mass."

Recalling those events as she sat in her poorly lit living room a decade later, Agnès turned to stare silently at a wall on which hung some old pictures of Jesus and the Virgin Mary—and an image of the balanced "scales of justice." She used the hem of her multicolored skirt-wrapper to wipe the tears that began to drop from the corners of her eyes. "That was the final day," she whispered. "The stone can't fight the gun. They swarmed the complex from every direction. The few survivors entered the church. The militias threw petrol around the building and set it on fire."

She clearly did not like to recite the details of those moments. The hundreds of broken skulls and other human bones still displayed as a memorial in a building at the church complex help fill out the picture of what happened next.

I was in the church. I don't know how I got out of it before it was torched. I had my youngest child with me. We ran to the Home Saint-Jean [a guesthouse run by the nuns next to the Convent]. I had a feeling it would be safe there since it was run by a Muzungu [White person]—and the militias would fear her. She hid us in the basement. I had no idea where my husband and our other two children were. I was almost certain they had been killed.

Later that evening, they came and sprayed tear gas into the basement. All of us came out of it. A militiaman called Luveto held me and told me to sit on the ground. A certain policeman who was with Luveto asked him not to kill me. I knew I was going to die anyway, so I asked the policeman to shoot me. This would be less painful and quicker than being hacked with a machete.

"Move! Let's go!" the policeman shouted at me. He shoved my son and me ahead of him and followed behind us.

Her voice fell quieter still.

We skipped, stepped, and stumbled over the dead bodies and a few dying survivors lying all over the compound. I'm always haunted by the moment when we passed by my little niece, covered in blood, lying between many bodies. My son pulled my hand and pointed at her, asking me to take her with us. "She's dead. Let's go," was my cold response. I couldn't tell whether or not she had died. But she looked like one who would die anyway. It turned out that she hadn't died and she's alive. In fact she lives nearby. I can't believe I acted that way. Fortunately she has forgiven me.

Several hundred meters after the church, the policeman stopped us. I knew that it was our turn to die. I held my son close. Then, surprisingly, the policeman told us to run into a nearby bush. "God willing, I will see you again," he told us. I don't know why he did it. I didn't know him.

For Agnès and her son, that was the beginning of two months of cold, rainy nights spent in bushes or abandoned houses and scavenging for leftovers under cover of nightfall. Along the way, they had a horrifying encounter with a ruthless, self-styled executioner nick-named "Pilate." Agnès and her son were taken to a mass grave to be buried, but the militiamen taking them there discovered that the grave in question was full—"full of living relatives and neighbors of mine, waiting to be buried alive," as she described it. She and the boy were made to wait while a new mass grave was dug.

They survived that, somehow. Agnès, a devout Christian, attributed their miraculous escape to God. "Then we learned that French soldiers had reached a neighborhood close to here. We all knew that the French were on the side of the government and the militias. But I immediately worked on reaching them since they would at least kill me with a gun. Fortunately, they didn't kill me."

She learned later that her husband and daughter had survived by hiding in a ruined building. Their other son was saved by the "White lady" at the convent.

She pointed to a bundle of old, dog-eared papers. "I tried to count how many members of my family survived," she said. The papers carried lists of about 180 hand-written names. She explained that she had put a cross beside the name of each person killed in the genocide. The pages contained fewer than a dozen names that stood alone, without crosses.

André Sibomana, a Hutu, was born in 1954 in the central Rwandan province of Gitarama. He became a Catholic priest, and worked as editor of *Kinyamateka,* an influential, church-founded newspaper through whose pages he sought to raise readers' awareness of human rights and corruption issues. In 1990, he helped found the Rwandan Association for the Defense of Human Rights and Public

Liberties (ADL). Then came the genocide. In 1996, Sibomana traveled with two Francophone researchers to Israel, where he talked at length about what he had experienced in his homeland. The text of those conversations was published in English under the title *Hope for Rwanda*.[3] The material that follows is taken mainly from that book. (In 1998, Sibomana died from the recurrence of a childhood disease.)

On April 7, 1994, the morning after the presidential plane was downed, Sibomana tried to go to his office at *Kinyamateka* to retrieve some files. Snipers made the road unsafe, so he went instead to a Catholic complex called the Centre Saint-Paul to wait out the disturbances in safety. While there, he persuaded the elderly Belgian priest in charge to admit the numerous Tutsi families who also came begging for refuge. Soon, the number of refugees there rose to 2,000 adults and "many" children.

On April 12, the fiercely anti-Tutsi radio station Radio et Télévision Libre des Milles Collines (RTLM) broadcast an announcement that an "important accomplice" was hiding at the Centre Saint-Paul. Sibomana understood that to mean him. Judging his life in danger, he fled the Center by car. As he describes it:

> I took with me two Tutsi nuns and a priest called Valens (all three survived). We tried to leave Kigali on the road going south. Everywhere along the road, we saw dead bodies. Men, women, children, old people, they were lying there, in clumps, killed in groups or individually. Some bodies were dismembered. The militiamen were laughing, drunk on beer or under the effect of narcotics. For them, it was a celebration: they killed and looted without restraint.[4]

He knew he had been openly identified by the leaders of the genocide as a "Wanted" person. Twice as he fled, his car was stopped at roadblocks—but each time one of the people staffing the roadblock helped him get through. He finally arrived at his home village, where he hid in his father's house for a while. "Then I changed my hiding place regularly. No place was safe."

Sibomana spent the weeks that followed continuing to work in his (mainly Hutu) parish. "I used this time to 'pacify' the people in my parish, to persuade them by every means to refuse to resort to violence. Then the war caught up with us. Apparently, money and machetes were distributed in the village. In any case, the massacres which started then were not at all spontaneous. From that moment onwards, it became impossible to live normally—and very difficult to survive. In my own parish, at Muyunzwe, I almost died from drinking poisoned communion wine."[5]

His village saw just one attack by the *génocidaires,* on June 12. They attacked during a church service, abducting five local Tutsis, whom they assaulted and mutilated. The victims were thrown down a deep pit latrine and left for dead. Two of them managed to survive, though both were badly injured. Sibomana said:

> I looked after these two young people as best as I could. They survived....
>
> It was extremely difficult to save Tutsi, to hide them and feed them. In Rwanda, in normal times, everyone sees and knows everything immediately. So in this context, where everyone is spying on each other, you can imagine! *For many people, not killing was in itself an act of resistance. Peasants were killed because they refused to beat the dead bodies of their Tutsi neighbors. There are brave people, people of integrity, who could not or did not have the courage to save their neighbors and who are still living with that guilt today.*[6]

He wrote, "[M]ost of the massacres were carried out using ... basic weapons: machetes, knives, axes, hoes, hammers, spears, bludgeons, or clubs studded with nails (known as *ntampongano* or 'without pity'). I don't need to dwell on the horror of these deaths, the frightful noise of skulls being smashed in, the sound of bodies falling on top of each other."[7] He continued:

> You can't explain everything or understand all forms of human behavior....
>
> The killers took the trouble to invent the worst kinds of cruelty. There were militiamen who traveled long distances to go and kill in person a Tutsi that they knew. I mentioned some people were forced to kill under threat. But others reveled in it. They inflicted horrific injuries without going as far as killing the victims, simply to intensify the cruelty of death and to prolong the suffering. They did it just like that, without any worries, in complete indifference. They stood around drinking beer calmly, watching their former friends literally dying in agony at their feet. ...
>
> Where did it come from, this hatred of others? I can only explain it by an insurmountable hatred of one's self. Indeed, some killers committed suicide after they had killed.[8]

Sibomana remained in his home village until early June. By then, the fighters of the mainly Tutsi, exile-based opposition force, the Rwandan Patriotic Front (RPF), were coming close. He recalled, "On June 5, three bishops, including the Bishop of Kabgayi, and around ten priests were shot dead by an RPF squad."[9] Scared for their lives, he and some of his parishioners fled west, into Kibuye province, where they stayed until early August.

During July, Kigali and most of the rest of the country fell to the RPF's generally well-disciplined and well-led units. (In mid-July, the RPF announced the formation of its new government in Kigali.) From nearly every region into which the RPF advanced, massive waves of Hutus fled before them: to the west, the south, and the east. For his part, Sibomana was eager to take his (mainly Hutu) parishioners *back* to their home village, even though it was under RPF control. But because his advocacy of basic human rights was so well known, he felt he had reason to fear reprisal actions *not only from the leaders of the génocidaires but also from the RPF.* At the end of July he wrote to the RPF's minister of the interior, telling him he intended to return to his home village, Muyunzwe, with the 230 parishioners who were with him, and asking for a guarantee of their safety. On August 5, they started walking home:

> After walking for three days, we arrived in Muyunzwe. It was a distressing sight: everything had been looted. The following day, I went to Kabgayi.... On the road leading to Mukingi commune, there was a choking smell of pestilence. Revenge had not spared these poor peasants who were at peace with their conscience and had thought the nightmare was over.... [I]t was on 19 June that RPF soldiers massacred hundreds of peasants there.[10]

RPF soldiers made one half-hearted attempt to persuade Sibomana to leave the region, but he insisted on staying. On August 11, the Pope's representative in Kigali appointed him the new bishop of Kabgayi. He recalled what he did next with his loyal parishioners: "Together, we started rebuilding from the ruins."

Dimensions of Atrocity

The anti-Tutsi genocide in Rwanda in 1994 was an extraordinary episode in human history. Genocide itself—the implementation of a project designed to wipe out all or part of a targeted ethnic, religious, or national group—is not an unprecedented phenomenon.

But the way in which the Rwandan genocide was pursued seemed unique in its combination of lengthy, detailed preplanning with subsequent broad public participation by many members of the Hutu community in the killings and many other brutal acts that marked it.

Because of the Rwandan and Burundian presidents who were killed in the presidential plane in April 1994 were both Hutus, the bloody spate of killings of Tutsis that followed may at first have looked like exaggerated acts of revenge. But even some weeks before April 6, considerable evidence was amassed indicating that a genocidal project had already been meticulously planned and prepared. Members of the country's Hutu-dominated armed forces and the extremist "Hutu Power" militias had been acquiring and distributing weapons. They had drawn up and circulated lists of those to be killed: Members of the Tutsi intellectual elite and Hutus thought to be pro-Tutsi topped these lists. Also listed by name, down to the level of individual neighborhoods and villages, were members of Tutsi families—men, women, elders, and children. For months, the extremists had used the country's printing presses and airwaves to disseminate hate-filled propaganda that routinely referred to Tutsis as "cockroaches" (*inyenzi*) who should be eliminated in the interest of national "hygiene"—and to any Hutus who might disagree with this program as "traitors" (*ibyitso*).

In the ten weeks that followed April 6, some 800,000 people, around 10 percent of the country's population, were killed. Around 90 percent of the victims were Tutsis. These killings were carried out intentionally and systematically—in churches, hospitals, and local government buildings where terrified Tutsis had fled for sanctuary; and in homes, in public places, and at roadblocks throughout the country where groups of drunken *interahamwe* militiamen used their generally primitive, often quotidian tools to torture and kill their targeted victims.

It was so routine, so sustained, that the perpetrators called it simply "work." It was so well organized, and so efficient, that the rate of killing was three to five times that at which, at the height of the Holocaust in Europe, Adolph Hitler's industrialized killing system was able to dispatch its victims.

Unlike the European Holocaust, however, this genocide was—according to its very design—a highly public affair: one whose organizers sought to enlist in its deadly "work" the maximum possible number of Hutu participants. Human rights researchers have documented much evidence of this broad, public mobilization.

One researcher interviewed Jean Bosco Bugingo, a married father of five who lived in the Gitaziga sector of Muhazi commune. "I personally macheted five people to death," Bugingo acknowledged. But he also underscored the role that some of the local officials, called "councilors," played in mobilizing the killers:

> Our councilor, Joseph Munyaneza, told the Hutus to rise up and defend ourselves.... At the meeting the councilors said Hutus must kill Tutsis and everybody who was against the government, so that when the RPF came they would not have anyone to rule. Many Hutus pointed out that they had lived with and intermarried with these people they are being told to kill. Munyaneza said: "Either you kill them or you will be killed." He told us that we would be moving around with soldiers and "They would see to it that either you killed or you die." In the end, even those who had hesitations had to kill too. They killed with less zeal, but they killed.[11]

The compilers of this account judged that descriptions like Bugingo's contained "no special pleading: many survivors readily admitted that some of the participants were reluctant murderers."[12] It is important to note the many cases of Hutus who withstood the enormous pressure to participate in the killing, or who even ran great risks to save the lives of those targeted. But still, the organizers of the genocide clearly aimed—for whatever reason—to secure the broadest and most public popular participation in the implementation of their plan; and they were remarkably successful in meeting this goal. The mass-participatory aspect of this genocide gave it a psychosocial context significantly different from that of the European Holocaust with its more "sanitized," mechanized, and hidden methods of killing. This fact would significantly complicate the task of postconflict reconciliation.

Dimensions of the Conflict

How did relations between Hutus and Tutsis in Rwanda deteriorate to the point that so many Hutus were ready to participate with seeming enthusiasm in the genocide against their Tutsi neighbors? That so much hatred could be whipped up in such a relatively short period of time is all the more remarkable (and disturbing) if we remember how many attributes were shared by members of the two groups. Indeed, according to most of the traditional markers of "ethnicity," Hutus and Tutsis in Rwanda are not members of two distinct ethnic groups. They speak the same mother tongue, Kinyarwanda, and follow nearly all the same social customs. They are members of the same churches—or, in the case of a small minority of them, the same mosques.[13] By many criteria, indeed, the distinction between them seems to be one of caste, more than ethnicity.[14]

The division of the population into Hutus and Tutsis is not unique to Rwanda; it is found also in Burundi—where, as in Rwanda, it frequently dominates expression of the nation's political life—and in broad areas of eastern Congo and southwestern Uganda. Among Rwandans, the proportion of Hutus to Tutsis is roughly 6:1. There is also a third, much smaller local group, the Twa, whose members historically lived nomadic lives in the country's rain forests. In general, though, the designation "Tutsi" was more associated with cattle herders; and the term "Hutu," with people who cultivated the country's extremely fertile—though very hilly—land. But in precolonial times there seems always to have been some fluidity between the two groups.

That started to change when, in the 1885 Treaty of Berlin, Germany was "given" the right to exercise colonial rule over Rwanda by the other European powers. It changed even more after World War I, when Belgium won control over Rwanda from Germany. In 1935, the country's Belgian administrator issued identity cards to all Rwandans that identified each person as "Tutsi," "Hutu," or "Twa": Families that owned ten or more head of cattle were listed as "Tutsis," and families that owned fewer than ten cattle were listed as "Hutus." In classic colonial fashion, the Belgian administration then happily played "divide and rule" by giving privileges to members of the (much smaller) Tutsi group so they would act as its enforcers against the Hutus. In the 1950s, however, it became clear to the Belgians that they would soon have to divest themselves of their African colonies, and they started quite cynically to shift their favors toward the Hutus. When independence came to Rwanda in 1959, the Hutus were "top dog"; and they soon started carrying out a series of anti-Tutsi massacres, motivated by the resentment many Hutus still felt at the role some Tutsis had played as Belgium's enforcers.

During the anti-Tutsi campaigns of the postindependence years, tens of thousands of Tutsis fled Rwanda, establishing a Tutsi diaspora that spread through many neighboring countries. Those Tutsis who remained in the country were meanwhile subjected to quotas that strictly limited the numbers of Tutsis who could enroll in the national university or other state institutions. But still, because they had relatively high educational levels and links with relatives living elsewhere, many Tutsis remained well positioned to engage in occupations like trading or financial services.

One significant gathering of Tutsi refugees was the group that found itself in Uganda, to the north. During the 1970s, when the infamous dictator Idi Amin ruled Uganda, a network of Rwandan Tutsi refugees, headed by Fred Rwigyema and Paul Kagame, played an important role in an anti-Amin movement in Uganda, headed by a man called Yoweri Museveni.[15] Rwigyema and Kagame had grown up together in a UN-sponsored refugee camp in southwestern Uganda. They were still teenagers when they joined Museveni's movement.

In 1986, Museveni seized power in the Ugandan capital, Kampala. The following year Rwigyema became Uganda's deputy defense minister; and Kagame, the chief of military intelligence. Thousands of other Rwandan Tutsi refugees served at different levels in the army and movement that now ruled Uganda. Then in 1987, Rwigyema and Kagame were both involved in the founding, in Kampala, of a new organization called the Rwandan Patriotic Front (RPF). The RPF's leaders started organizing the worldwide diaspora of (mainly Tutsi) Rwandan refugees, raising money for weapons, and planning the creation of a guerrilla army that could take them back to their homeland.[16]

On October 1, 1990, Rwigyema led an RPF force of some 2,500 fighters over the border into Rwanda. (Kagame was in the United States at the time, taking part in an officers' training course at Fort Leavenworth, Kansas.) The RPF gained some advantage from the strategic surprise their attack achieved, and they won control of a swathe of land inside northern Rwanda. But on the second day, the charismatically popular Rwigyema was killed, and the Kigali government started to regain some ground. Kagame hurried from Kansas to the front line inside Rwanda, where he reorganized the RPF into a sturdier, long-term guerrilla force. Though he remained in the political shadows until 2000, from late 1990 on Kagame was the effective leader of the RPF.[17]

The RPF managed to keep control of a strip of land inside Rwanda running along the eighty-mile border with Uganda. Kagame's old ally, President Museveni, allowed them to run all their supply lines through Uganda. For its part, the Rwandan government could count on significant military and political support from France, whose president, François Mitterand, apparently saw Rwanda as a bastion of "*la francophonie*" in the region.[18] (Uganda, like most East African countries, had long used English as its main "international" language. Many of the Rwandan refugees who grew up in Uganda, including Kagame, were more familiar with English than they were with French, or even Kinyarwanda.)

Between October 1990 and April 1994 northern Rwanda was the scene of a significant civil war. The authorities on each side of the war's front line committed significant rights abuses, though these abuses were not symmetrical. Human Rights Watch reported that "the government killed approximately 2,000 Tutsi between 1990 and 1992." It also noted that in February 1993, "[a]ccording to information collected by local human rights groups and the clergy, the RPF killed more than one hundred civilians."[19]

Those 1993 events were connected with a new RPF offensive that brought broad new stretches of land under the guerrillas' control: One of the main abuses the RPF reportedly committed in the newly occupied area was a form of anti-Hutu ethnic cleansing. In May 1993, French researcher Gérard Prunier visited the RPF zone, which he described as "eerily empty of life." He noted that "[t]he RPF admitted that only 1,800 Hutu peasants were left in an area which had had a population of about 800,000 before the war."[20]

The RPF's February 1993 offensive damaged the Rwandan army significantly. Soon afterward, representatives from the Habyarimana government, the RPF, and Rwanda's domestic opposition parties started meeting in Arusha, Tanzania, to negotiate a peace settlement. This settlement, the Arusha Accord, was concluded in August 1993, and gave the RPF a number of crucial political victories. It was basically a power-sharing agreement. The United Nations would send a small supervisory force into the country, after which a twenty-two-month transition period would begin. During the transition, Habyarimana would remain as president, but a leader of the country's internal opposition would become prime minister. The 40,000 soldiers in the national army and the 10,000 fighters in the RPF would be combined into a single, much smaller, national force. One other valuable victory the RPF won was the Accord's stipulation that *all Rwandan refugees would be allowed to return to their homeland.*

In October 1993 the UN Security Council established the United Nations Assistance Mission for Rwanda (UNAMIR), to "help the parties implement the [Arusha] agreement, monitor its implementation and support the transitional Government."[21] UNAMIR sent an advance party into Rwanda in early November, but it took the UN headquarters in New York several further months to send in UNAMIR's full complement of troops. That tardiness delayed the implementation of the political parts of the Arusha Accord—and the promised transitional government was never installed.

Understanding what happened between February 1993 and April 1994 helps to explain the broad popularity that the mobilization for genocide won among the Hutu population in late spring of 1994. Ugandan American researcher Mahmood Mamdani has written that

> it was not greed—not even hatred—but *fear* which was the reason why the multitude responded to the call of Hutu Power the closer the war came to home. Hutu Power extremists prevailed not because they promised farmers more land if they killed their Tutsi neighbors—which they did—but because they told farmers that the alternative would be to let RPF take their land and return it to the Tutsi who had been expropriated after 1959.... The war, said the government, was about keeping the threat of Tutsi Power at bay.[22]

Mamdani wrote, too, that the pre-1994 civil war "created widespread hunger and starvation. In addition, the war displaced a substantial minority, so large that it came to include *one out of every seven Rwandans*. ... Living in camps scattered around the country, the internally displaced and the [Hutu refugees from Burundi] were like so many bundles of dry tinder wood, awaiting but a spark."

The downing of the presidential plane was that spark.

At War's End

At the beginning of July 1994, the positions still held by the Rwandan government forces started to disintegrate under the pressure of the RPF's systematic and generally well-disciplined military operations. (Anthropologist Christopher Taylor has noted that the attention that the progovernment forces paid to pursuing the genocide hindered their ability to resist the RPF's advance, principally by diverting so much progovernment manpower into the maintenance of huge numbers of anti-Tutsi roadblocks.[23]) On July 4, RPF forces seized control of Kigali and the southern provincial capital of Butare. On July 15, the U.S. government announced that it no longer recognized the now-ousted Rwandan government. On July 17, the RPF captured the last redoubts held by forces loyal to the old government; and two days later, an RPF-led "government of national unity" was sworn in in Kigali. The President was a pro-RPF Hutu called Pasteur Bizimungu, and the prime minister was a leader in the country's former internal opposition. Staying in the shadows as vice president was Paul Kagame.

Kagame and his colleagues engaged in no political negotiations over this transition with any representatives of the former government, or any outsiders. The RPF had been fighting for an outright victory on the battlefield that all of Rwanda had become; and that was what it won.

The main outside actor present in Rwanda was the UN peacekeeping force, UNAMIR. It was hopelessly weak, having barely survived the attempts of various Security Council members (including the United States) to *disband it completely* during the genocide.[24] Separate from UNAMIR, the French government had, at the end of June, won a two-month mandate from the Security Council for a "humanitarian" expeditionary force of its own called "Operation Turquoise." France inserted this force into three provinces of southwestern Rwanda in early July.[25] The UN mandate for Turquoise ran out on August 22. The new government in Kigali was adamant that the French should leave exactly then; and they did.

The country the RPF found itself ruling over had been devastated by at least three separate waves of human-engineered catastrophe: the 100 days of outright genocide, which had killed more than 800,000 citizens, badly mutilated scores of thousands, and left a trail of horrifying physical destruction throughout the land; the preceding four years of civil war; and, finally, a mass exodus from their homes of around half of the country's entire population, organized by the Hutu Power politicians as the last vestiges of their hold on the central government collapsed.

Nearly all these latest refugees had fled on foot, taking only what they could carry. Between 1.3 million and 2.1 million of them ended up outside the country, with the greatest concentration in President Mobutu's Zaire (today known as the Democratic Republic of Congo, or DRC). Others ended up in Tanzania, Burundi, or Uganda. Many who fled their homes in this chaotic mass migration never made it outside the country, ending up adrift in other areas inside Rwanda: These "internally displaced persons" (IDPs) numbered between 1.3

million and 1.8 million people. As Gérard Prunier wrote, "[O]ne could say that in a population of slightly over 7 million about half were displaced in one way or another, at a tremendous cost in human suffering."[26]

In 2002, in Kigali, I talked to a Hutu woman who—along with her husband and six children—had been a part of that flight in 1994. She told me that the whole family fled their home in Kigali, walking westward with a human wave of other refugees, "because we were afraid of the RPF—and also because our government leaders told us to go." She and her family walked for days before they reached Zaire. Once there,

> [w]e had to live in the forest for two years. For some weeks we had no shelter at all, and after that our only shelter there was a piece of plastic tied in the trees. It was like a prison. Everything we did was completely controlled by the armed men [the Hutu Power militias]. No one was allowed to leave the refugee camp there. Anyone who tried to leave, they shot. It was impossible for us to escape, especially with six children.

The situation inside Rwanda was little better. As Prunier described the scene:

> Those people still "in Rwanda" were in a complete state of disarray. Many were displaced and living some distance from their *ingo* [home community]. A large number (especially among the Tutsi survivors) had lost all they possessed including their houses. Many were hiding in the hills.... Psychologically most people were in various states of shock, and many women who had been raped were now pregnant with unwanted children. Most of the infrastructure had been brutally looted, with door and window frames removed, and electric switches pried from walls. Almost no vehicles were left in running order except RPF military ones, in the towns running water and electricity did not work any more and although the crops on the hills were ripe, nobody was there to pick them. ... [27]
> Psychologically, the place was full of walking wounded; traumatized Tutsi survivors who had lost everything—their friends, their relatives, their houses—and were wandering around like ghosts, and traumatized Hutu survivors who could not believe what had been done to them.... There were 114,000 children without parents trying to survive with nobody to care for them.[28]

While many Hutus were fleeing the country in those weeks, significant numbers of other people were coming back in: These were the Tutsi refugees who had been living in the surrounding countries—some, since 1959. Describing the area along one border alone, that with Burundi, Prunier wrote: "In the first two weeks of August, 13,000 new Hutu refugees crossed the Burundi border southwards [toward Burundi], while probably three or four times that many *former* Tutsi refugees were crossing it northwards."[29] During the thirteen weeks of the genocide some 600,000 to 800,000 Tutsis had been killed in the country. By the end of November 1994, some 400,000 former Tutsi refugees had moved into the country from various portions of the Tutsi diaspora—and they kept on coming. Many of these returnees summarily evicted Hutus from properties the returnees claimed had belonged to their families some thirty-five years earlier.

A number of those who came back and some Tutsi survivors from inside the country were bent on taking physical revenge against Hutus whom they encountered. Prunier noted that the RPF had undertaken a huge, rapid mobilization after April 6, and that "[m]any young boys from inside Rwanda and even more from Burundi had been taken in and superficially trained. They found themselves with a uniform, a gun, and none of the fighting tradition and discipline of the "Ugandan" veterans.... Boys from Rwanda had lost their families and understandably harbored strong feelings of revenge."[30] Compounding the problem of revenge actions was the fact that many of these recent recruits into the RPF had never been paid. So, as Prunier wrote, "they tended to contract themselves out to private parties who needed a gunman, whether to scare off the owner of a coveted property or to murder somebody one wanted to get rid of."[31]

Dealing with the Legacies of the Genocide

As the new government consolidated its hold on the country, it faced many daunting tasks. Cleaning up whole neighborhoods where bodies had been left lying in the streets and on dirt paths, in the burned ruins of houses, or in pit latrines was a matter of basic public health. In some churches where the "sanctuaries" were full of grotesquely decaying human remains, all that people could do in the first instance was throw lime on the bodies to prevent the spread of disease. Homes and public buildings had been ransacked, and with the rainy season just ahead, the problem of providing shelter from the country's famous rains loomed large. Corrals and hedges had been trampled; livestock roamed freely, as did wild dogs that feasted on the amply available human and animal remains. Many of the country's hill-based neighborhoods (*collines*) remained sparsely populated and very insecure. The country had, in effect, no economic activity. Meanwhile, in the refugee camps just to the west, in Zaire, the *génocidaires* were starting to regroup and plan their return.

Given the extreme vulnerability of the situation inside Rwanda, the response of the international community had a huge effect on what happened next. Most people at the United Nations and in the rich, powerful Western nations recognized that during the lengthy and much-televised agonies of the 100-day genocide, the "international community" had failed Rwanda's people very badly. There was a huge amount of guilt motivating Western and other decisionmakers at that point. In addition, the Genocide Convention of 1948, of which all major Western powers were signatories, specifically obligates signatories to intervene to "prevent" or "suppress" any genocide, anywhere—wherever in the world it occurs. But these countries and the United Nations had failed to do this. It was, instead, the thin-stretched guerrilla troops of the RPF who had successfully suppressed the genocide. As soon as that task had been achieved, the UN and the rich Western nations were eager to undertake whatever actions they could think of that might help to restore their own essentially liberal, beneficent self-image.[32]

One such action was the decision to send massive humanitarian aid to Rwanda, and to Rwandan refugees, in the immediate aftermath of the genocide. That decision was evidently well-intentioned. But much of the aid was sent to help the *new* waves of refugees who streamed out of Rwanda in advance of the progressing RPF forces; and aid workers in the refugee camps rapidly came to realize that the primary effect of this aid distribution was *to enable the génocidaires to regroup in the camps.* This fact posed searing ethical dilemmas. Conditions in the camps were often terrible, with the weakest refugees—women, children, the elderly—ravaged by disease. The aid workers, their bosses in humanitarian organizations, and Western governments struggled to find ways to distribute aid that, instead of benefiting the *génocidaires,* would support the new Rwandan government's efforts to disarm the refugees and attract them back to their homes.[33] Some, despairing that this was possible, eventually "folded their tents" and pulled out. Others did not.

The miasma of guilt that hung over Western governments in the late summer of 1994 resulted in another major policy initiative that was, perhaps, just as poorly thought out as the rush to pump humanitarian aid into eastern Zaire. This was the strong—and again, well-intentioned—drive to extend to the perpetrators of atrocities in Rwanda the new norms of "accountability" and "ending impunity" that the United Nations was trying to apply to gross rights abusers in the Balkans. In Rwanda, this drive took two forms. At the strong urging of Western governments, the Security Council established a new ad hoc international tribunal for Rwanda, parallel to the ad hoc court for former Yugoslavia that it had set up the preceding year. The International Criminal Tribunal for Rwanda (ICTR) was established in November 1994.

Throughout the negotiations over ICTR's establishment, the new Rwandan government expressed reservations about many aspects of its work. As noted earlier, Rwanda had a seat on the Security Council in 1994 and in November of that year, the new Rwandan ambassador at the United Nations cast the only vote there *opposing* the creation of ICTR. Broadly speaking, the Rwandans objected to the idea that officials of the new international court, and not the Rwandan government, should make the very important decisions on *who* should be tried in cases related to the genocide carried out in their country, and *how* this should be done.[34] The Rwandan government therefore continued with its plan to prosecute as many participants and planners of the genocide as possible in its own national courts; and, as noted above, it received considerable support from the Western governments for this project.

By the end of 1994, it was clear that, in attempting to deal with the legacies of the genocide, both the new Rwandan government and the international community would be focusing their efforts on prosecutions. There would be little room in Rwanda for other approaches to dealing with the aftermath of grave political violence—like the community healing approach that Mozambique's people were using at that time to deal with the aftermath of their own recent, atrocity-laden civil war, or the truth-seeking approach that South Africa's new government was adopting in 1994–1995 to deal with the legacies of apartheid. Instead, Rwanda would be a test case for a new world order based on the strict application, at both the national and the international levels, of the norms and practices of Western-style criminal justice. Over the years that followed, the efforts pursued at both these levels would reveal much about the effectiveness of such a system in a postatrocity society that was still reeling from mass traumas, pauperized and deeply polarized by the very recent (and ongoing) violence.

The International Criminal Tribunal for Rwanda

An International Courtroom in Africa

Fast forward to April 2003. We were in a UN-run courtroom in the heart of Africa. The man at the witness table wore a gray suit, a too-blue shirt, a checkered brown tie, and gold-rimmed glasses. His coffee-colored face was heavyset, shining with sweat. He was the defendant in this trial, now giving his own testimony. He was sitting very close to the floor-to-ceiling Plexiglas that separated the long and thin courtroom from the similarly shaped public gallery, with his back to the public. (But a video image of his face was shown on the large monitors suspended above our long rows of seats here.) The defendant spoke directly toward the elevated blond-wood "bench," some ten feet in front of him, where three judges sat, presiding over the hearing with varying degrees of attentiveness.

On the far left of the courtroom, the row of blond-wood desks for the defendant stood empty. They faced to the right, as did the two rows of desks for the defense attorneys located to their right. In the courtroom's midsection the judges' bench and the witness box faced each other across a narrow space where a pair of black-robed clerks hunted for documents in file boxes stacked three high on metal carts. Farther right, facing leftward now, were two or three rows of desks for prosecuting attorneys and at the far right, still at ground level, the glass-walled booths for the interpreters. The scene looked like a long, thin diorama in an old-fashioned museum and emphasized through its very layout the implacable opposition between accusers and defendants.

Outside this building, in the Tanzanian city of Arusha, market women in gaily colored cloth wrappers hawked fresh produce on the dusty sidewalks; clerks hurried to work on rickety bicycles or crammed into raucous *dalla-dalla* ride-share vans; children in skimpy uniforms danced through the crowds on their way home from school. But inside the stark, concrete boxes of this sprawling conference center a set of intriguing and tightly choreographed rituals was being enacted. Attorneys and judges in this bland, wood-paneled space wore capacious robes patterned on the gowns of medieval European clerics. The judges' robes were mainly black, though with broad, red satin reveres and cuffs. For the attorneys: black, with occasional streaks of color. Judges and attorneys all wore white "European-style" legal neckwear ("jabots") Velcroed around their necks and had headsets for linguistic interpretation jammed down over their hair. Some of these headsets had tiny, curled British barristers' wigs perched on top of them. (In one of the courtrooms here, the air was thick with quaint-sounding British courtroom locutions.) When the judges filed in or out, a clerk would bark, "All rise; *il faut se lever,*" and we all did. If anyone should enter or leave while the judges were sitting, that person was supposed to pause and bow gravely to the bench.

I was observing the proceedings in Chamber 2 of the International Criminal Tribunal for Rwanda (ICTR). In June 1994 the defendant, Juvénal Kajelijeli, had served as *Bourgmestre* (mayor) of Rwanda's Mukingo commune; he was accused of having founded and led the genocidal *interahamwe* militia in Mukingo. I was observing "Day 69" of his trial on eleven counts of genocide, crimes against humanity, and war crimes.

Kajelijeli was arrested in Benin, West Africa, in June 1998. His first ICTR trial day, in front of a bench of three UN-appointed judges, came in mid-March 2001. But one of those judges died not long after, and another was reassigned to the court's Appeals Chamber, in The Hague. So, four months later Kajelijeli's trial was started again from scratch, with Tanzanian judge William H. Sekule presiding, assisted by judges from Lesotho and Madagascar.

On Day 69, defense lawyer Lennox Hinds of New York City was conducting the principal examination of his client, the last part of his presentation of the defense case. Hinds, a distinguished, bearded African American, would peer down over his reading glasses and ask his questions in English. One interpreter would then render the question into French, and another from French into Kinyarwanda, in a process known as "relay translation." Kajelijeli would answer in Kinyarwanda, and his answer would undergo "relay translation" back into English for the benefit of Hinds and the many other English-speakers in the court. (English, French, and Kinyarwanda are the three official languages of the court.)

Hinds was asking Kajelijeli about a questioning he had been subjected to five years earlier, in June 1998, by people working for the Office of the Prosecutor (OTP) in Benin. Suddenly, on my earphones an anguished cry came from one of the interpreters: "The French is not coming through!" A lengthy on-air discussion ensued between the interpreter and Judge Sekule in which the increasingly distraught interpreter explained that *yet again* they had problems with the relay between the two sets of interpreters.

After the trial resumed, a question arose about two audiotapes that the OTP people had made during the 1998 interrogation. Judge Sekule mused at length over whether the whole tapes, or just excerpts compiled by the defense, should be played in court. A confused, trilingual discussion ensued over how to handle the tapes. Soon, everyone in the courtroom was discussing the issue together, like neighbors around a kitchen table. Even the defendant offered some suggestions. Judge Sekule had lost control of the courtroom. Finally, he suggested a break. A clerk called out, "All rise; *il faut se lever,*" and out the judges filed, robes billowing.

In early 2001, the United Nations introduced a time-tracking system that required judges and courtroom administrators to post a daily report on how each courtroom's time got used that day. The reports are posted on ICTR's website (www.ictr.org): In Sekule's courtroom precisely three hours and thirty-six minutes of work got done that day.

The court would hold its last substantive day of this trial ("Day 78") in July 2003. In December 2003, Kajelijeli was found guilty on three of the eleven counts on which he was charged: genocide, direct and public incitement to commit genocide, and extermination as a crime against humanity. For the first and third of these crimes Kajelijeli was sentenced to two terms of life imprisonment; and for the second, an additional fifteen years.[35] He then filed an appeal. In May 2005, the Appeals Chamber in The Hague issued a 120–page final judgment in which it overturned his convictions for genocide and extermination, leaving standing only the incitement conviction. The chamber also found "that the Appellant's fundamental rights were seriously violated during his arrest and detention." Taking all things into consideration, the chamber reduced his total sentence to forty-five years of imprisonment.[36]

Building a New Court from Scratch

One aphorism by which many legal scholars set great store warns that "justice delayed is justice denied." There were many reasons why—in all the cases it tried, not just Juvénal Kajelijeli's—it took ICTR so long to complete its trials. One was, obviously, the difficulty the court had gaining custody of its indictees, since all of them had fled Rwanda as the RPF surged to power, and they had networks of supporters throughout the world that helped them to evade justice.

In addition, it took the new court some time to become established, and along the way the people responsible made a number of missteps. Many of the ICTR judges were legal scholars who had never before run a courtroom; and many of the people who, as a result of the highly politicized UN system of hiring, ended up establishing and running ICTR's infrastructure had little experience of efficient and accountable public administration.

Laïty Kama of Senegal was the first presiding judge of ICTR, and the renowned Italian legal scholar Antonio Cassese was the first presiding judge of the Appeals Chamber that ICTR shared with its sister court for former Yugoslavia, ICTY. They and their fellow judges, along with the people named by the UN to head ICTR's "Registry" (administrative section), were the ones most responsible for creating and supervising ICTR in its early years. But almost inevitably, much public attention was drawn to the role of the chief prosecutor, the person who—acting in his or her own name but also on behalf of the "international community"—would fashion the indictments brought against the accused. When the Security Council established ICTR, it stipulated that the court's chief prosecutor should be the person already playing that role at ICTY. At that point in late 1994, Richard Goldstone had been ICTY chief prosecutor for just four months. Now, he had to scramble to fulfill his duties for the new court as well.

Goldstone had previously been a judge on South Africa's Supreme Court. A genial, bespectacled man, he has written frankly of his surprise when he was invited to become ICTY's chief prosecutor: "Although I had read of the establishment of the tribunal, I knew little about it. Furthermore, I had no knowledge of humanitarian law and had never before acted as a prosecutor."[37] He had spent many years practicing commercial law, but during the declining years of South Africa's apartheid system he had spent three years heading a government commission that uncovered some of the most serious rights violations committed by the regime's security forces. He brought to the ICTY/ICTR prosecutor's office a strong commitment to human rights, as well as an activist mindset.

Security Council resolution 955 made clear that ICTR should *not* be headquartered inside Rwanda, since it was generally—and probably correctly—held that Rwanda right after the genocide could not provide adequate access and protection for any witnesses the court's defendants might call.[38] But after his appointment, Goldstone made a point of visiting Kigali as soon as he could—to work out a *modus operandi* with the Rwandan government, and to set up his office's in-country investigations unit.[39] One organization already conducting forensic investigations there was the Boston-based group Physicians for Human Rights, which had a team of forensic anthropologists helping to map and exhume bodies from mass graves in Kibuye and Kigali. The work that Goldstone's investigators and PHR did in Kibuye provided vital evidence for Goldstone's first indictment, issued in late 1995: It accused Clément Kayishema, the prefect of Kibuye, and seven other officials of having organized the genocidal killings that Agnès had lived through.

It took the other parts of ICTR much longer than the Office of the Prosecutor to become operational. ICTR did not even have a proper budget from the United Nations until July 1995.[40] Initial negotiations with Kenya over locating the court there fell through, so the UN negotiators had to start over with Tanzania. The court was eventually headquartered in Arusha, the small town near Mount Kilimanjaro that had been the site of the key (but aborted) 1993 political accord between the RPF and the Habyarimana government. In November 1995, a temporary courtroom and ICTR's administrative offices were installed in one wing of Arusha's International Conference Center.

The court's judges were named in May 1995. At the beginning, they did not have much to do. They had to await requests from the OTP to have indictments confirmed, and then wait even longer till the OTP could bring its indictees to Arusha for trial. Like ICTY, ICTR had no law enforcement capabilities of its own. Both courts remained dependent on the willingness of national governments to arrest suspects and hand them over for trial. Goldstone reported to the Security Council that his priority as prosecutor was "investigating and prosecuting individuals who had held important responsibilities in the events which occurred in Rwanda in 1994."[41] As he and others in his office explained, this strategy was molded on that pursued by the prosecutors at Nuremberg fifty years before. OTP attorney Simone Monasebian told me in Arusha in April 2003, "Our strategy was ... to bring indictments against the most culpable people, but also people from broad sectors of society. The idea was, very much like Nuremberg, to make an example of all those who carried high responsibility in society." A good part of the intention here was didactic: to teach people around the world more about how leaders in different sectors of society helped create the climate in which the atrocities had been committed. To underline this intention, at ICTR as at Nuremberg, many of the cases were grouped, and often tried, according to "occupational" categories—the "Media" group, the "Military Leaders" group, the "Religious Leaders" group, and so on.

As the OTP teams traveled the world searching for and seeking custody of their indictees, they sometimes found their efforts contested by the Rwandan government, which claimed that *it* should be the one to try them. One such tussle occurred in the case of Théoneste Bagosora, the man frequently described as the genocide's mastermind. Bagosora was arrested by the authorities in Cameroon, West Africa, in 1996. Goldstone presented the government there with a request for his extradition based on Article 8 of the ICTR Statute, which reads: "The International Tribunal for Rwanda shall have primacy over the national courts of all States." According to Goldstone's memoir, the Rwandan government asked him to withdraw his claim to Bagosora, but, "[u]nwilling to compromise, I said I would prefer the tribunal to cease its activities rather than defer to the national courts of Rwanda."[42]

Goldstone won. In January 1997 Bagosora was transferred to the UN detention facility in Arusha. He and three other members of the "Military I" group of indictees went on trial in April 2002. At the end of 2005—nearly ten years after Bagosora's arrest—his trial was still nowhere near completion.

ICTR's Philosophy and Practice

It was not just the strategy pursued by ICTR's prosecutors that was modeled consciously on precedents from Nuremberg. The jurisprudence and judicial practice used by ICTR (and ICTY) also built heavily on those pioneered by the post–World War II military

47

court. Indeed, the underlying legal philosophy of the new courts—including the key idea that *people should be held responsible as individuals for all their harmful actions, including those perpetrated in a time of war*—was also drawn directly from the list of seven "Nuremberg principles" adopted by the UN International Law Commission in 1950.[43] Regarding judicial practice, the two new ad hoc courts built on many of the precedents Nuremberg established when it integrated some aspects of a continental (civil law) legal system of law into a blended system of "international" justice that was based heavily on the philosophy and practice of the Anglo-American (common law) system.[44] The national governments of both Yugoslavia and Rwanda used the civil law system.

The ad hoc tribunals of the 1990s also built on—and adapted—precedents that Nuremberg established in its categorization of the crimes it tried. In ICTR's statute, prosecutable crimes were listed under the headings "Genocide," "Crimes Against Humanity," and "Violations of Article 3 Common to the Geneva Conventions and of Additional Protocol II" (i.e., war crimes). At Nuremberg, the four categories of crimes tried were war crimes, crimes against humanity, crimes against peace, and conspiracy. Genocide had become prosecutable as a type of crime only after the UN Convention Against Genocide came into force in 1948. ICTR's definition of the crime of genocide, based on the Convention, was as follows:

> Genocide means any of the following acts committed with intent to destroy, in whole or in part, a national, ethnical, racial or religious group, as such: (a) Killing members of the group; (b) Causing serious bodily or mental harm to members of the group; (c) Deliberately inflicting on the group conditions of life calculated to bring about its physical destruction in whole or in part.

The law of genocide is distinguished by its insistence on the need to prove a "double intentionality." That is, to be found guilty of genocide, a person must be found not only to have had the intention to commit the harmful act in question, whether killing, maiming, or whatever; but he or she must also be found to have committed that act with the additional intention of destroying "in whole or in part" one of the groups of the specified kind. At ICTR, charges involving crimes of genocide (as well as the other two types of prosecutable crime) were brought against just about all the defendants. In October 1998, ICTR pronounced the first conviction on a charge of genocide ever issued by an international court. The person so convicted was Jean-Paul Akayesu, a *Bourgmestre* from Rwanda's Gitarama province.[45]

Another way in which ICTR's officers sought to replicate the experiences and achievements of Nuremberg was in their desire that the new court leave behind *an incontestable record of the atrocities committed in Rwanda in 1994.* In postgenocide Rwanda, as in postholocaust Germany, there were plenty of people prepared to deny or minimize the extent of the atrocities committed. In Rwanda, in addition, there was an attempt by many *génocidaires* to say that what they had done may have been bad—but that it was only one-half of a "double genocide," with the other side having been committed by the RPF against the Hutus. But the truth-establishment efforts of the prosecutors in Arusha were much harder to carry out than those of their Nuremberg predecessors, for two reasons. First, Nuremberg was established by an alliance of armies running a military occupation, and was explicitly a "military tribunal"; as a result, its judicial processes lacked many of the protections defendants would have to be afforded in any modern-day nonmilitary tribunal. Second, Rwanda's *génocidaires* never left behind them anything comparable to the detailed trail of written records that the Nazis kept of their actions. The OTP at Arusha therefore had to build its cases—and establish its historical record—by relying heavily on witness testimony, and this in a multilingual situation in which much of the testimony had to be subjected to simultaneous or even "relay" interpretation. In addition, at Arusha, the defendants had the right not only to undertake rigorous cross-examinations of all prosecution witnesses but also to call an equivalent number of witnesses of their own.

In the Kajelijeli case, the prosecution brought 14 witnesses and the defense attorney 28 (including Kajelijeli himself). Kajelijeli's case, it should be noted, had been expected by ICTR administrators to be one of their simpler, more straightforward cases on the docket. Many others were far more complex. For example, in the "Military I" trial, which involved Bagosora and three other military leaders, the OTP originally informed the court that it wished to call *800* witnesses. The court's second president, Norwegian judge Erik Møse, was presiding in this high-profile case. He urged the OTP to reduce the number of its witnesses. After the trial began in April 2002 the OTP finally brought 82 witnesses. By the end of

2005, defense attorneys had presented 54 witnesses, and there were still many more to come.[46]

Court time, and the associated out-of-courtroom work, is very expensive indeed. The OTP had its own sizeable cadre of Arusha-based trial attorneys, who were compensated as fairly high-level UN staff and undertook any court-related air travel by flying Business Class. One senior trial attorney told me in 2003 that her salary was $80,000 per year, tax free, with a housing allowance on top of that. Because the defendants all claimed indigence, their attorneys' fees were also paid by the United Nations. In 2003, a Lead Defense Counsel received $220 per hour, and a co-counsel, $80 per hour; they could be remunerated for up to 175 hours per month. Defense attorneys received an additional $100 per day for time spent outside their home countries, along with reimbursement (though only at coach class) for travel to and from Arusha. One defense attorney, a high-ranking barrister back home in England, told me, "For many advocates at the Tribunal, I understand the rates of pay compare very favorably with the remuneration they would receive in their home countries ... though as far as I am concerned, I could earn significantly more in England."

These "very favorable" salaries for defense attorneys came with their own temptations. At the end of the 1990s, the UN Office of Internal Oversight Services (OIOS) launched an investigation into accusations of "fee splitting" between defense attorneys and their clients—at both ICTY and ICTR. It found some evidence for the exchange of favors between attorneys and clients, if not for actual direct payments. It also found evidence of what it claimed were linked activities, including "the use of frivolous motions and other delaying tactics before the Trial Chambers."[47]

Still, ICTR's costs continued to mount, year after year. In December 2005, the General Assembly adopted a budget for ICTR for 2006–2007 of $269.76 million, up a little from the budget for the 2004–2005 biennium.[48] By the end of 2005, the court had consumed *considerably more than $1 billion worth of international funds.*[49] *It had completed the trials of first instance of precisely twenty-six individuals.* By comparison, in 2003 $331.6 million was given in foreign aid to all of Rwanda's 8.8 million people. Many extremely needy and populous countries in Africa receive considerably less foreign aid than that.

Politics and the Court

In spring 2003, I discussed the court's performance with Martin Ngoga, a Rwandan diplomat then assigned there to monitor ICTR's work.[50] We talked in the small office he maintained in Arusha International Conference Center just across from ICTR's offices.

"Our relations have always been up and down," he said. "Right now, it's not so bad." He said his government's main criticism of the court was still, "as always," over the issue of witness protection, and argued that what he called the witnesses' psychological security needed to be protected, along with their physical security. "What is security? The woman who's a victim of rape needs much more than physical security. Especially, she needs HIV treatment. But she doesn't get it—while the accused people who are in the UN Detention Facility get it. Witnesses are dying of AIDS!"

He referred, too, to the retraumatization that witnesses who are rape survivors frequently suffer when undergoing cross-examination as witnesses. "This trauma is an indisputable medical issue. You see witnesses subjected to questioning and harassment.... They say it is what the common law system demands." Like many practitioners in civil-law systems, he seemed to find the strongly adversarial nature of common law trials quite shocking.

Ngoga argued that even regarding physical protection of witnesses, the steps the court took were insufficient. "Their identities are protected from the public—but not from the defendants and their teams. Maybe it would actually be *better* if European journalists at least knew who they are. Maybe that would give them better protection? We have had cases of witnesses being threatened and killed after testifying. Not so many; but some."

He complained bitterly about the slow pace of the trials.

Right now, they have completed an average of one case per year since they started. Remember, three of their cases were not even contested. And they have 800 employees and a budget of more than $100 million a year. It looks like a job creation program for foreigners!

Also, look at the number of witnesses they call. Recently, there was a prosecutor who called 100 witnesses. That does not make it a better case than one with five or 15 witnesses ... Judges need to have rules to limit the number of witnesses.

He said there was still a problem of genocide suspects being "on ICTR's payroll," by working as investigators on defense teams funded by the court. "Is this allowed at ICTY? Do they allow it here because the Rwanda genocide was 'unimportant'?" He said that his office had identified seven defense investigators as suspects: Two had been arrested by ICTR, and two by the Tanzanians; the other three were simply sacked from their jobs. "But we're telling them there are more," he said.

I asked if he thought that, on balance, ICTR's work was helping or harming the reconciliation process inside his country. He said that in 1994, when Rwanda voted against resolution 955, it did so primarily because "[w]e needed it inside Rwanda to contribute to peace and reconciliation. The concerns we had then have now been vindicated. Yes, the mere existence of the court is important because it has undercut the prospects for genocide denial. But has it been harmful to peace and reconciliation as well?"

He referred to some meetings then-Prosecutor Carla del Ponte had recently held in Europe with Rwandan opposition figures who were urging her to issue indictments against some of the RPF people accused of committing war crimes or crimes against humanity. "These were political leaders of the former armed forces and the *interahamwe* she met with!" he protested.

> She told them, "I can't be held [the] hostage of Rwanda's domestic agenda." But what she calls that is what makes Rwanda survive today and builds up peace and reconciliation. She is effectively denouncing our process! ...
>
> We've always felt betrayed and neglected by the UN ever since it abandoned us in 1994. We see ICTR as having been driven by UN guilt. We may tolerate it not doing its job—but not if it harms our own process.

For the first nine years of ICTR's existence, the possibility that the OTP might indict people associated with the RPF—though on charges other than genocide—continued to loom large over the court's relationship with the Kigali government. Among court officials, these possible cases were always referred to as the "special investigations." When I talked with Carla del Ponte in Arusha in April 2003, she assured me she was determined to proceed "wherever the special investigations might lead."[51] But Martin Ngoga said that if indictments were brought in these cases,

> they would put the genocide perpetrators in the driver's seat....
> There are not *two* sides to the story. There was only one genocide.
> Yes, in the RPA [the RPF's guerrilla forces] there were some excesses and acts of vengeance. But we dealt with those. We *executed* some of

those who carried out such acts—both before 1994, and right up to two or three years ago. The ICTR is satisfying nobody!

In summer 2003, as del Ponte's four-year term was coming up for renewal, the Rwandan government lobbied hard against her, primarily because of her insistence on pursuing the special investigations. She, like both of the ICTR chief prosecutors who preceded her, had held that position for ICTY, as well. But when the Security Council renewed her term in September 2003, it was *only* for the ICTY job. The Council named a new prosecutor for ICTR: Hassan Bubacar Jallow of Ghana. He quietly dropped the "special investigations." The Rwandan government had won a significant victory.

Reactions from Rwandans

Most of the early reactions to ICTR's work expressed from inside Rwanda were highly critical. The RPF government, as we know, entertained grave reservations about the court all along. Philip Gourevitch quoted Justice Ministry official Gerald Gahima as saying in 1995, "If the international community really wants to fight impunity in Rwanda, they should help Rwanda to punish these people.... It makes it harder to forgive the ordinary people if we don't have the leaders here to be tried in Rwandan courts before the Rwandan people according to Rwandan law." Gourevitch noted that Rwandan investigators had by that point drawn up a list of some 400 top *génocidaires*. "But all of them were in exile, beyond Rwanda's reach."[52]

It was not just the Rwandan government that was critical of ICTR. Veteran human rights activist André Sibomana told his interviewers in 1996 that ICTR's main effect had been

to enable the international community, or rather the countries within it, to save face and give the impression to the public that the crime they watched without intervening would not go unpunished....

I have met some of the ICTR officials; I am amazed by their incompetence. They are very intelligent people, but completely incapable of carrying out research. They don't speak Kinyarwanda—which is understandable—but nor do they know how to employ competent interpreters. I agreed to talk to the ICTR investigators. I spent a lot of time with them. When they presented me with an account of our meetings translated from Kinyarwanda into English and transcribed in French, there was only a remote link between the text and the subject matter of our discussions in French. I was angry with them for this flippant attitude and I refused to sign what was intended to be my deposition. Do you think the investigators tried to rectify the mistakes? They simply put me in the category of those who refused to cooperate with the ICTR. That was the last straw. *They are incapable of approaching those who lived through the genocide. They don't ask the right questions.* People are offended by their attitudes and their discourse. Rwandans had invested great hope in the ICTR. They are very disappointed.[53]

Most Rwandans remained critical of ICTR, even after the judges in Arusha started handing down their sentences. In February 2003, the court found 78-year-old Elizaphan Ntakirutimana, the former chief pastor of the Seventh Day Adventist church in Rwanda, and his son, physician Gerard Ntakirutimana, guilty of genocide.[54] Elizaphan received a ten-year sentence, and his son a twenty-five-year sentence. Two days after the sentencing, reporter Mary Kimani visited the district in Kibuye province where many of the two mens' crimes had been committed, to seek the reactions of people there to the sentences. "Our questions soon drew a crowd around us, leading to a heated debate on the sentence," she wrote.

She found some people—mainly, apparently, survivors of the genocide—arguing vigorously that the sentences were too low, and others who noted mitigating factors such as the pastor's advanced age as well as the claim that he had actually tried to save the lives of some Tutsis. She added this:

Perhaps the most disturbing comment came from a woman who refused to give her name. "The genocide was organized by the leaders. We know that the leaders of that time, the mayors, the councilors and the gendarmes were all determined to carry out the killings; the pastor had no authority to say no. *Even now, if the government told us to go and kill, who would refuse?*" she asks.[55]

One person following ICTR's work closely was Christine Murekatete, a woman who lost her husband, her parents, and all her siblings during the genocide. She herself was also gang-raped and had her thighs mutilated; she learned later that she had contracted HIV from the rapes. When Mary Kimani interviewed her in 2003, Murekatete was sick, destitute, and responsible for the care of twelve children—three of her own and the others orphans of the genocide.[56]

Murekatete was paying much attention to ICTR's trial of Pauline Nyiramasuhuko, who was its only woman defendant. Pauline, a Hutu, had been Rwanda's Minister for Gender Affairs, but the ICTR prosecutor charged her with genocide and orchestrating the rape of Tutsi women.[57] Murekatete said, "Pauline played an important role in what happened to me. Pauline came with a driver to our place in Kiduha, they took my brother away and killed him.... She is the one that gave an order [that] all women of Tutsi descent were to be raped." The reporter noted, "Murekatete's health is frail, and with no access to medical care, it is likely she could die before the end of Nyiramasuhuko's trial.... The long wait for justice both at the local and international level is proving a bitter experience for most survivors who are also aware of the relatively comfortable facilities provided by the ICTR to its detainees."[58]

The Rwandans quoted by Mary Kimani all seemed fairly well informed about ICTR, and to have definite opinions about the way it had dealt with various cases. With other Rwandans, however, ICTR's work appears to have left only an indistinct impression. In one 2002 survey of the opinions of 2,000 Rwandans in four different parts of the country, the researchers found that on a majority of the ten questions they asked about ICTR's performance, a majority of respondents said they were either "not informed" about the issue or "uncertain" about the answer. In that survey only 29.2 percent of respondents said they agreed or strongly agreed with the statement "Overall, the Arusha Tribunal has performed well," while 54.4 percent said they were uncertain or not informed about that issue; 16.3 percent disagreed or strongly disagreed with the statement.[59]

One possible indication that many Rwandans *were* following ICTR's work with interest came in February 2004, when a crowd estimated at 10,000 turned out in the southwestern Rwanda provincial capital of Cyangugu to demonstrate against ICTR's acquittal of two senior leaders from the province on genocide charges. One journalist reported that the demonstrators carried placards denouncing the "revisionist ICTR" and the "useless UN," among other slogans. The demonstrators, who were addressed by representatives of genocide survivors' organizations, called on ICTR to reconsider the judgment.[60] However, the involvement of government bodies and nongovernmental groups close to the government in planning this demonstration meant that the large popular participation could not necessarily be taken as an indicator of people's true degree of commitment to this cause.

Ibuka (which means "Remember!") is an organization that links many nongovernmental survivor groups. In May 2002, I talked with Philibert Gakwenzire, the head of Ibuka's department of "memory and documentation," in its offices in central Kigali. He explained that Ibuka was created in December 1995 with three main aims: to preserve the memory of the genocide and its victims, to defend the interests of the survivors, and to carry out socioeconomic projects with and for the benefit of survivors. He estimated that, nationwide, there were around 280,000 immediate survivors. Ibuka—which has generally, though not always, had good relations with the Rwandan government—has expressed great concern with the way that genocide survivors who go to Arusha to testify have been treated there; and it has often coordinated its protest actions against the court closely with the government.

Some months before I met Gakwenzire, Ibuka took the step of "suspending its relationship" with ICTR. Because of the broad support Ibuka and its sister organizations enjoyed among the genocide survivors, this dried up, almost overnight, the supply of survivors willing to go to Arusha to testify. For some months the court was forced almost to halt its work.

Gakwenzire told me that the suspension of relations "would only be temporary." The main reason he gave for it was an infamous incident the preceding October, when a rape survivor and prosecution witness known as "TA" faced a bench of judges who were apparently laughing at her plight. "She was definitely mistreated," Gakwenzire said. Like the Rwandan diplomat Martin Ngoga, Gakwenzire also accused the court of having people known to be *génocidaires* still on the payrolls of the defense teams.

Resources—and Benefits?

During my discussions with Rwandan citizens inside and outside their country, many of them expressed very strong criticisms of ICTR— and particularly, of what they saw as the huge amount of money its work was costing. Antoine Rutayisire is an Anglican priest and a genocide survivor who heads a very effective social-development organization headquartered in Kigali. (He is also vice chair of the quasigovernmental National Unity and Reconciliation Commission.) "When I see what they are spending on those trials there at ICTR," he told me in 2003, "and the small number of the accused there, I regret that. If that same amount of money went into social programs here, it would have been so much better for us all."[61] Rutayisire's very skeptical assessment of the UN court was also tightly linked to his memories of the fact that, during the genocide itself, "I saw with my own eyes how the international community stood idly by while my neighbors were being killed."

In Arusha, one successful Rwandan business executive, whom I'll call "BV," told me he saw ICTR as "far removed from the real, concrete needs of the people in Rwanda. We have women survivors of the genocide who come here to Arusha and they're *still bleeding*," he said. "But no one gives them anything."[62]

"Whose interest is it that ICTR serves?" he asked. "If they just took one year's worth of the budget from there and put it into social programs inside Rwanda—even if they freed all the ICTR's detainees!—it would still be much more helpful than what they're doing here." He stressed that inside Rwanda, "[w]e ... need to have a big process of continuing education and re-education, in order to build peace and reconciliation."

I heard that same criticism of the court's work—that it was irrelevant to the real needs of the Rwandan people—from most of the people I talked to inside Rwanda. The 2002 survey of Rwandan opinion cited earlier found that 35.1 percent of respondents agreed or strongly agreed with the statement "The Arusha Tribunal is there above all to hide the shame of foreigners," while only 12.1 percent expressed any disagreement with that statement (and once again, most respondents professed to have no informed opinion on the matter.)[63]

There was one moment in all the years of ICTR's work that gave many Rwandans real satisfaction. That was in 1998 when Omar Serushago, who had pleaded guilty on four different counts, made a confession in open court.[64] BV said he saw Serushago making his confession on television, and he recalled the incident quite clearly, even five years later: "Serushago cried. He pleaded for forgiveness. He showed remorse," he said. (The ICTR judges were also moved by Serushago's statement, and despite the severity of the crimes he confessed to they gave him a sentence of "only" fifteen years.)

BV said, "Rwandese liked to see the way Serushago acted." He contrasted Serushago's behavior—and the popular reaction to it—with that of the most prominent suspect to plead guilty at ICTR, Jean Kambanda, who was Rwanda's genocide-era prime minister. Kambanda pleaded guilty to counts of genocide and crimes against humanity. But in his presentencing hearing, also in 1998, he notably failed to express remorse.[65] "Kambanda just coldly admitted he had committed the crimes, and thought that was enough," BV said. "And he didn't even understand why, after he had done that, he still got a life sentence."

In May 2002, Gerald Gahima, by then his country's attorney general, sat with me over lunch in a hilltop restaurant in Kigali. The criticisms he voiced of ICTR were scathing. "It has made no contribution!" he exclaimed at one point. "It is just a way for the international community to act out its shame over what it did in '94. How else can you explain it? That they pour such huge resources into it without being concerned at all about its performance? ... It has nothing to do with Rwanda. They excluded Rwandans!"

Justice and Rebuilding Inside Rwanda

Detentions, Battles, and Politics

In the late summer and fall of 1994, while Rwanda's new RPF rulers were still trying to consolidate their hold on the ruins of the country, they faced the urgent challenge of how to treat those scores of thousands (or possibly even *millions*) of their countrymen who had participated in, or knowingly profited from, the genocide. As these two parallel processes proceeded, there were—as even Rwandan government officials were ready to admit—some vengeance-driven "excesses" committed by people on the RPF side. But the new government moved quickly to end any anarchic settling of scores. What it ordered its forces to do instead was to *imprison* as many genocide suspects as they could, with a view to later bringing them to trial.

The first problem that government officials faced as they attempted this was a shortage of prisons. Of seventeen prisons operating prior to the genocide, only four could be used after it. Canadian journalist Carol Off reported that, as a result, "[t]he arrested prisoners were first placed in local *cachots,* or makeshift jails, where the overcrowding quickly became acute.... In one of them, local police had forced sixty people into a tiny room, closed the door and locked it.... When the cell was finally opened again the next morning, twenty-two people had suffocated; four others had to be put in a hospital, where two more died."[66] And in Chapter 1, we read André Sibomana's description of the conditions inside Gitarama Prison, where 1,000 of the 7,000 detainees died within nine months, simply from overcrowding and damp. Sibomana noted that as soon as his diocese gained permission to intervene in the prison in spring 1995, the mortality rate started dropping: The church distributed makeshift sandals to the prisoners, which allowed them to avoid gangrene just by keeping their feet dry. "As a human rights defender and as administrator of the diocese of Kabgayi, it was my duty to think of actions which would ensure that prisons did not turn into death traps," he said. "The prison guards accused me of wanting to help the *interahamwe*. In their minds, even before they had been tried or simply heard, these people had ceased to be human beings."[67]

In any normally peaceful country, detained suspects can expect that their case will be brought before a preliminary hearing fairly rapidly, and that this hearing will cull out cases of clearly mistaken identity, evidently false accusations, and so on. In postgenocide Rwanda, no such mechanism existed: The court system had also been a major victim of the genocide. As noted in Chapter 1, in the years immediately after the Rwandan genocide, the country had no capacity at all to process the enormous volume of cases it was faced with.

The number of detained genocide suspects continued to rise. Nearly all the detainees were able-bodied people of breadwinning age; most were men. Each could, in normal times, have been expected to support some five or more family members. (In Rwanda, families are large.) Quite aside from questions of guilt or innocence, the continued detention of such large numbers of people placed a heavy economic burden on an impoverished society comprising around 8 million people altogether.

Why did the government persist in its detentions policy? An important part of the context in which it did so was the tough campaign its leaders felt they needed to sustain—first within Rwanda's borders and later also outside them—against the remnants of the former regime.

In the last days of the genocide, hundreds of thousands of Hutus fled to the parts of western Rwanda where France had sent its troops under Operation Turquoise. The French left in August 1994; and the concentrations of Rwandan internally displaced persons (IDPs) who remained in western Rwanda were thereafter given some relief services by UN agencies. But the government was very eager to close down these IDP camps, which it feared were becoming focal points for *génocidaires* trying to regroup inside the country. Units of the new national army were sent into the camps, starting with the smaller ones, to dismantle them and send the IDPs back to their home areas. As Philip Gourevitch described the campaign: "[P]eople were evicted from their shanties, then the shanties were torched." By early 1995, some 250,000 IDPs remained in just a few camps, of which Kibeho camp was the largest.[68]

As the Hutu IDPs returned to their homes—walking, or in UN-supplied trucks—they were sometimes harassed by Tutsis living along the roadside. Then, once they reached their homes, local administrators would screen each group for suspected *génocidaires* and send these suspects to places of long-term detention. Many returnees also found that their homes and crops had been taken over by Tutsi families who, after the RPF's victory, had returned to Rwanda from their multiyear exile outside the country.

Soon, Kibeho was the last IDP camp left; and in mid-April 1995, the government decided to clear it out as well. It used the same approach it used to clear the other, smaller camps. But Kibeho was big. The process of "registering" the IDPs for their transport home became swamped. RPF troops around the camp's perimeter started firing into the air, trying to force the IDPs toward the registration tables; a deadly mêlée ensued. Human Rights Watch later reported that, for two days, Rwandan troops "fired directly into the crowd, using machine guns as well as rocket-propelled grenades, killing thousands of people. On April 23, they chased and shot at unarmed civilians, including children, who were attempting to flee the carnage. During the nights of April 20 and 21, unidentified assailants killed and wounded dozens of camp residents in attacks with machetes."[69]

The final casualty toll was hotly contested. UN troops and observers who were present (but unable to do much to stop the carnage) later helped bury the dead, whose numbers they first estimated at 8,000. The government challenged that figure, and the United Nations later reduced it to 2,000.

After Kibeho camp had been cleared out, the major security threat the government perceived was that posed by the presence of *génocidaires* among the even larger concentrations of Hutu refugees *outside* Rwanda—primarily, in the refugee camps in Zaire, to the west. Zaire is a much larger country than Rwanda. By 1995 Mobutu Sese Seko had been in power there for thirty years, during which his rule became ever more corrupt and authoritarian. Zaire's capital, Kinshasa, was hundreds of miles from Rwanda, and the portions of Zaire bordering Rwanda were very underdeveloped, thickly forested, and almost inaccessible to Mobutu's control. In 1996, the Rwandan government sent troops into eastern Zaire to clear out the huge, *génocidaire*-dominated refugee camps there in the same way they had cleared out Kibeho. The troops encountered no significant presence of Zairean troops and indeed, for many years after 1996, found they could use eastern Zaire as a virtual free-fire zone in which they could chase down the ragtag battalions of Rwandan-Hutu *génocidaires* as violently as they chose. Before long, Rwanda's troops occupied an area of eastern Zaire that was *sixteen times as large as that of Rwanda itself*. Over the years that followed, the Rwandan military set up large networks to extract mineral and timber wealth from the occupied area.[70]

(In May 1997, amidst the turmoil that plagued Zaire after the Rwandan invasion, the veteran Zairean opposition figure Laurent Kabila—a longtime ally of Paul Kagame's—seized power in Kinshasa. It was he who renamed the country the Democratic Republic of Congo, DRC.)[71]

The battles in eastern Zaire/DRC between Rwanda's Hutus and Tutsis took place far from the eyes of the international community. They also ignited old hatreds between the sizeable Hutu and Tutsi groups *within* eastern DRC's own native population. In eastern DRC, it was even harder than in Kibeho for anyone to count the casualties. Gérard Prunier, an experienced French specialist on the region's affairs, estimated in a conversation with me in 2001 that "more than 200,000" Hutus disappeared there in 1996 during massacres carried out by the Rwandan army. In June 2001, Amnesty International wrote that "2.5 million people have died in eastern DRC from war-related causes in the last four years. Since August 1998, Rwandese government forces have occupied most of this part of the DRC."[72] In those years, hundreds of thousands of Rwandan Hutus who had been refugees in eastern DRC since 1994 came back to their former homes in Rwanda. For them, as for the IDPs who survived the Kibeho killings, a return home was often followed by having some family members detained on suspicion of having participated in the genocide.[73] Rwanda's jails and lockups continued to fill.

In 1996 and the years that followed, a notable level of armed conflict also continued inside Rwanda—mainly in the northwest of the country, where attacks by regrouped *interahamwe* forces met with tough countermeasures from the Rwandan army. In fall 1997, Amnesty International was reporting that "armed opposition groups have intensified their attacks during 1997—sometimes attacking in groups of more than 100—and ... in turn, the RPA has adopted a tougher line to crack down on the insurgency, amounting in some cases to a 'scorched earth' policy, using the legitimate need to combat the insurgents as a pretext for massacring unarmed civilians." That report also cited the "life-threatening conditions" inside Rwanda's prisons, judging that they "constitute an extreme form of cruel, inhuman or degrading treatment." It estimated the number of detainees then in Rwandan jails at "above 120,000."[74]

Criminal Trials and Their Limitations

It was in those circumstances of continuing conflict that, in 1996, the government adopted new legislation on how Rwanda's scores of thousands of genocide suspects should be prosecuted. The 1966 Genocide Law divided the cases into four categories as follows:

Category 1: Planners, organizers, instigators, supervisors and leaders of the crime of Genocide or of a crime against humanity; persons who acted in positions of authority; notorious murderers ... [and] persons who committed acts of sexual torture or violence.
Category 2: Perpetrators, conspirators or accomplices of intentional homicide or of serious assault against the person—causing death.
Category 3: Persons whose criminal acts or whose acts of criminal participation make them guilty of other serious assaults against the person.
Category 4: Persons who committed offenses against property.[75]

The law also sought to encourage confessions by stating that offenders who confessed fully would receive reductions in their sentences.[76]

The government was eager to start holding trials under this law. Canada, Belgium, and other nations were helping the government rebuild its court system. According to Carol Off, any Rwandan who could pass a fairly rudimentary, one-hour aptitude test was admitted to a fast-track training program lasting between one and five months. "At the end of it, successful candidates were declared to be qualified prosecutors, investigators, and judges.... Many of the newly minted judges were realistically afraid of the consequences of rendering any verdict other than guilty."[77]

The first trials under the new law opened in Kibungo in December 1996, when two men were tried on charges of genocide and crimes against humanity. Amnesty reported soon afterward that the trials lasted only about four hours; the defendants had no access to legal counsel; defendants were denied the opportunity to summon their own witnesses or cross-examine prosecution witnesses; and the defendants were reportedly booed, and prosecutors applauded, during the trial. "On 3 January 1997 the two men were pronounced guilty and sentenced to death."[78]

Throughout 1997, as the turbulence continued in northwest Rwanda and eastern DRC, the Kigali government continued holding trials of genocide suspects. By April 1998, prosecutors had won a few hundred convictions, and more than 100 people had received death sentences. On April 24, 22 of those sentenced to death were publicly executed. They included the first two men convicted under the Genocide Law, who were executed in Kibungo. But most of that day's executions were performed by a firing squad in Kigali's main sports stadium, in front of a crowd of 30,000.[79]

One high-ranking Rwandan judge later said to me, about these executions:

> It was right to do it in the open air, because people believed that we could not impose any penalties, they thought we were merely making the motions of operating a legal system.... *When we executed those people, people started to take us seriously,* and since then, the confessions started increasing....
>
> Then too, it was educational. It showed the population that those kinds of acts would not be ignored. Because you know that was not our first genocide [in 1994]. Before that, there had been many earlier genocides and nobody had been punished for them. So people thought, well, there are so many criminals, they can never be convicted, never be executed.... But after we had that execution, all of a sudden people realized we were serious about things.[80]

Rwandan and international human rights groups continued to criticize the trial procedures the government was using, but the government was in a tough bind. If it tried to implement all the changes the human rights groups urged, in order to increase the *fairness* of the trials, then the *length* of each trial would certainly have grown (even if not to the proportions of ICTR's trials). But meanwhile, the caseload continued to be mind-bogglingly large: A quick calculation revealed it would take between 160 and 200 years of nonstop trials to clear the backlog of genocide cases—even if the courts heard no other kinds of cases in the interim. Many of the detainees had anyway already been deprived of their liberty since 1994 or 1995: Any further period of detention prior to their cases being tried would constitute a further massive denial of their rights.

To the government's credit, its leaders fairly quickly came to understand that their single-minded pursuit of a Western-style prosecutorial approach to the events of 1994 was unworkable, or even counterproductive, in practice. In addition, the people running the government—most of whom were Tutsis—realized that as a matter of great political urgency they needed to reach some kind of *modus vivendi* with the majority of Rwandan citizens who were Hutus. They sought to meet this challenge in a number of ways, including working through a body called the National Unity and Reconciliation Commission (NURC) and running a systematic "re-education" campaign to promulgate among Rwandans a worldview in which the concepts of "Hutu" and "Tutsi" no longer had any place, and even the words "Hutu" and "Tutsi" would not be spoken.

Meanwhile, so long as many or most Hutu families had a relative languishing in detention, that fact would undermine the government's search for internal reconciliation. But, again, the government did not want to alienate the—relatively small, but politically significant—communities of Tutsi genocide survivors, or to tarnish its own reputation as the savior of the Tutsi remnants. Figuring out what to do about the 100,000–plus Hutu detainees must have seemed, all in all, to be a tricky political balancing act.

In 1997–1998, Kagame and his colleagues started to consider alternatives to their previous plan to hold criminal trials of all the detainees. Following the large-scale public executions of April 1998, they engaged in a year-long leadership-level deliberation on what to do about the detainees. "Many problems were debated," the Rwandan Supreme Court's Augustin Nkusi later recalled, "including the problems of justice, the problems of the national economy, the problem of national reconciliation, the problem of national security, etc., etc. So this debate resulted in the formation of a commission headed by the Minister of Justice … and they prepared a project."[81] This project was adapted from a traditional, community-based hearing mechanism used in Rwanda called *gacaca*—literally, justice "on the lawn" (see Chapter 1).

In 1999, Kagame and his circle launched a public discussion on the idea of formally incorporating aspects of *gacaca* into the country's response to the genocide. In June 2000, researchers at the National University of Rwanda followed up this discussion by conducting a nationwide survey on issues related to *gacaca* and the genocide. It found that 36 percent of respondents reported the loss of at least one member of their immediate family during the genocide, and that "[a]wareness about [proposed] gacaca jurisdictions is high but actual knowledge [of how it would work] is low." Among the other findings of this survey were these:

- "More than three-fourths of the respondents mentioned poverty as the major social problem in the Rwandan society. Moreover, most of the problems of poverty are perceived to be directly linked with the genocide and thereby expected to be resolved through the gacaca."
- "The data indicate that Rwandans have major expectations vis-à-vis the Gacaca law.... [I]t is widely believed that the law will lead to sustainable peace in the country."
- "In the opinion of most (89%) respondents, lasting peace can only be ensured when the authors of genocide recognize their faults, ask for forgiveness, and show the desire for reconciliation."[82]

The *gacaca* courts' proposal rapidly came under fire from Western rights organizations. In April 2000, Amnesty International protested that "Fundamental aspects of the gacaca proposals do not conform to basic international standards for fair trials guaranteed in international treaties which Rwanda has ratified."[83] But the Rwandan government stuck to its plan. Later in 2000, Gerald Gahima—then the justice minister—told an interviewer that "[w]e have to put the genocide behind us."[84] The Gacaca Law was adopted by parliament in early 2001.

Understandings of the 1994 Violence

In most of the world outside Rwanda, the main lens through which observers viewed the 1994 violence was that of international atrocities law. Indeed, the most burning question for most outsiders was *whether the violence met the internationally agreed legal definition of a genocide, or not.* This was a matter of great potential policy impact; for if any of the governments that had ratified the 1948 Convention Against Genocide should determine that what was happening in

Rwanda *was* genocide, then they were legally obligated to intervene to suppress it.[85] In addition, the vast majority of supporters of the politically powerful international human rights movement based their view of what was happening in Rwanda on a strong presumption that each of the perpetrators of the violence could and should be held individually responsible for his or her part in it; and based on this view, rights activists called loudly for the prosecution of all perpetrators in national or international criminal courts.

Within Rwanda, some people shared this view of what was happening in their country. But other Rwandans had different explanations—different lenses, if you will—with which they understood the events. One aspect of the violence that seemed very clear to Rwandans who studied it closely was the difficulty, especially in a situation where many people were making decisions in a climate of all-embracing fear, of making any hard-and-fast distinction between "perpetrators" and "victims" of the violence. For example, Sibomana had noted that "some people were forced to kill under threat;" and Jean Bosco Bugingo was far from the only killer who testified that those were indeed the circumstances under which he had acted.[86]

In 2002, I discussed this question with Rwanda's attorney general, Gerald Gahima. He told me how complicated he found many of the decisions he had to make as the official responsible for all the prosecutions of genocide suspects. One case he mentioned was that of a young priest in charge of a church called the Sainte-Famille (Holy Family) church. "This man saved maybe 25,000 people in that church complex," Gahima noted.

> But along the way, he gave up some groups of 100 or so people each to the militia. Plus, there were many reports he ran around with the militiamen in uniform, and he probably had sexual relations with a number of women and even girls who came under his care. ...
>
> But he saved so many lives! In addition, those girls are probably now married women. If the prosecution proceeds with a case against him they would be subjected to subpoenas to come and testify. It would break up their families. It's almost impossible to find the best thing to do.

I asked him about an explanation I had heard about the nature of mass violence from survivors of atrocities I had talked to in Mozambique—namely, that in some times of mass violence it is most helpful to look at the violence as having been caused by some form of generalized, malevolent spirit rather than by any human agency that could be held accountable on a strictly individual basis.

"How else can you explain it? These people were their neighbors, their friends!" Gahima replied.[87]

Others in Rwanda also, like Gahima, dwelt on the disturbingly "intimate" nature of the genocide and what that indicated about the causation and nature of its violence. Augustin Nkusi, who by then was counselor to the *gacaca* court system, told me in 2002:

> A genocide was something that came and it didn't have Rwandan sources. Rwandans speak the same language; there is nothing that designates one Rwandan as different from another; there is nothing that makes one Rwandan look at another and obliges him to cut off his head. What happened was that this came upon us accidentally, but in reality there were no substantial causes that made one Rwandan kill another. So above everything we have to discover what made it so that people would kill each other? More than that—what happened that caused people to kill their *neighbors,* their *relatives*—because that was what happened: a cousin would kill a cousin; there were even dads who killed their children, a husband would kill his own wife. ...
>
> Oh, there were causes, but the causes were not something in the root of the Rwandan experience; the reasons came from elsewhere. The reasons came from *le pouvoir,* the reasons came from colonization.

For his part, Christopher Taylor is an American anthropologist who has studied Rwandans' traditional cosmologies, and their traditional understandings of the role of the individual in society. He has written that "[t]he Rwandan [concept of the] person is fractal, less than one, perennially incomplete. He or she is ever involved in the process of being added to, built upon, and produced by the gifts of others. Through his or her own gifts such a person is habitually adding to and producing others. Rwandans relate to one another through various aspects of themselves and not as integrated bounded unities."[88] This strongly suggests that many Rwandans would find it hard to think of responsibility for acts of violence always to be exactly distributable among a number of bounded individuals.

Gacaca Then and Now

Filip Reyntjens is a Belgian expert in Rwandan and international law who has studied *gacaca* since the 1970s. He has written a lively description of one *gacaca* hearing that he observed, in a rural area of Rwanda in 1986. The dispute in question was a disagreement between two women over the size of a debt. It was generally agreed that their fighting over the issue had disturbed the local peace, and that was why the dispute had been brought to the local "lawn" (*gacaca*) for resolution.

According to Reyntjens, about sixty men and women of varied ages took part in the hearing, joining in with shouts to express support of or opposition to the different arguments made. Nine local elders seated on a bench directed the proceedings. After an hour of discussion, the "defendant" said that the other woman's account of the debt was indeed accurate, and that she would repay the whole amount. The people gathered around them debated what "damages" she should additionally pay to the community for having caused a disturbance of the peace. The size of this fine was later set at ten bottles of banana beer, which would be contributed *to the community*. "The reconciliation would then be celebrated later in the course of a little feast," Reyntjens wrote.[89]

He reported that in one Rwandan canton that he studied, around 1,200 cases were heard in *gacacas* during an eight-month period in 1986, compared to only 83 in the canton's formal court system. He wrote that, at times, parties dissatisfied with a judgment made at *gacaca* would take an "appeal" against it to the formal court, and all judgments rendered by *gacacas* were registered with the local authorities.

When I talked with Reyntjens in Antwerp, Belgium, in 2001, he argued that using a *gacaca*-type system to hear cases of alleged genocide would be a significant departure, because it had seldom previously been used for cases involving murder or severe bodily harm. Rwanda's ambassador to the United States, Richard Sezibera, made the same point when I talked with him in his embassy a couple of weeks earlier.

Sezibera recalled the categories into which the 1996 Genocide Law had divided the accused *génocidaires* and explained that under the Gacaca Law the "worst" (Category 1) detainees—some 2,000 to 3,000 people, in his estimation—would still be handled by the criminal courts. Suspects from Categories 2 through 4 would now be dealt with in new *gacaca* courts. He referred to the need to end the "culture of impunity" in Rwanda: "If you committed a crime, you will be punished proportionately. Not *commensurately*, of course. But proportionately. We need to send the message: if you committed a crime, there will be consequences." He said it was also important that survivors of the genocide should "feel they are a part of the process of healing."

Up to that point, he admitted, survivors had sometimes caused "problems" when the government tried to reduce the sentences of accused *génocidaires*. "So we have to make sure that they are a part of the process.... We can't replace the people who were lost. But we must replace the property that was lost, and the whole community must take part in that. Rehabilitation has to be both a moral and a physical undertaking."

He also emphasized the parallel need to construct a determinedly *national* identity for all Rwandans. "Our system should not be polarizing," he said. "We should not end up entrenching the rigid identities that had been promoted in the past." (Here as elsewhere in our discussion, Sezibera abstained from mentioning the suspect identities in question, which both of us understood to be "Hutu" and "Tutsi.")

"Taken together," Sezibera concluded, "the Genocide Law and the Gacaca Law are designed to pick out the small numbers of perpetrators that society can't deal with, and to reintegrate the rest."

Starting the Gacaca Courts

Creating and running the *gacaca* court system was a truly massive undertaking—one in which the Kigali government sought to involve all adult Rwandans. Rwanda has for many generations been a highly hierarchical society.[90] At the base of its pyramid of tight social organizations are the more than 9,000 "cells," each containing some ten to twelve families. Each group of six to ten cells constitutes a "sector"; the sectors are grouped into "districts," and the districts into provinces. The *gacaca* courts were designed to operate at all four of these levels. First of all, cell-level *gacaca* courts would *establish the facts* of what had happened in that cell during the genocide; then they would sort into the right "categories" the suspects who had been active there in 1994. Later, hearings for the Category 4 suspects would be held at cell level, while hearings for Category 3 and Category 2 suspects would be sent to *gacaca* courts working at the sector and district levels.

The first step, in October 2001, was to elect the judges. All Rwandans were given a day's holiday so the adults could take part in these elections. Each cell elected 19 judges to work at its own level, and a further 6 to work at the "district" level: This process resulted in the election of more than 170,000 judges![91] The main qualifications for judges were that they be "people of integrity" and "free from the spirit of sectarianism and discrimination" (Article 10). There was no requirement that they be literate, and many were not. A few hours of training was all they received.

According to the Gacaca Law, each cell would then hold a large number of public sessions, attended by all local adults, with the judges sitting in front and running the proceedings. The sessions would run through a number of assigned tasks. First, the judges would draw up lists of the people who had lived in the cell before the genocide, those who had been killed there during the genocide, and so on. Then, they would sort the local suspects into the four "categories." Finally, they would resolve the cases of the Category 4 suspects right there in the cell. It was envisaged that many of the punishments meted out by these *gacaca* courts, especially for "lower-category" offenders, would take the form of reparative community service. Jail sentences would be halved for all offenders who had confessed their crimes, and in most cases the time participants had already served in detention would be enough (or more than enough) to cover their final sentence. The process was thus intended to bring about the peaceable return to their home communities of nearly all the genocide suspects apart from Category 1 suspects.

The logistical challenge of holding these hearings was enormous. All Rwandans were expected to give up one day a week, for the numerous weeks it would take to get through the process—and to do this in a society where there was already one day a week of obligatory "community service" (*umuganda*) for everyone, one day for church, and, traditionally, one day for going to market. Farmers and small tradespeople would end up with only three days a week in which to work! The *gacaca* judges faced an even greater time burden, since they would need to spend additional time in their (closed-session) deliberations and in fulfilling their many administrative tasks. One genocide survivor I talked to in Kigali in 2002 sighed when he told me he had been elected a *gacaca* court judge. "It's far too much work!" he said.

The government planned to test the process by first holding a small number of pilot *gacaca* courts around the country. But even organizing these pilot projects took much longer than expected. I planned a trip to Rwanda in May 2002, hoping to observe some of the pilot hearings—but they had not started by then. I was, however, able to have some good discussions with Rwandan officials tasked with setting up the new system. One was Augustin Nkusi. Talking with me (in French) as he worked late into the evening in his office in central Kigali, he said the *gacaca* courts had three main goals: speeding up case management, establishing a strong historical record, and contributing to reconciliation. Regarding reconciliation he said:

> You know that the classical justice system doesn't bring about reconciliation, ever. But with the *gacaca*, one is aiming at a reconciliation between the people, because in fact it is a system which offers a reduced penalty, which proposes to the criminals that they confess, and that they ask for forgiveness for what they have done. You understand, that [in the *gacaca* system] if I confess what I have done, I describe exactly what happened, and I ask forgiveness, then I can obtain a reduced sentence within the legal limits, within the limits that the law defines.
>
> From the other side, we have the survivor, that is, the victim of the genocide, who waited and waited for justice to be done so that he could be rehabilitated. But with the delays of classical justice he could still die with his misery.

In Nkusi's description of the goals of the *gacaca* courts, timeliness was ranked very high. How long, I asked, did he see the *gacaca* process taking? "It's difficult to say precisely," he said, "but we could say somewhere between five years and eight or ten years.... If it goes on longer than ten years, that would not in my opinion be a good thing."

When I talked with Attorney General Gerald Gahima, he described the goal of the *gacaca* project, in broad terms, as "to balance accountability with stability." The only thing, in his view, that could prevent the process from working as planned was "lack of resources." What would happen then? I asked. He replied, "Amnesties, I guess."[92]

Problems Dogging Gacaca

From the very beginning, the *gacaca* project encountered numerous challenges. The London-based organization Penal Reform International (PRI), which monitored the project closely, noted in a September 2003 report that the small number of pilot hearings held until then had been plagued by low popular participation—this, in what was supposed to be an inclusive, community-wide process. Also, two other linked programs—establishing systems for victim compensation, and for the performance of community service by the guilty—had experienced serious delays.

Regarding participation levels, the PRI report stated:

> The low level of participation is felt both in terms of physical presence (delayed sessions, most of the population not showing up) and contributing towards difficulty in establishing the truth.... People are afraid of testifying or assuming their responsibilities; the rumors and confrontations during the sessions create a strong feeling of insecurity (real or imaginary). Only the prisoners have no hesitation in confessing. However, the latter, who are often perceived to be arrogant for many reasons, only increase the feelings of unease and mistrust that the population may have in relation to the *Gacaca*. In these circumstances, the lack of training and sometimes of motivation of the judges is felt even more strongly.[93]

This report, like others from PRI, gave a wealth of detail about the workings of the *gacaca* courts. It also presented some thought-provoking case studies that challenged any assumption that people who have gone through an episode of violence as pervasive and complex as the Rwandan genocide could ever be easily divided into (innocent) survivors and (guilty) perpetrators. The report described a small number of instances in which the hearings had a seemingly good effect on intergroup relations within the participating cells. But overall, its assessment of the effect the hearings had on relations among cell members seemed gloomy:

> At the outset of the *Gacaca* sessions, the survivors and nonsurvivors used to mix, but since the meetings of the 6th and 7th sessions, their segregation is more and more noticeable, especially before and after the meetings. The moment accusations are made, tensions arise between the two groups. ...
> [M]istrust between members of these two groups is still very great and appears to be reactivated by the confrontations that take place during the *Gacaca* sessions.[94]

As the government pushed on toward its goal of holding *gacaca* hearings in all the 9,000–plus cells in the nation, the logistical and political problems caused by the project continued to multiply. At the end of 2003, the country was rocked by reports that three genocide survivors who planned to testify in one rural *gacaca* hearing had been maimed and killed. Other murders, as well as acts of intimidation against survivors planning to testify, were reported from elsewhere around the country. "If this doesn't change, very few people will come forward to testify," one *gacaca* judge was reported as saying.[95]

The nationwide opening of the *gacaca* courts finally took place on June 24, 2004. President Kagame himself launched the process by going to the *gacaca* court in his home neighborhood in Kigali. Hirondelle News Agency reported that "[a]fter the inauguration ceremony, President Kagame then took part, together with other inhabitants, in the Cell's first general assembly."[96] But even while he was participating in a process that supposedly aimed at national reconciliation, Kagame's regime was becoming markedly more authoritarian. A committee of the Rwandan parliament—over which Kagame exercised strong influence—was finishing work on a report that accused a dozen local civil society organizations of promoting a "genocide ideology." The accused organizations included some of those most dedicated to providing an impartial monitoring presence at the *gacaca* hearings, like the respected Rwandan human rights organization, Liprodhor. On June 30, parliament accepted the committee's report. The government then asked the attorney general's office to investigate its accusations, and to prosecute the malefactors whom it named. Around the world, human rights organizations (and a handful of other governments) cried foul. Amnesty International protested that "[t]he Rwandese National Assembly is inappropriately manipulating the concept of genocide to silence not only organizations and individuals critical of the government but organizations who have a close relationship with the Rwandese people and whose loyalty the government questions."[97] By January 2005, Liprodhor had been forced out of business.[98]

In March 2005, some 100–plus of the pilot *gacacas* entered the crucial "trial" phase of their work. On the first day of these trials, thirty suspects were convicted and one was acquitted. Those convicted were given sentences of between one and thirty years. A spokeswoman for the National Service for Gacaca Jurisdictions (NSGJ) said that in most cases the sentences given tallied with the amount of time these people had already spent in jail, and they would be released.[99] That month, the Rwandan media gave a lot of play to some politically prominent participants in the *gacaca* process. One political bombshell concerned sitting Defense Minister Marcel Gatsinzi, who was named as a genocide suspect in the *gacaca* in his home district.[100]

Gatsinzi was not alone. The public naming of large numbers of new suspects, as a result of the "full confession" provision of the

Gacaca Law, was something of which observers had long warned. In the spring of 2005, this process started to have evident political and human consequences. In Butare province and other border provinces of the country, individuals fearing broad new campaigns of detention (or worse) fled their home areas in large numbers, crossing into neighboring countries. In mid-April 2005, reports from Burundi—the country that borders Butare—spoke of "at least 2,000" Rwandans having sought refuge there from the feared actions of the *gacaca* courts.[101]

By fall 2005, the ballooning of the suspect list as a result of *gacaca* was becoming alarmingly clear. In October, after interviewing a NSGJ spokesman, a Hirondelle reporter wrote that "Rwanda now expects over 700,000 people—almost one tenth of its population—to be brought before genocide courts," whether in the *gacaca* system or the regular courts. "Category One suspects alone are expected to hit the 50,000 mark some time before the end of the year," he added.[102] Quite an increase from Ambassador Sezibera's 2001 estimate that Category 1 suspects numbered between 2,000 and 3,000!

The whole *gacaca* court experiment, which earlier seemed to have great potential as a visionary, culturally appropriate, and politically astute way of dealing with the legacies of the genocide, had now fallen prey to many of the same problems that the policy of mass prosecutions in the regular courts had encountered before it. Meanwhile, a dozen years after the genocide, many Rwandans still found themselves forced to engage in repeated and detailed public discussions of the events of those days, seemingly trapped in the atmosphere of divisiveness and fear that the genocide had engendered.

Politics, Society, and Reconciliation

Immediately after the RPF's victory in July 1994, its leaders named Pasteur Bizimungu as president of Rwanda, while Paul Kagame stayed in the shadows as vice president. Bizimungu was a veteran Hutu politician who had been a key ally of Kagame's since 1990. Throughout the years after 1994, Bizimungu's presence in the presidency and his significant personal stature gave crucial reassurance to many Hutus that they could expect fair treatment inside the country even if it continued to be dominated by the RPF. In early 2000, however, Bizimungu started expressing increasingly strong criticisms of Kagame. In March 2000, he resigned from the presidency, joining a stream of other top government officials—both Hutus and independent-minded Tutsis—who were resigning or being ousted from their jobs at that time. Kagame then dropped the fig leaf in which he had shrouded his increasingly tight control of the country and became openly the president.

Most of the numerous political figures who had resigned from the RPF government since 1994 immediately fled the country. But Bizimungu stayed in Rwanda, where he tried to found a new political party, the Party for Democracy and Renewal (PDR). The PDR was targeted by the government from the beginning. In June 2000, it was officially banned. In December 2001, one of the PDR's co-founders was shot dead in Kigali by unidentified assailants. In April 2002, Bizimungu and another former PDR leader were arrested on charges of "threatening state security."[103] In August 2003, Kagame held nationwide "elections" for both the presidency and the Chamber of Deputies. The odds in these polls were stacked heavily in his and the RPF's favor; to no one's surprise, Kagame won 95.1 percent of the votes for the presidency, and the RPF and its allies won forty of the fifty-three races for the Chamber of Deputies.[104] In June 2004, as a footnote to the story of Kagame's consolidation of power, Pasteur Bizimungu was sentenced to fifteen years in jail.

It was in the context of this trend toward increasing authoritarianism that Kagame and his allies continued their campaign for their own particular brand of Tutsi-Hutu reconciliation. This form of reconciliation rested on two main pillars:

1. trying to erase any traces of the (long fateful) division between the country's Tutsis and Hutus, primarily by implementing a strong (though never explicitly legislated) ban on public use of either of those two words, and by pursuing a strong campaign against anyone accused of "divisionism"—that is, of drawing attention to inequities between the two groups;[105] and
2. promulgating a view of Rwanda's history that was, in fact, extremely Tutsi-centric, primarily by keeping citizens' attention focused on the harms done to the country's Tutsis since 1959 (but particularly in 1994), while suppressing any public mention at all of harms done by Tutsis to their Hutu compatriots and any mention of the RPF's extensive and very damaging military operations within the DRC.

The main body charged with promulgating these views among Rwanda's (majority Hutu) population was the government-backed National Unity and Reconciliation Commission (NURC). The NURC implemented its public education (or "re"-education) campaigns at many different levels and in many different ways. Among its projects were the re-education camps to which many of the (Hutu) refugees returning from DRC and elsewhere were consigned, and the "solidarity camps" (*ingando*) that were designed as halfway houses in which detained genocide suspects spent time before being sent back to their home cells to take part in *gacaca* hearings.[106]

The RPF government's desire to control the public discourse in the above ways was perhaps understandable; and many of the steps it took to prevent intergroup violence, official discrimination based on group membership, and genocide denial seemed like good ones. For example, one of its early steps was to change the nationwide identity cards that all Rwandans carry, to take out the line listing the bearer's affiliation as Hutu, Tutsi, or Twa. But many other aspects of the "reconciliation" campaign waged by the government and the NURC ended up having a strongly "Big Brother"-ish effect that, over the long run, could not be expected to build a strong basis for stability and human rights in the country. Indeed, as we saw in the cases of Liprodhor and Pasteur Bizimungu's political party, the campaign against "ethnic divisionism" was used to silence both political opponents and independent, nonpolitical critics of the government.

The strategies the post-1994 government used as it dealt with the scores of thousands of detained genocide suspects were designed as an integral part of the broad (and essentially political) campaign outlined above. For example, in the detentions and prosecutions policies pursued by the country's regular court system, no attention at all was paid to accusations of atrocities committed by Tutsis against Hutus. Even if we agree (as I am prepared to do) with the government's argument that no Tutsis ever planned or implemented a *genocide* against the Hutus, still, the title of the key legislation that is generally called Rwanda's 1996 Genocide Law was actually "Prosecutions for Offences constituting the Crime of Genocide *or Crimes against Humanity* committed since October 1, 1990." But no prosecutions were pursued under this law against Tutsis accused of committing "crimes against humanity" during the period in question, even though such crimes were almost certainly committed—for example, at Kibeho.

In the *gacaca* court hearings that have been held since 2002, mention of atrocities committed by Tutsis has similarly not been allowed. PRI, in its description of how the pilot *gacacas* operated in some cells in Gisenyi province, noted that several people involved in those hearings wanted to talk about the genocide survivors who reportedly killed a large number of the Hutu refugees who had returned *en masse* to Rwanda in 1997–1998. But no one was allowed even to mention those killings in the *gacaca* courts.[107]

Finally, though as mentioned above much of NURC's work has been ethically problematic, we should note that there are numerous more independent, mainly faith-based groups in the country whose efforts to build intergroup reconciliation have been more soundly conceived than NURC's, and which seem to have some chance of being more successful at building long-term reconciliation than that often heavy-handed governmental body. Given the role that many church leaders had played in supporting the genocide, this judgment may seem a strange one. But I discovered during my visit to Rwanda that the orientation (and even the identity) of the country's principal Christian-based organizations had changed a lot since 1994. In the postgenocide years many of these organizations have run some innovative and apparently successful reconciliation efforts; and the 5 to 10 percent of Rwanda's population who are Muslims have made their own contribution to reconciliation, too.[108]

One notable development in postgenocide Rwanda was the apparently explosive growth of Protestant Christianity in the country, at the expense of its older Catholic congregations. Prior to the genocide, Protestants were estimated to form less than 10 percent of the population. But one careful June 2000 survey found that 44 percent of the adults surveyed described themselves as Protestants. Those researchers found that Muslims made up "not quite 5%" of their sample.[109] The vigor of various Protestant denominations was very evident during my 2002 visit to Rwanda. A Pentecostal congregation had erected a massive prayer tent near the center of Kigali, which would fill to overflowing on Sundays. I talked with a number of Protestant ministers who described ambitious programs they were running that combined faith-based development projects with an emphasis on intergroup healing. Many Protestant evangelists were running active prayer groups inside the country's overcrowded prisons. From my discussions with Protestant ministers and laypeople, I concluded that two notable things that Protestant ministry brought to the challenge of reconciliation inside Rwanda were its emphases on sincere confession and on forgiveness.

One of the social-activist ministers I met was Michel Kayetaba, an Anglican (and a genocide survivor) who headed an organization called "Moucecore." Moucecore organized regular, two-week-long training seminars for engaged laypeople ("evangelists") from different denominations on issues like conflict resolution, community development, and trauma counseling. In the seminar that I visited, some forty men and women from different parts of the country were learning how to launch and run grassroots economic development projects. During the seminar, Hutus and Tutsis were learning, praying, living, and working enthusiastically together.

Kayetaba, a gentle man with a ready smile and an infectious laugh, told me:

> Change is possible, if there is the political will to make a change after an incidence of violence.... It's true that the government can't do everything. It can't change people! So where is the power to bring about change nowadays? The power to bring about change is in civil society, the NGOs, the church: it is they who—if they want to bring about change, also—they can do so, in support of the government's plan, and together we'll see the changing of the community.

I asked whether he thought a Western-style system of justice that attempts to hold each individual strictly accountable for his or her misdeeds could succeed in a situation like Rwanda's genocide. He replied:

> What I have discovered, as someone who does a lot of training of people in reconciliation work, in the work of building unity, in the work of bringing people to a condition of reconciliation after so much violence—is there *is* no justice, that is, in the sense of western-style justice. It demands instead, sacrifice. Because in our country, for example, when one asks a person to pardon the perpetrator, that is to ask him to accept that he has lost everything, even any [moral] advantage he may have. ...
>
> In general, the concept of justice is that the guilty one should be punished, and the punishment should be comparable to the crime. But in a case like that of the genocide, there is no punishment that could be equal to the wrongs they committed.... No one is going to kill a million!

Therefore, speaking of western-style justice, it won't work here. Especially because—justice is what? Justice is ... to keep the peace. So first of all, let us bring back peace, and then keep it. And to keep the peace, at this level, one should not be "just." For example, look at the kids, say, a child whose father was a killer, but he, the child, is not a killer—So the child has to be recovered. People shouldn't go around saying, "Oh, he's the child of a killer." No, the child should be recovered, rehabilitated, and be given his rights. *That's* what justice is. Or, if we have some orphans from the genocide, then they need to be supported, helped by all the community. And if one does that, *that* is justice. But it's not "equal"—it's not "equal" to what one has lost. And we have found that mercy is more than justice.

These are the difficult issues that Rwanda's ministers and other community leaders have been dealing with. Antoine Rutayisire is, like Kayetaba, an evangelical Anglican minister and a genocide survivor who runs an ambitious social-development organization.[110] He is also, however, vice president of the commission that supervises the work of the government's NURC; and he articulated a view a little different from Kayetaba's. He wrote to me in June 2004:

It is difficult to couple "full accountability" with reconciliation, but a certain level of justice needs to be done if we are to eradicate the impunity that had become a culture and that has served as an incentive to the sporadic killing of Tutsis since 1959. For sure, the kind of justice and punishment applied will not be proportionate to the crimes committed but at least they will send a signal that such practices will no longer be tolerated in the future.

All in all it is not easy but we are sure we will succeed to live together!

At the end of 2005, however, this result still seemed sadly far away.

3
South Africa
Amnesties, Truth-Seeking—and Reconciliation?

From Conflict to Peacemaking

Two Participants

Rejoice Mabudhafasi can fit in time to meet only during a stopover at Johannesburg's airport. "Come to the VIP lounge at 11:30," she says. She is South Africa's deputy minister for the environment and tourism. She is a hurricane of energy, but she sits long enough to talk a little about her life and her view of the TRC's record.

In 1965, then a young teacher, she moved from Johannesburg's vast, Black-populated Soweto "townships" to become a librarian at the ("Blacks only") college that would later become the University of the North. Throughout the 1970s the university acted as a lively incubator for many young Blacks who went on to become leaders of the nationalist movement.

The government had banned the African National Congress (ANC) and the more militant Pan Africanist Congress (PAC) in 1960. Because of the intense repression aimed at political organizers, much of the antiapartheid activity in the following decades was conducted through networks of community groups: youth groups, women's groups, church and mosque organizations, labor unions, and so on. Mabudhafasi was involved with many such groups. She was arrested for the first time in 1976.

In the early 1980s, the pro-ANC groups nationwide started co-ordinating their activities through a network called the United Democratic Front (UDF). "I was a founder member of the UDF in the Northern Province," she told me proudly. "From 1983 through 1986 I was the Secretary of the UDF there. I was arrested so many times! We would organize strikes, and consumer boycotts. One consumer boycott was so successful that I was arrested three times for helping organize it."

In 1985, she helped found the National Education Coordinating Committee (NECC), which addressed the crisis that had faced the Black community since 1976, when school students in Soweto and other parts of the country launched a stay away from school to protest the inferior education they were receiving. In those years, too, the government was trying to implement its ill-fated "homelands" policy, an attempt to force all the country's Black citizens to live and exercise their (severely constrained) "rights" only in a bizarre archipelago of quite nonviable "Black Homelands." The University of the North was situated in a "homeland" called Lebowa.

The NECC held its first big organizing meeting in the north in a Lutheran church building. Mabudhafasi told me:

> They sent in the Homeland Police. The police used big *sjamboks* [whips] and dogs to break up the meeting. It was pandemonium! I just managed to get out in time before I was arrested. After that, I stayed underground for two months, moving from house to house among our supporters. That October, though, they managed to arrest me.
>
> They didn't keep me very long that time. Soon after that, though, I learned from my students that I was on a government hit list. My colleague Peter Mokaba was on it, too. The students said the orders to the Homeland Police were to torture us until we were dead.
>
> In April 1986, the police bombed my house by throwing a hand grenade onto the windowsill. One of my children was sleeping in that same room. The children were quite traumatized. They used to come and raid our house once a week. Each time it was a horror for the kids.
>
> I was in jail from 1986 through 1989. Sometimes, we'd say we were safer inside the jails than outside, because of the activities of the hit squads all around! We developed pretty good survival skills inside the prison. We figured how to speak to people in other cells through the toilets. We kept our spirits up by singing. We learned how to smuggle letters in and out....

We organized a hunger strike in that prison. They put me in an isolation cell for that, for two weeks. But the Lutherans in Germany knew about the hunger strike and they helped pressure the government to release me. Still, even after they released me, they gave me a "banning" order which meant I had to report to the police at 7 A.M. and 5 P.M. every day, and I couldn't travel away from home or attend meetings.

Nowadays, Mabudhafasi is busy. She has a plane to catch, a development conference to attend, projects to organize. We talk quickly about the TRC. But she becomes most animated when she remembers this about the old days: "Every time they put us in jail, when they released us we'd go out more angry than when we went in!"

Eugene de Kock was on the other side. He was born around 1950 to an Afrikaner father who was a public prosecutor in Springs, in the East Rand region. In 1998, de Kock published a memoir in English, from which most of the following account is taken.[1]

When still a boy, de Kock became aware of his parents' increasingly frequent and loud arguments:

> The day the bubble burst for me was after my parents had a massive quarrel and my mother climbed into her car and drove off, with my father doing nothing to stop her. My brother ... started crying and I, though not crying, suddenly realized that we might be alone from then on. This was an unknown fear. I experienced nothing like it before or since, and no other fear, not during battles, not during riots, not during fistfights, not during any other situation in my life, has been as frightening for me. ...
>
> I stuttered from birth and it grew worse as I grew older and became more self-conscious. By my adolescent years I had pretty much given up taking part in conversations.... I have never forgotten the ridicule to which I was subjected, both to my face and behind my back.

De Kock did his national service in the army, then joined the South African Police (SAP) where he became a specialist in counterinsurgency. He wrote, "In 1977 the government was in a swamp of trouble. The eruption of Soweto in 1976 underlined, thickly and in Black, the country's internal problems. Across the borders, the United Nations was making moves to wrest South West Africa [Namibia] from South Africa's tight grasp. White power was crumbling in Rhodesia. Marxist-Leninist states had been set up in Mozambique and Angola." In 1977, Defense Minister P. W. Botha responded to this situation with something called the "Total Strategy." De Kock wrote, "Its underlying argument was that the country was the target of a Marxist-driven Total Onslaught. Only a Total Strategy—a coordination of the state's activities in the military, economic, psychological, political, diplomatic, cultural and ideological fields—would be strong enough to combat it."

In June 1983, newly promoted to captain, he joined a counterinsurgency unit at a farm called Vlakplaas near Pretoria.

> The unit consisted mainly of askaris—that is, former ANC and PAC operatives who had been "turned" and now worked for the police.... In June 1986, some seven askaris under my command infiltrated a group called the Chesterville Youth Organization, a UDF-affiliated group, in Chesterville township near Durban. The idea was that they gather information, not kill anyone. I gave them AK-47s [semiautomatic rifles] to enhance their image as freedom fighters. But something went wrong and the askaris killed [four Black men.]

De Kock recalled that sometime during 1986 or 1987 a colleague asked him to help kidnap a citizen of neighboring Swaziland. The other officer wanted to interrogate the man to learn about ANC activities in nearby portions of South Africa. "I instructed four of my members to kidnap the man.... They carried out the mission and handed him over.... I was told the man was badly hurt during the interrogation. He was then, according to Van Dyk, killed and his body blown up by Gert Schoon on the missile range adjacent to the sea."

In August 1988 an officer at the central police station in Johannesburg asked De Kock to blow up Khotso House, the headquarters of the South African Council of Churches. He wrote, "A meeting was held at the safe house in Honeydew. [General Gerrit] Erasmus later joined the meeting.... I remember being appalled when I asked Erasmus what we ought to do if challenged by other policemen who were not in the know. He said we should simply shoot them. The operation took place two or three nights later, when I went into the building with a number of my men and others."[2] He did not mention having been appalled at the broader instruction to blow up Khotso House.

Atrocities and Their Context

For 350 years prior to 1994, colonies established by people from both Britain and the Netherlands had systematically expropriated the land and other resources of South Africa's indigenous peoples. Throughout the first portion of that colonial period the region's rulers also imported enslaved captives from the East Indies and indentured people from India and elsewhere. These (quite voteless) individuals of non-European origin were forced to work in plantations and mines run by colonial corporations. The colonial processes of land expropriation, ethnic cleansing, enslavement, indenturehood, and forced labor constituted a huge, entrenched system of structural violence that killed untold millions of people and badly blighted the lives of its survivors.

In 1948, the National Party (NP) came to power through elections for the country's Whites-only parliament. ("Whites" made up less than 12 percent of the population then, as has been the case since then.) The NP represented mainly the interests of the Afrikaans-speaking White people, and fervently advocated the perpetuation of White domination of the country.[3] Over the years that followed, the NP tried to replace direct colonial control over the lives of the country's non-White citizens with a new system called "apartheid," which is Afrikaans for "segregation." The main aim of the apartheid project was to deflect the political aspirations of the Black citizens, who made up more than 75 percent of the population, away from the national capital, Pretoria, to newly created centers of Black administration inside what had previously been the country's "reservations" of tribal land.

From 1948 on, the Whites-only parliament put the legislative building blocks of the apartheid system into place. A 1950 law required all citizens to be registered from birth as belonging to one of four distinct racial groups: White, Coloured (a group composed of mixed-race individuals and ethnic Malays), Asian, or African (Black). The Group Areas Act mandated that different areas of the country be designated for the exclusive use of one racial group and required everyone to move to an area designated for "their" group. A 1959 law transformed the tribal reservations into Black Homelands ("Bantustans") and divided Blacks into a dozen separate, ethnically discrete groups. A 1970 law stripped Blacks of their South African citizenship, designating them instead as "citizens" of various Bantustans: All the Blacks still living in "White" areas—including those whose families may have lived there since time immemorial—were summarily transformed into "aliens" in those areas. A 1971 law paved the way for the Bantustans' (always quite nominal) "political independence."[4]

The longstanding system of colonial rule in South Africa and the system of apartheid that was its modern manifestation were sustained only through the government's large-scale application of direct physical and administrative violence against those 87 percent of the country's people who were not classified as White. In 1973, the UN General Assembly quite justifiably ratified a treaty that declared that "apartheid is a crime against humanity." The treaty's text also "declare[d] criminal those organizations, institutions and individuals committing the crime of apartheid."[5] However, the treaty never had any implementing mechanism. Indeed, given that China was the only one of the five veto-wielding members of the Security Council that supported it, it was clear the Security Council would not be acting to prosecute or punish the perpetrators of this particular crime against humanity.

The ANC had been founded in 1912. In 1955 it adopted the Freedom Charter, which called for the establishment of a unitary, one-person-one-vote democracy that would include all of South Africa's people in the governance of the country on an equal footing.[6] This stance was uniquely inclusive among those of the many anticolonial movements then roiling Africa. However, the government was quite unresponsive to the Charter; so in 1961, urged on by a youthful Nelson Mandela, the ANC leadership established a military wing to fight for the Charter. Headed by Mandela, this military apparatus was named Umkhonto we Sizwe ("Spear of the Nation," often called MK). The government counterattacked: Mandela and other MK leaders were arrested and sentenced to life imprisonment on Robben Island. Over the thirty-two years that followed, MK and a handful of smaller nationalist organizations maintained a low-level armed struggle that targeted mainly economic and security targets, although it also resulted in the deaths of noncombatants.

In the mid-1970s, various developments inside and outside the country (as described by Eugene de Kock) led the government to launch a Total Strategy against perceived attackers at home and abroad. At home, the political part of the Total Strategy involved accelerating the establishment of "governments" for the ten Black Homelands whose territories formed a leopard-spot pattern throughout the infertile east and north of the country. Four homelands ended up with a virtually contentless "independence" that was recognized by almost no outside powers. The others—including the Zulu homeland, KwaZulu—remained as "self-administering" areas under the central government. The security part of the Total Strategy involved stepping up the repression of nationalist sympathizers.

In 1983, after pro-ANC groups founded the UDF (as described above by Rejoice Mabudhafasi), the government's response was brutal. In 1985, the number of people reported as killed by the police exceeded 500; and that annual total never went below 100 between then and 1994.[7] The security forces also, all along, engaged in the gross mistreatment of detainees. For example, Laloo Chiba, an early member of the MK, was arrested in April 1963. He later testified that when taken in for interrogation that time he was beaten, punched, and kicked for about half an hour:

> But what was to follow was far more serious.... From behind someone threw a sack, a wet hessian sack over my body so that half my body was covered and I was partially strait-jacketed. I was then flung onto the floor. My shoes and socks were removed and I could feel electric wires being tied to my toes, to my fingers, my knuckles and so on.... Every time I resisted answering the questions, they turned on the dynamo and of course, violent electric shocks started passing through my body. They did so every time I refused to answer. All I could do was to scream out in pain.... After the electric torture was over, I was unable to walk.[8]

After the Soweto Uprising of 1976, the security forces became even more brutal. In September 1977, renowned Black Power activist Steve Biko died in police custody after sustaining brain injuries. The uproar that followed his death persuaded the government's "securocrats," as they were called, to start keeping many of their suspects *outside the formal criminal justice system;* and security force members operating in that legal "black hole" became correspondingly more lawless and savage. For example, in 1981, the police formally arrested Gcinisizwe Kondile and tortured him so badly that they believed he might die. Fearing "another Biko," the securocrats decided that Kondile "should be killed and all evidence of his existence destroyed." To bring this about, they released him from custody and immediately *rearrested him secretly*. Members of the security forces testified that Kondile was taken to "an isolated spot" and drugged with a powerful narcotic. He was then "shot and cremated over a log fire for seven hours until all traces of his body had been destroyed." One police captain testified that "[t]he burning of a body to ashes takes about seven hours, and whilst that happened we were drinking and even having a braai [barbecue] next to the fire."[9]

By 1986, the security forces were vigorously seeking out activists whom they would abduct and then hope to "turn," so they would agree to act within the nationalist movement as agents for the police. One means they frequently used to "turn" people was extreme torture, but in these cases, too, the torture often resulted in death. Lethal (though often painfully drawn-out) torture to the point of death was also used to "punish" various Black individuals.[10]

In that era, the security forces were conducting their violent operations against not only suspected members of MK but also suspected UDF grassroots organizers in the populous and often openly insurgent townships. The UDF activists who were sustaining the insurgency—under a general slogan of "making the country ungovernable"—developed their own, often violent, means of rooting out and punishing suspected police agents. In 1984 some UDF activists started using a new method to punish suspected collaborators: They would place a tire around the suspect's neck, fill it with gasoline, and then burn the individual to death. This grisly means of killing was given the name "necklacing," and for a few years it was used quite frequently around the country. The TRC later reported a high of 306 necklacings in 1986, but indicated that by 1989 the number had fallen almost to zero.

Other forces also used atrocious violence in this period. The most significant group in the Black community that collaborated with the government was the Zulu nationalist organization Inkatha; indeed, the period in which the country was traversing the last, difficult steps of the march toward democracy also saw the most extensive and violent fighting between Inkatha and the ANC. Between 1990 and 1994, bitter battles between them erupted in parts of KwaZulu-Natal and the "Reef" area around Johannesburg.

One notable episode in this conflict occurred in 1990 in KwaZulu-Natal. The communities in two lower valleys in this region had been very strongly pro-ANC. Then, as the TRC report later noted, in late March 1990 the communities were invaded by thousands of heavily armed male Inkatha supporters. "Over seven days, 200 residents in the lower valley were killed, hundreds of houses looted and burnt down and as many as 20,000 people forced to flee for their lives."[11] Altogether, between incidents of ANC–Inkatha violence and the activities of the SAP-backed "askaris" and of pro-ANC vigilantes, much of the violence of the late-apartheid era was "Black on Black"; it left a huge need for healing *within* the Black community, as well as between Whites and non-Whites.

The TRC would later estimate, very conservatively, the numbers of killings attributed to various actors during the years 1985–1994. These figures are listed in Table 3.1.

Ending the Conflict

The small minority of "Whites" in South Africa's population hung onto power for several years after colonial rule had disappeared from the rest of Africa. They managed to do so because the extractive industries and plantations that they organized squeezed such high profits out of the subjugated non-White workforce that Pretoria had no dependence at all on outside governments. It was also for many decades able to cover from its own accounts the financial cost of massively applying force to non-White communities in South Africa and several neighboring countries. By the mid-1980s, however, some voices in the country's Afrikaner elite were asking whether it was time to try to negotiate a peace with the ANC.

The Afrikaners were, in the main, descendants of fervently Protestant Dutch colonists who began settling in the country as farmers ("Boers") in the seventeenth century. The other main group of Whites—those of British origin, who spoke English, not Afrikaans—dominated the country's very profitable business and mining sectors. Long into the twentieth century many Afrikaners nursed resentful memories of their own victimization at the hands of the country's earlier, English-speaking colonial rulers.[12] But then, after

Table 3.1 TRC Report on Killings, 1985–1994

Killed by	1985	1986	1987	1988	1989	1990	1991	1992	1993	1994
South African Police	500	400	140	150	100	310	150	160	170	30
Inkatha	70	120	160	200	170	700	650	750	900	600
Sub-total: pro-government forces	*570*	*520*	*300*	*350*	*270*	*1,010*	*800*	*910*	*1,070*	*630*
ANC and pro-ANC	40	100	40	50	100	210	150	240	200	100
Total	*610*	*620*	*340*	*400*	*370*	*1,220*	*950*	*1,150*	*1,270*	*730*

Source: Data from *Truth and Reconciliation Commission of South Africa Report*, vol. 3, Chart E2.1-1, p. 9.

the strongly Afrikaner NP came to power in 1948, many good jobs opened up for Afrikaans-speakers in the country's large government administration. The major institutions influential in Afrikaner life in the twentieth century included the three branches of the Dutch Reformed Church; the NP itself, along with a number of smaller spin-offs from it; the leadership of the country's security forces (the securocrats); and teachers and others who were seen as guardians of the much-vaunted Afrikaner culture. Leaders in all those institutions were linked together through a national network called the Broederbond ("band of brothers"). In the 1930s and 1940s the Broederbond, which was strongly anti-English, maintained numerous contacts with the Nazis. After 1948 it continued in operation, acting as a shadowy force that helped the NP to consolidate power over many areas of national life.

There were always some individual Afrikaners—such as the poet Breyten Breytenbach or the sociologist Frederick van Zyl Slabbert—who questioned the Afrikaner leaders' pursuit of a tough, no-holds-barred defense of White power. Voices that criticized apartheid were more numerous among English-speaking Whites than among Afrikaners. Yet, most English-speaking Whites remained passive but grateful beneficiaries of the apartheid system. Several factors accounted for this situation, including the influence of corporate interests that reaped great benefit from the perpetuation of a disfranchised Black workforce, the desire of many English-speaking Whites to hang onto the lovely lifestyle that apartheid allowed them, and feelings of unabashed racial superiority over the country's non-White peoples.

When an effective change of political heart came in the White community, it arose *from within the Broederbond.* One former member of the organization's youth wing told me that it was in the early 1980s that he first heard Broederbond members say it might be a good idea to start talking to the ANC.[13] In 1985, Broederbond member Kobie Coetzee, the country's justice minister, used his ministerial power to arrange a first, tentative meeting with long-jailed ANC/MK leader Nelson Mandela. (Afterward, Mandela was moved to new prison quarters that isolated him from his ANC cellmates.) Coetzee held further meetings with Mandela, one in 1986 and another in 1987—years in which, on the streets, the government was battling the ANC with great violence. Then, from May 1988 on, the meetings became more frequent. They were authorized by the conservative state president (and former author of the Total Strategy) P. W. Botha. Coetzee went to those meetings along with three other government officials; Mandela was forced to participate alone.

In January 1989, Botha had a stroke. In July, still state president, he had his first personal meeting with Mandela. Mandela recalled it as short but friendly.[14] But more important, this encounter legitimized the idea of such meetings for Frederik W. de Klerk, who succeeded Botha as president in August 1989.

The ANC was also ready to talk. Late that same month, its exiled leadership issued a statement in Zimbabwe saying that if Pretoria showed itself ready to engage in genuine negotiations to end apartheid, then perhaps the time for these negotiations had arrived. It further stated that the outcome of this process should be "a new constitutional order," based on these principles:

- South Africa shall become a united, democratic and nonracial state.
- All its people shall enjoy common and equal citizenship and nationality, regardless of race, colour, sex or creed ... [and] shall have the right to participate in the government and administration of the country on the basis of a universal suffrage ... under a common voters roll.[15]

In October 1989, de Klerk freed six leading ANC political prisoners. They did not include Mandela. In mid-December he held his first meeting with the still-imprisoned Mandela. Though the two still disagreed over the issue of "group rights," each concluded that he could continue to "do business" with the other.[16]

That meeting was one of many steps de Klerk took in his early weeks in office as he started to formulate a radically new policy for his government. On February 2, 1990, he announced the new approach publicly to parliament. In that speech he committed his government to the following actions: releasing Mandela and many other ANC prisoners, unbanning all the previously banned antiapartheid organizations, repealing the Separate Amenities Act (which had kept many aspects of "petty" apartheid in place), and commissioning a proposal for "a charter of human rights with a view to a future constitution." He told the country that "[t]he time for negotiation has arrived."[17]

Nine days later, Mandela was released from jail to a tumultuous welcome from his own people and from millions of other supporters around the world. Other leaders of the at-last-legal ANC and PAC started joyously to return to their homeland after lengthy years in exile. In early May, an eleven-person ANC delegation led by Mandela started the party's first-ever formal negotiation with a government delegation. (The ANC team comprised two Whites, one Coloured person, one Indian, and seven Blacks. Two of its members were women. The government team had nine Afrikaner men.)

The ANC had long been led by the exile-based Oliver Tambo. But Tambo had suffered a bad stroke in 1989; Mandela was elected ANC president in July 1991. He and the rest of the ANC leadership faced many challenges. They had to (re)build a unified national political organization out of the different strands of the ANC that previously had to operate under very different circumstances. They had to clarify the ANC's relationships with the other groups in the Black community. And, meanwhile, the ANC leaders were plunged directly into the most momentous negotiations ever held over their country's future.

From the NP side, the political tasks were more straightforward. The NP was already an established political party. Like the ANC, it faced tough challenges from hardliners inside and outside its ranks who criticized its readiness to make concessions in the negotiations—but its leaders could nearly always rely on solid support for their new policy from the country's Anglo-White community.

The negotiations proceeded bumpily. In August 1991, the ANC agreed to suspend its armed actions (but, notably, not yet to disarm). It and the NP then called on all parties to commit to peaceful negotiations. But the violence still continued, including escalating clashes between Inkatha and the ANC and many continuing attacks by security forces people against pro-ANC activists and communities. In September 1991, the NP, the ANC, Inkatha, and various other parties concluded an agreement called the National Peace Accord. One outcome was the establishment of an independent commission to investigate the causes of the ongoing violence. Its head was Richard Goldstone—the man who would later become ICTR's first chief prosecutor. In South Africa, the main role his commission played from 1992 through 1994 was to slowly shed increasing light on the involvement of some shadowy government branches in the continuing acts of anti-ANC violence. And still, the violence continued.

In late December 1991, the parties held the first round of the Conference for a Democratic South Africa (Codesa-1). Over the months that followed, one key Codesa working group reached a crucial agreement on *the reincorporation of the Bantustans into a unitary Republic.* But when the full Codesa reconvened in May 1992 it deadlocked over another issue; and with negotiations in deadlock, violence flared again throughout the summer. In September 1992 the ANC and NP got into a new round of direct, bilateral talks: They announced an agreement to engage seriously in renewed negotiations, along with any other parties that would join them. The hard-line Afrikaner parties, Inkatha, and the "governments" of three of the homelands rejected that invitation, forming an antitalks bloc called the Concerned South Africans Group (COSAG).

During that violent summer of 1992, MK's longtime military commander, Joe Slovo, a Communist, proposed a mechanism for the transition to democracy whereby, for a fixed number of years, a coalition government would continue to run the country using the existing, Afrikaner-dominated bureaucracy, and the NP would retain a central role in the government.[18] He proposed, secondly, that during this transition the civil service (including the security forces) should be restructured in a way that would take into account existing personnel contracts, or offer early retirement buyouts, or both; and thirdly, that *a general amnesty be offered* to all those who had perpetrated politically motivated crimes, in return for their full disclosure of their activities. Historian Richard Spitz wrote, "Slovo's three offers were carefully designed to buy off three critical sectors of the government—leading NP politicians, the security forces, and ... civil servants."[19] In November 1992, the ANC leadership adopted Slovo's proposal, which thereafter formed the basis of their negotiating stance.

In December 1992 and January 1993, ANC and NP leaders made two trips to a remote game reserve to hold talks-about-talks in a place far from the public eye.[20] In March 1993, they and two dozen smaller parties convened near Johannesburg in a new gathering called the Multi-Party Negotiating Process (MPNP). Participants now included the PAC, but still not the COSAG parties. Shortly after the MPNP's second session started in April, a right-wing extremist killed the charismatic Communist Party leader Chris Hani. But even that act failed to derail the negotiations. On April 30, the MPNP's negotiators committed themselves to holding the nation's first fully democratic elections *no later than April 30, 1994,* and shortly afterward they set April 27, 1994, as the election date.[21]

From then on, the transition process gathered steam. In September 1993, the Whites-only parliament adopted laws that established a Transitional Executive Council (TEC), an Independent Electoral Commission, and other bodies essential to the transition. All parties represented in the MPNP would be represented in these bodies, provided they continued to renounce the use of violence. In November, the MPNP adopted the text of an Interim Constitution that would remain in force until the soon-to-be-elected democratic parliament—functioning as a Constitutional Assembly—could promulgate a new permanent Constitution for the country. The Interim Constitution would also guide and constrain the content of the permanent Constitution. In December, the TEC took office, at which point it started functioning *in tandem with de Klerk's cabinet*. At that point, Black South Africans were able, for the first time ever, to exercise some executive power in their own country.

Inkatha and most other COSAG parties continued to stay outside the transition; and they ramped up their violence in an attempt to block it. But in January 1994 the "government" of Ciskei broke ranks with the rest of COSAG and joined the TEC, and two months later the anti-TEC "government" in Bophuthatswana collapsed. Inkatha leader Mangosuthu Buthelezi continued to refuse to join the election. A stream of international figures (including Henry Kissinger) traveled to KwaZulu to beg him to do so. But he hung back until April 19, when a little-known Kenyan politician finally persuaded him. Four days later, an extremist Afrikaner party led by influential retired general Constand Viljoen, whose goal was the creation of an ethnic Afrikaner ministate in a portion of the country, was brought into the process by a promise that if his party should win "substantial support" in the election, then the ministate proposal would be "taken into consideration" by the incoming parliament.[22]

But there still remained much concern about the willingness of the country's security forces to undertake the extensive measures needed to ensure the safety of the elections. On April 8, the TEC issued a statement reminding all public employees, including members of the security forces, that their jobs and pension prospects would be unharmed by the coming of democracy. But another, linked issue—the possibility that security force members *might be prosecuted for rights abuses they had committed in the course of their jobs*—still loomed. On April 25, Mandela and de Klerk finally agreed to add a new "Postamble" to the Interim Constitution, spelling out that an amnesty would be available to these people.[23] The language for this was ready by April 27—as the elections entered their second day. Inserted into the Interim Constitution as Chapter 16, it was titled "National Unity and Reconciliation." It read in part:

> [T]here is a need for understanding but not for vengeance, a need for reparation but not for retaliation, a need for ubuntu but not for victimization. In order to advance such reconciliation and reconstruction, amnesty shall be granted in respect of acts, omissions and offenses associated with political objectives and committed in the course of the conflicts of the past.... With this Constitution and these commitments we, the people of South Africa, open a new chapter in the history of our country.[24]

Thus—building on the ideas proposed by Joe Slovo in 1992—was sown the seed for what would become the TRC.

The elections of April 1994 were a watershed event, celebrated around the world, that terminated both the centuries of minority rule in South Africa and the lengthy and damaging conflict waged to end it. Voters of all skin colors, ethnicities, and income levels lined up for hours, constituting by their participation in the vote a unified citizenry for the first time in the country's history. Under the rules designed by the Independent Electoral Commission (IEC), they voted for a two-house parliament. One house was a 400–member National Assembly, whose members were directly elected. The other was the 90–person Senate, composed of ten representatives elected by the legislatures of each of the country's nine new provinces. The provincial legislatures were also elected in the April poll. A proportional representation system was used throughout, in an attempt to prevent any winner from "taking all."

Prisoners and sick, disabled, and elderly voters cast their ballots on April 26. Then, on April 27, two days of general voting began. So great was the crush of voters that the army had to hurriedly print and distribute millions of additional ballots; the polling places had their opening hours extended until late each evening; and on April 28 de Klerk announced that the polls would open for a third day of voting in KwaZulu and five other "homeland" areas.[25]

On May 2, de Klerk conceded to the ANC. In his concession speech, he paid numerous compliments to Mandela. He also said with apparent pride: "After so many centuries, we will finally have a government which represents all South Africans. All South Africans are now free."[26] Four days later, the IEC announced the results. Voters had cast more than 19.5 million valid votes. The ANC won 62.6 percent of them, giving it 252 of the 400 seats in the parliament. The NP won 20.4 percent (82 seats); Inkatha won 10.5 percent (43 seats). In the provincial races, the ANC won large victories in seven of the nine new provinces, but Inkatha won in KwaZulu-Natal and the NP won in the Western Cape. Mandela would be president. He announced that the first deputy president in his Government of National Unity would be ANC national chairman Thabo Mbeki, and the second deputy would be de Klerk.[27]

On May 10, Mandela delivered his inaugural address to the new democratic parliament. It was a potent call for healing and reconciliation:

> We deeply appreciate the role that the masses of our people and their political mass democratic, religious, women, youth, business, traditional and other leaders have played to bring about this conclusion. Not least among them is my Second Deputy President, the Honourable F.W. de Klerk. We would also like to pay tribute to our security forces, in all their ranks, for the distinguished role they have played in securing our first democratic elections and the transition to democracy, from bloodthirsty forces which still refuse to see the light. The time for the healing of the wounds has come. The moment to bridge the chasms that divide us has come. The time to build is upon us.

Dealing with the Perpetrators of Atrocities

The perpetrators and organizers of most of the atrocious violence in the years before 1994 had been members of the South Africa Defense Force and the SAP; but substantial atrocities had also been committed by members of Inkatha, the MK/ANC, and other Black organizations. In May 1994, Mandela appointed Joe Modise, a veteran ANC and MK leader, as the country's first-ever Black minister of defense. His job was to integrate the existing South Africa Defense Force, MK, the defense forces of five homelands (including KwaZulu), and the PAC's armed force, APLA, into a single new military structure, the South African National Defense Force (SANDF). Planning for the SANDF had been under way for a while. It came into existence at midnight on April 26, 1994.

Some 136,000 individuals from the former fighting forces had their names placed on the SANDF's roster, coming from the following formations: former SADF, 90,000; homelands defense forces, 11,039; MK, 28,888; and APLA, 6,000.[28] The SANDF's commanders had to integrate into the new force fighters who had previously operated according to very different doctrines—and in many cases, against units and individuals who were now their comrades-in-arms! They had to develop new priorities for the SANDF now that the old army's mission, fighting the insurgency, was no longer applicable. They also sought to downsize the total force, to free up resources for the huge reconstruction tasks that awaited the new government. The campaign to build the new, racially integrated army was generally successful.[29] But this success—like that of the project to hold democratic elections—was possible only because the members of the apartheid-era armed forces (and police) all understood clearly that *amnesties would be available* to those who had committed politically motivated crimes in the struggle to uphold (or oppose) apartheid.

The way the applications for those amnesties ended up being processed was in combination with another transition-related proposal that ANC leaders had been considering for some time: one that would establish a "truth commission" to uncover and put on the public record the truth about the violence of the apartheid years. This idea had been advocated in South Africa primarily by Alex Boraine, an English-speaking White man who had previously been (among other things) a Methodist minister and a member of the Whites-only parliament. In the early 1990s, Boraine and his colleagues at a prodemocracy think tank became intrigued with the role that truth commissions had played in Latin America in buttressing the implantation of democracy in countries reeling from recent dictatorships.

The idea of an investigatory commission of some sort was already familiar to the NP, which over the years had formed a number of (often fairly toothless) judicial commissions to investigate claims of security force abuse. It was also familiar to the ANC, whose National Executive Committee had three times formed internal commissions to investigate allegations of the abuse of recruits in MK training camps.[30] In 1993 the third of these enquiries reported back to the ANC leaders that gross rights violations *had* taken place in some of the camps. The ANC leaders accepted those findings. But in an August 1993 statement they argued that those abuses had been committed in the context of the ANC's fight against the much broader rights violations committed by the government; and they called on the government to establish a nationwide "Commission of Inquiry or Truth Commission into all violations of human rights since 1948."[31]

In July 1995, these two ANC projects—its promise of an amnesty to apartheid's rights abusers and its pursuit of a nationwide truth commission—came together in new legislation called the Promotion of National Unity and Reconciliation Act, 1995. The Act established a Truth and Reconciliation Commission to carry out the following tasks:

(a) establishing as complete a picture as possible of the causes, nature and extent of the gross violations of human rights ... committed during the period from 1 March 1960 to the cutoff date. ...
(b) facilitating the granting of amnesty to persons who make full disclosure of all the relevant facts relating to acts associated with a political objective. ...
(c) establishing and making known the fate or whereabouts of victims and restoring the human and civil dignity of such victims.
(d) compiling a report.[32]

In November 1995, Mandela named seventeen commissioners for the new body. Anglican Archbishop Desmond Tutu would be the chair. The vice chair was Alex Boraine. Of the other commissioners, seven were women and eight were men. Tutu and six other commissioners were Black Africans; Boraine and five others were Whites; two were Coloured, and two were Indians. Four were Protestant ministers, five were lawyers, and three or more were health professionals.

The TRC's mandate was to investigate "gross human rights abuses," which were defined as acts of gross physical or mental abuse directed *against persons*. It notably did not include violations of social and economic rights as defined in, for example, the UN's Covenant on Social and Economic Rights. Thus, all the hardships suffered by non-White communities in the course of, for example, the massive relocations (ethnic cleansing) undertaken by the apartheid regime, or through the application of its extremely abusive labor laws, fell outside the TRC's mandate. Some of the excluded issues, such as violations of land rights, were supposed to be addressed through other government initiatives. Others remained unaddressed.

The focus on gross human rights violations (as defined in the law) may have left many grievances from the apartheid era unaddressed. This focus did, however, provide a single, recognizable, and politically neutral benchmark for the TRC as it investigated acts committed by all parties. This "evenhanded" aspect of the TRC's work drew the frequent ire of members of the ANC and other antiapartheid groups, who claimed loudly that at least their struggle—unlike that pursued by the defenders of apartheid—had been waged *for a just cause*. But the TRC tried hard to stick to the principle of using in its work only politically neutral criteria well grounded in international humanitarian law. The commissioners hoped the TRC could thereby strengthen respect for human rights and humanitarian law norms in postapartheid South Africa. The events of the years that followed indicated the degree to which they succeeded.

How the TRC Worked

Rapid Change and the TRC

The TRC was established in 1995 as one part of a much broader effort by the ANC's leaders to pull the country free from the legacies of its past. The first years after the 1994 elections were busy, truly transformative ones for South Africans and their leaders. Hundreds of new parliamentarians had to establish ways of working together in the country's first democratic parliament. (Its early proceedings were conducted in a broad bouquet of the country's eleven now-official languages, before members of parliament settled down to communicating with each other mainly in English.) Civil servants in all the national ministries—nearly all of whom were holdovers from the past—had to redesign their programs completely and start delivering services to all the country's people *on an equal basis*. In the country's businesses, schools, media, churches, and other institutions, people of all races were dealing with the new facts of political equality. And the newly enfranchised non-Whites were coming to terms with the fact that civil and political equality made little immediate difference to a socioeconomic situation still marked by glaring interracial disparities and thus—for many or most Black South Africans—by a continuation of the grinding poverty that their families had known for several generations.

At the same time, previous "national" symbols—the national anthem, the flag, even the famed Springboks rugby team—were being redrawn or recontextualized in a way that would more accurately represent the whole new nation. The new flag combined the red, white, and blue of its predecessor with the ANC's green, gold, and black. The new national anthem combined verses from the ANC anthem *Nkosi sikelel' iAfrika* ("God Bless Africa") with verses from the White state's anthem, *Die Stem* ("The Call"). The new coinage had the name of the country in a different official language on coins of each denomination. New names were chosen for most of the country's nine new provinces, including one—"Gauteng"—that was a completely new word, designed to sound compatible with local languages like Zulu and Afrikaans. As for the rugby team, which had been a potent symbol of group belonging for White South Africans for decades: One day in mid-1995, at the beginning of its all-important World Cup final against New Zealand, President Mandela transformed the whole "meaning" the team had in national discourse by walking onto the field with the team members, wearing a Springboks shirt and cap. The crowd, 95 percent of whom were White, went wild, shouting "Nelson! Nelson!" Then, buoyed by a national outpouring of enthusiasm, the team went on to crush the Kiwis.[33]

The fact that the Rugby World Cup was being played in South Africa at all was indicative of another big change South Africans were then undergoing: the reopening of links with the outside world that had been largely severed during the lengthy international boycott of the apartheid order. This opening was a breath of fresh air for South Africans in many ways. But at the economic level, the protectionism with which the apartheid regime had previously approached the economy now quickly gave way to the neoliberal demands of IMF-imposed "structural adjustment"—this, at a time when the price of the country's main export commodity, gold, was sinking fast.

It was in that broad context of rapid national reconfiguration that, between 1995 and 1998, the TRC carried out most of its work. It did so using procedures very different from those of a court of law. One early indicator of this different approach: The very first activity the commissioners embarked upon—presumably, in deference to Tutu—was to go on a spiritual retreat.[34]

The TRC had three main committees: the Human Rights Violations Committee (HRVC), the Reparation and Rehabilitation Committee, and the Amnesty Committee. The first two operated completely as subdivisions of the TRC, but the Amnesty Committee

(AC) had a somewhat separate constitution: Of its five members—all lawyers—three, including the chair and vice chair, were not TRC commissioners.[35] The term of the TRC was originally defined as eighteen months, but parliament later gave it until October 31, 1998, to complete its task.

In the TRC's early months the most publicly prominent of its committees was the HRVC. The HRVC placed its main focus on the victims/survivors of rights abuses. It rapidly developed a standard "victim statement" form and started training "statement takers" who fanned out around the country, gathering statements from members of the public who claimed to have been the victim of a gross human rights violation between March 1, 1960, and May 10, 1994. Meanwhile, the HRVC started planning the first of the public hearings that were designed to provide a sympathetic forum in which a small subset (chosen by the HRVC) of those who had presented victim statements could deliver public accounts of their sufferings. These hearings were designed to be educational, performative enactments of a broad, intergroup healing ritual rather than, as a criminal trial is, to "prove" or "test" the truth of the testimony given. Members of the TRC's Investigative Unit would work elsewhere, less publicly, to verify the claims made in the victim statements.

The Reparations and Rehabilitation Committee had two main tasks. One was to suggest principles according to which, in line with a provision in the legislation, the government might provide reparations to the victims. The TRC had almost no power and no budget to make reparations on its own account; all it could do was authorize tiny "emergency" payments to some victims. But it could, and did, formulate a recommendation for the president on broader aspects of the reparation issue. The committee's other task was to provide psychosocial support for the victims participating in the public hearings.

These two committees had gotten their work well under way by the middle of 1996; but the Amnesty Committee's work was badly delayed by legal challenges. Under the terms of the Promotion of National Unity and Reconciliation Act, any person who wanted to apply for amnesty, "in respect of any act, omission, or offense ... associated with a political objective," needed to submit his or her application to this committee. The committee would firstly determine whether the action in question had been sufficiently "political" (if not, it was summarily rejected), and also whether it had been a less than "gross" violation, in which case the committee could grant amnesty without holding a hearing. But if the action did appear to have been political, and to have involved one or more gross violations, then the committee would schedule a public, judicial-style hearing in which all participants would receive due-process protections.

It is often forgotten in the West that large numbers of antiapartheid activists benefited from the TRC's amnesties. Numerous amnesty applications came from people who had been convicted and imprisoned by the old regime. Those individuals were understandably eager to regain their freedom if they were still in jail and, in any case, to have their records expunged of any reference to acts of violence committed in the course of the struggle. As for the people who had committed abuses on behalf of the old regime, they were expected to apply for amnesty motivated largely by a now-lively fear of being prosecuted in the criminal courts. But in October 1996 the Durban Supreme Court *acquitted* former Defense Minister Magnus Malan and a number of other formerly high-ranking individuals on charges that they bore responsibility for a massacre that had killed thirteen UDF supporters near Durban in 1987. That acquittal, the broad effort undertaken by security personnel to destroy the records of their earlier misdeeds, and the many legal challenges the Amnesty Committee faced from all sides slowed the committee's work considerably.

The Human Rights Violations Committee

The most visible part of the TRC's early work was the series of open hearings held by the HRVC—primarily those at which individual victims like Nomonde Calata came and publicly told their stories of victimization, but also those in which representatives of major national institutions explained the role they had played during the apartheid era. Archbishop Tutu signaled the importance he gave to the HRVC's work by chairing this committee himself. He also, along with fellow minister Alex Boraine, had a large say in designing its proceedings.

The TRC decided from the get-go to publicize the HRVC's hearings as widely as possible. It established a Media and Communications Department that worked with media representatives to ensure broad dissemination of the hearings throughout the nation and the world. Having the ever-newsworthy Tutu chairing many of the hearings helped win wide attention for them. Given existing media consumption patterns in the country, the Media Department focused initially on gaining good radio coverage. The government-backed South African Broadcasting Corporation (SABC) already provided radio broadcasts in six or more local languages. It assigned radio journalists to provide live coverage of the hearings on one channel as well as weekly "wrap up" programs in all its broadcasting languages. The TRC also allowed full television coverage of the hearings: SABC-TV broadcast these images through frequent nationwide news bulletins, as well as through a weekly wrap up called *TRC Special Report*. At least nine South African newspapers—most of them White-owned—appointed full-time "TRC correspondents," and correspondents from the foreign media flocked to the hearings.[36]

In addition to the hearings at which individual victims spoke, the HRVC invited representatives of key national institutions to take part in public deliberations in connection with its "institutional" investigations, which were grouped into a number of different themes. There was an "armed forces and police" group, a "business and labor" group, and investigations (and hearings) in the areas of youth, health, law, the media, political parties, and religion. The aim in all these institutional investigations was, as the TRC's Final Report put it, "to understand how, over the years, people who considered themselves ordinary, decent and God-fearing found themselves turning a blind eye to a system which impoverished, oppressed and violated the lives and very existence of so many of their fellow citizens."[37] This didactic purpose paralleled almost exactly that pursued by the prosecutors at Nuremberg and, more recently, at ICTR, though in the TRC's case the strategy was pursued more even-handedly than in those two court projects since the TRC was looking at rights abuses committed by *all* sides in the earlier conflict, not just one.

While some citizens and organizations hurried to present their statements to the Commission, others did not—and for a range of reasons. Former UDF activist Rejoice Mabudhafasi, for example, told me that she had simply been "too busy with my work as a parliamentarian" in the mid-1990s to think of acquiring and filling out a TRC victim statement. Others refrained from contacting the TRC because perhaps they had something to hide; but in these cases, the TRC did have the power to subpoena "witnesses." It twice subpoenaed former President P. W. Botha to come and answer questions about his responsibility for the worst excesses committed during his presidency. Botha refused to comply with the subpoenas, and was prosecuted for his noncompliance.[38]

Some of the most notable moments of the TRC's work occurred during the HRVC's public interactions with willing participants in its process such as Nomonde Calata; and others, during interactions with more reluctant participants such as Nelson Mandela's wife, the ANC parliamentarian Winnie Madikizela-Mandela. (She was called to discuss murders committed by leaders of a soccer club that operated under her patronage while Nelson Mandela was in jail. The HRVC had heard much evidence about the club's activities that undermined her claims of ignorance about the events. Madikizela-Mandela put in a reluctant appearance near the end of that HRVC hearing, and Tutu pled with her at least to apologize to the relatives of the victims. All she could manage to say was "It is true: things went horribly wrong and we were aware that there were factors that led to that. For that I am deeply sorry.")[39]

Day after day between April 1996 and June 1997, the parade of witnesses continued, in the church halls and other public places around the country that were quickly transformed into HRVC hearing rooms. There were women who had lost their husbands, brothers, or sons. There were survivors of torture, male and female. There were Black men who had been tortured by the regime, then "turned" by the police and forced to become torturers themselves. There were people who had been tortured in ANC training camps abroad. There were White people disfigured by bombs delivered by the liberation forces, and White people disfigured by bombs delivered by the regime. There were prayers and wailing and crying and hymn singing. There were people whose emotions were on the surface and freely shared, and people who seemed unable to show any emotion at all. And much of it was broadcast nationwide.

Antjie Krog was a distinguished Afrikaner poet and percipient observer who covered the hearings for the SABC. For her, these interactions were emotionally searing and deeply informative. "What gradually becomes clear," she wrote,

> is that the apartheid system worked like a finely woven net—starting with the Broederbond, who appointed leaders. In turn these leaders appointed ministers, judges, generals. Security forces, courts, administrations, were tangled in. Through Parliament, legislation was launched that would keep the brutal enforcement of apartheid out of sight....

Now that people are finally able to tell their stories, the lid of the Pandora's box is lifted; for the first time, these individual truths sound unhindered in the ears of all South Africans.[40]

She noted, however, that

[t]he black people in the audience are seldom upset. They have known the truth for years. The whites are often disconcerted: they didn't realize the magnitude of the outrage, the "depth of depravity," as Tutu calls it. ...

"For me, justice lies in the fact that everything is being laid out on the same table," says my [Black] colleague Mondli. "The truth that rules our fears, our deeds, and our dreams is coming to light. From now on, you don't only see a smiling [B]lack man in front of you, but you also know what I carry inside of me. I've always known it—now you also know."[41]

Only around 1,000 of the people who submitted victim statements got the chance to appear at public hearings. But a total of 21,297 victim statements were submitted to the HRVC in all.[42] HRVC staff members used them as raw material for the final report that the TRC was due to submit before the end of October 1998.

The 1988 Report

Five volumes of the *Truth and Reconciliation Commission of South Africa Report* (hereafter referred to as "the Report") were written, printed, and ready to be delivered to President Mandela before the end-of-October deadline defined by parliament. All the commissioners except one concurred on the content of these volumes; the dissenter was Wynand Malan, an Afrikaner who had formerly been an MP for the NP. Volumes 2, 3, and 4 of the Report contained much of its "meat." Largely the product of the HRVC's labors, they presented a broad and detailed picture of the rights violations of the apartheid era.

In Volume Two, one lengthy chapter covered violations committed by the state outside South Africa over the period 1960–1990. These included atrocities the state had committed during a lengthy counterinsurgency campaign in Namibia and during large-scale armed incursions into Angola and Mozambique, as well as others it committed in Zambia, Rhodesia/Zimbabwe, Lesotho, the Seychelles, and elsewhere. Three other chapters covered violations committed before 1990 by the state *inside* South Africa, by the liberation movements, and by the central government and its proxy forces inside the "Bantu Homelands." One chapter carried reports of the "special" inquiries the Investigations Unit had conducted into such issues as the suspicious October 1986 death in an airplane accident of Mozambican president Samora Machel (no definitive finding there), the state's activities in chemical and biological warfare, secret state funding of propaganda and other activities, the activities of Mrs. Madikizela-Mandela's soccer club, and the results of the fifty-four exhumations carried out by the TRC. (Nearly all the bodies exhumed were of ANC/MK activists who had been secretly murdered by the security forces.) The volume's seventh and last chapter surveyed political violence committed during the transitional period, 1990–1994.

Volume Three covered the violations committed by the various parties inside the country in much greater detail, grouping these by region. Volume Four summarized the results of the HRVC's "institutional and special hearings."

Volumes One and Five summarized the work of the whole TRC. In Volume Five, the crucial Chapter 6 presented the TRC's "Findings and Conclusions." This chapter included detailed findings relating to the responsibilities of two individuals (P. W. Botha and F. W. de Klerk) and a number of key institutions for having committed, organized, ordered, or condoned large numbers of gross rights violations. The institutions cited included the apartheid state, Inkatha, the KwaZulu police, all the main liberation movements, and many parts of apartheid-era civil society. Regarding the state, it found that

> [t]he predominant portion of gross violations of human rights was committed by the Former State through its security and law enforcement agencies.
>
> Moreover, the South African State in the period from the late 1970s to the early 1990s became involved in activities of a criminal nature when, amongst other things, it knowingly planned, undertook, condoned and covered up the commission of unlawful acts, including the extrajudicial killings of political opponents and others, inside and outside South Africa.
>
> In pursuit of these unlawful activities, the State acted in collusion with certain other political groupings, most notably the Inkatha Freedom party (IFP).[43]

Regarding the ANC, the TRC found that during the armed struggle many operations of the ANC-commanded MK "resulted in civilian casualties.... [T]he people who were killed or injured by such explosions are all victims of gross violations of human rights perpetrated by the ANC. While it is accepted that targeting civilians was not ANC policy, MK operations nonetheless ended up killing fewer security force members than civilians." The TRC also found that ANC units in exile, "and particularly its military structures responsible for the treatment and welfare of those in its camps, were guilty of gross violations of human rights in certain circumstances and against two categories of individuals, namely suspected 'enemy agents' and mutineers." Finally, regarding the violence of the 1990–1994 period, it found that, although that violence was neither initiated by nor in the interests of the ANC, "the ANC was responsible for ... killings, assaults and attacks on political opponents ... [and] contributing to a spiral of violence in the country."[44] Volume Five also contained Commissioner Malan's twenty-page "Minority Report" and a rebuttal to it by the TRC majority, as well as an intriguing chapter in which the TRC presented its claims that its hearings had promoted some significant national reconciliation.

Even after the Report had been printed, there continued to be doubts as to whether it could be made public. De Klerk and the ANC both filed last-minute lawsuits to try to prevent publication. In the de Klerk case, his lawyers and the TRC reached agreement on October 28 that the Report would contain no findings about him until after a full-court consideration of his case the following spring. (The TRC then replaced the two pages of Volume Five dealing with de Klerk with new pages with the relevant portions blacked out—an eerie echo of censorship under apartheid.)

In the case brought by the ANC, on October 29—while dignitaries were already gathering for the ceremony in Pretoria in which the Report would be handed to Mandela—the judge finally ruled in favor of the Commission.[45] But a legacy of distrust between the Commission and many ANC cadres (though not Mandela himself) had been building for a while, due to the TRC's insistence on "even-handedness" in its work. That distrust was exacerbated by the row over the findings presented in the 1998 Report, and it continued long after October 1998.

The Reparation and Rehabilitation Committee

In comparison with the work of the HRVC, that of the Reparation and Rehabilitation (R&R) Committee was carried out far from the limelight and consumed relatively few TRC resources. When the HRVC's activities got off the ground, the R&R Committee started to provide some basic emotional and psychosocial support to the HRVC's statement takers and those victims who appeared in its hearings. Meanwhile, the R&R Committee's ten members started planning a long-term policy to provide reparations to the victims.

It came up with following five-part proposal, as described in the TRC's 1998 Report:

1. Urgent interim reparation would be provided to victims in "urgent need." The TRC recommended that only limited resources be devoted to this.
2. Individual Reparation Grants would then provide more carefully calibrated cash payments to victims over a six-year period.
3. Symbolic reparation and legal and administrative measures could include steps like the expedited provision of death certificates to families, the declaration of a national day of mourning and remembrance, and the erection of memorials and museums.
4. Community rehabilitation programmes would include strengthening the provision of community-based rehabilitation services around the country.
5. Institutional reform would include measures (not further defined) designed to "prevent the recurrence of human rights abuses."[46]

While some action was eventually taken in line with all these types of reparation, it was the second one that—to the surprise of some—proved the most controversial. In this category, the R&R Committee proposed cash payments to victims based on a benchmark related to the median annual household income. The amount given would vary according to how many dependents the victim had and whether she or he lived in an urban or rural community, and payments would continue for six years. The annual grants would be as follows: for a rural dweller, from 18,330 Rand (about $2,300) for a single person to R23,023 for someone heading a nine-member household; and for an urban dweller, from R17,029 (single person) to R22,464 (nine in household). As calculated in the Report, if the roughly 22,000 victims who had submitted statements all received such reparations the cost would be R477.4 million annually, for a total of R2,864.4 million

($358 million) over six years. It recommended that these grants be funded by the government and administered by an existing body, the President's Fund.[47]

In the minds of many people on and beyond the Truth and Reconciliation Commission, these financial reparations were extremely important. The amnesties being provided to perpetrators by the TRC's Amnesty Committee were, it was argued, removing from the victims not only the satisfaction of seeing their tormenters prosecuted in a criminal court but also the possibility of suing them for damages in a civil court. Therefore, the provision of financial reparations to the victim-deponents was an essential complement to the provision of amnesties to perpetrators. Other South Africans, including many in the liberation movements, contested this on two counts. On the one hand, they argued that no one in the liberation movements had joined the antiapartheid struggle for monetary purposes. And, on the other, they noted that there were numerous victims of apartheid, including people who had been victims of gross rights abuses, who had *not*, for whatever reason, submitted victim statements to the TRC; therefore, to give cash grants to individuals based solely on whether they had submitted statements to the HRVC would be an unreasonable form of preferment.

In many respects, this dispute over giving cash grants to individual victims assumed the form of a contest between people (mainly White South Africans) who held a generally individualistic view of the human condition and those (predominantly non-White South Africans) who held a more communitarian view. That was certainly the impression I received during my discussions on this issue in South Africa. "We all suffered under apartheid, all non-Whites without exception," ANC Minister Rejoice Mabudhafasi told me firmly. "There is no reason whatsoever to pick out 20,000 people and give them cash grants. What we are committed to doing in the government is to lift up the condition of all the country's people, and particularly the most disadvantaged." Her views on this matter were widely shared within the ANC and among much of the Black public. (A chart that the R&R Committee itself presented indicated that only around 20 percent of the TRC's victim-deponents specifically requested monetary compensation for their suffering.)[48]

The TRC had the power to make "recommendations" to the government regarding a reparations policy; but as noted earlier it had almost no powers or budget to provide reparations on its own account. As for the government, despite the pleas of Tutu and other TRC commissioners as well as other individuals, for twenty-seven months after the 1998 Report was submitted it did nothing to fund the reparations program that the TRC had proposed. In the end, parliament appropriated sufficient funds to provide a one-time payment of R30,000 to each victim. By the end of 2004, more than 16,000 victims had received their payments, but a further 1,800 designated victims reportedly had not yet claimed theirs.[49]

The Amnesty Committee

As noted previously, the Amnesty Committee was made up completely of lawyers. Neither its chair, Judge Hassen Mall, nor its vice chair, Judge Andrew Wilson, were commissioners of the TRC. The work of this committee was always very controversial; indeed, almost immediately after the TRC was established, the AC's work became the subject of legal challenge. One of the first cases brought against it was filed jointly by the Azapo People's Organization and the families of Steve Biko along with those of four other prominent antiapartheid figures murdered by the security forces. The plaintiffs applied to the country's new Constitutional Court to have the TRC's amnesty-granting power declared unconstitutional. In July 1996, the Court ruled that since the Interim Constitution of April 1994 had explicitly allowed the granting of amnesties in cases like these, such amnesties were *not* unconstitutional.

Persons seeking amnesty were instructed to submit their applications to the Amnesty Committee; and by the September 1997 cutoff date, 7,127 applications had been received. By June 1998, 4,303 of these applications had been rejected—most of them because the crime in question had not been political in nature.[50] When the 1998 Report went to press, it listed the names of 150 people who had been granted amnesty; more than 2,500 applications were still outstanding. Of the amnesties granted, only 57 were judged to have concerned rights violations categorized as "gross." Those had required a public hearing. The rest, concerning lesser matters, had been decided by the AC in chambers.[51]

In designing its hearings, the AC decided to keep its options "flexible." In one of its reports, it wrote: "The guiding principle followed was to allow every interested party the fullest possible opportunity to participate in the proceedings.... Every party that participated in the hearings had the right to legal representation, and even those who were indigent were always afforded some form of legal representation."[52]

The AC's public hearings were, like the HRVC hearings, widely broadcast on both radio and television. Also like the HRVC hearings, many were conducted in halls decorated with big banners reading "Truth, the road to reconciliation." But in other respects, they were very different. They were much more lawyerly—due to the professional dispositions of the people responsible for conducting them and because AC members judged rightly that the results they reached were always likely to be challenged in the courts, so they sought to defend themselves from anything those courts would consider to be procedural flaws. As a result there were no hymn singing or prayers; no presiding archbishop empathizing with the witnesses or breaking into song at emotional moments; no Kleenex-armed "comforters" charged with holding the hands of the main actors. Instead, at the AC, just about everyone had legal representation; there were cross-examinations and lots of fine-grained legal argumentation. These hearings were thus extremely drawn-out and ended up consuming a large proportion of the TRC's resources. For example, the AC's hearings and other activities consumed 44,456 hours of interpreters' time compared to the 10,856 hours taken up by the HRVC's work.[53]

The AC hearings had many moments of drama. The veteran anti-apartheid lawyer George Bizos put in some noteworthy appearances on behalf of the Biko and Mxenghe families, who were challenging the applications submitted by their loved ones' killers. One of the most dramatic interactions at an AC hearing (or, indeed, any TRC hearing) occurred in July 1997, when SAP officer Jeffrey Benzien was applying for amnesty for some tortures (and one killing) he had perpetrated against pro-ANC activists in Cape Town, in the late 1980s. At the time he appeared, Benzien *was still an officer in the SAP.* One of the individuals who contested his application was a survivor of his earlier actions as a torturer: pro-ANC activist Tony Yengeni, now an African National Congress MP and chair of parliament's Joint Standing Committee for Defense.

Benzien had admitted to having used the notorious "wet bag" method of torture on Yengeni. In the transcript of the hearing, we see Yengeni reproaching Benzien, saying: "What kind of man … uses a method like this one of the wet bag, to people, to other human beings, repeatedly and listening to those moans and cries and groans and taking each of those people very near to their deaths, what kind of man are you?" Later, he persuaded Benzien to give a detailed description of the method. The transcript continues:

> Mr. Benzien: [I]t was a cloth bag that would be submerged in water to get it completely wet. And then the way I applied it, was I get the person to lie down on the ground on his stomach normally on a mat or something similar with that person's hands handcuffed behind his back. Then I would take up a position in the small of the person's back, put my feet through between his arms to maintain my balance and then pull the bag over the person's head and twist it closed around the neck in that way, cutting off the air supply to the person.

With the permission of the increasingly fascinated bench, Yengeni then persuaded Benzien to give an in-court reenactment of the method, using a volunteer from among the spectators and a pillow case as the wet bag. As Benzien did this—in a televised hearing—Yengeni and the members of the bench continued to question him:

> Mr. Yengeni: [A]t what point do you release the bag to give the person who is tortured, more air? Is there something, are you counting time or is there something that you feel and then you release the bag? What happens, what makes you to release the bag?
> Chairperson: I imagine that when you are in that position, you are asking questions? ...
> Mr. Yengeni: The question, Mr. Benzien, is, myself and others if we are under that kind of wet bag and we are being choked by that bag, how do we react at that point? How do we react, what is our physical reaction?
> Chairperson: What happens to the person [when] he is being choked? Can you describe? ...
> Mr. Benzien: There would be movement, there would be head movement, distress, all the time there would be questions being asked do you want to speak or what have you and as soon as an indication was given that this person wanted to speak, the air would be allowed back to his person to say what he wanted to say.
> Mr. Yengeni: Would the person groan, moan, cry, scream? What would the person do?
> Mr. Benzien: Yes, the person would moan, cry, although muffled, yes, it does happen.
> Mr. Yengeni: And you did this to each and every one of us?
> Mr. Benzien: To the majority of you, yes.[54]

By June 1998, as noted above, only 4,303 of the 7,000–plus amnesty applications had been finalized—and even that record was achieved only because the number of AC members had been increased from five to nineteen. But more than 2,500 cases remained outstanding; and these included a large proportion of cases more difficult than those already decided. The TRC therefore requested, and won, an extension of its mandate. The "final final" deadline for the completion of all the Commission's work, including that of the AC, was set as March 2003. (Throughout those additional years, the TRC's other committees disbanded almost completely.)

The final disposition of the amnesty applications is shown in Table 3.2.

The police torturer Eugene de Kock received amnesty for most but not all of his activities. Jeffrey Benzien received amnesty in the case of Tony Yengeni and six others tortured at around that time, and for the killing of antiapartheid activist Ashley Kriel. His application in another torture case was later refused.

The TRC Completes Its Work

In August 2002, the TRC published the final two volumes of its Report. Volume Six was, in many respects, an updating of Volumes One and Five. It carried short updates from the HRVC and the still-frustrated R&R Committee, a much fuller report from the AC, and updated sets of "Findings" and "Recommendations." The Findings section reexamined but essentially reconfirmed the major findings presented in the 1998 Report.

Table 3.2 Final Disposition of Amnesty Applications in South Africa, 2003

Amnesty granted (completely)	1,167
Amnesty granted for certain incidents but refused for others	139
Amnesty granted for certain incidents, application withdrawn for others	6
Amnesty refused after hearing	362
Amnesty refused administratively (i.e., without a hearing)	5,143
Application for amnesty withdrawn	258
Duplicate applications	40
Amnesty not applicable, applicant acquitted	1
TOTAL	7,116

Source: Data from Martin Coetzee, "An overview of the TRC amnesty process," in Charles Villa-Vilencio and Erik Doxtader, eds., *The Provocations of Amnesty: Memory, Justice, and Impunity* (Trenton, NJ/Asamara, Eritrea: Africa World Press, 2003), p. 193.

Volume Seven, by contrast, was something completely new. Nearly all of its 900-plus pages presented an alphabetical listing of all the victims that the HRVC process had identified, with a short description of how each had had her or his rights grossly violated. "This volume is a tribute to the victims of Apartheid and a living monument to those who sacrificed so much in order that we could all enjoy the fruits of democracy," the Foreword said. It acknowledged the fact that many victims "were not able to access the Commission," and also that "[t]here were other reasons why many people did not come forward to tell their stories.... [A]s a consequence, many cases that may be expected to appear here do not, including those of a number of well-known victims. Despite their exclusion from these summaries, we recognize that their stories too form part of this period of the history of South Africa."[55]

Throughout the six years of the TRC's operations, every single aspect of its work came under intense scrutiny and drew considerable and sustained criticism from one or more of the major political elements inside the country. Many Afrikaners complained that the HRVC hearings had turned into witch hunts against the whole of their community. Many non-White South Africans (and some Whites) continued to find it hard to reconcile themselves to the amnesties. The R&R Committee's work was intensely controversial, as noted above. Several of those who opposed the TRC's work had taken steps to try to block it. But perhaps the most serious campaign against the TRC was one in 1997 when Commissioner Dumisa Ntsebeza, a lawyer who was also head of the Commission's Investigative Unit, was accused of having driven the getaway car for a particularly nasty massacre in 1993. Ntsebeza's name was eventually cleared, and the accusation was shown to be part of an elaborate smear campaign. That discovery occurred in November 1997; but for the six months prior to it, the accusation hung over the Investigative Unit and the entire TRC, crippling many aspects of the unit's work and opening deep cleavages of interracial distrust even among the TRC commissioners themselves.[56]

The work of the TRC proved inspirational or otherwise helpful to many South Africans, but for others it proved unsatisfactory to a greater or lesser degree. Even Archbishop Tutu—whose general optimism about the prospects for reconciliation had helped keep the TRC's commissioners and staff going through some tough times—ended up expressing some disappointment in the Foreword he wrote to Volume Six:

I regret that at the time of writing we owe so much by way of reparations to those who have been declared victims.... I appeal to the Government that we meet this solemn obligation and responsibility. ...

It is something of a pity that, by and large, the white community failed to take advantage of the Truth and Reconciliation process. They were badly let down by their leadership.... Apart from the hurt that it causes to those who suffered, the denial by so many white South Africans even that they benefited from apartheid is a crippling, self-inflicted blow to their capacity to enjoy and appropriate the fruits of change.

But he ended the Foreword in an upbeat and characteristically theological way:

When we look around us at some of the conflict areas of the world, it becomes increasingly clear that there is not much of a future for them without forgiveness, without reconciliation. God has blessed us richly so that we might be a blessing to others. Quite improbably, we as South Africans have become a beacon of hope to others locked in deadly conflict that peace, that a just resolution, is possible. If it could happen in South Africa, then it can certainly happen anywhere else. Such is the exquisite divine sense of humour.[57]

South Africans Look Back at the TRC

Stakeholder Views

Thulani Mabaso is a very special tour guide. On Robben Island, the wind-swept piece of rock off the coast of Cape Town where Nelson Mandela and his colleagues were imprisoned for decades, Mabaso today leads the part of the tour that takes you right into the cellblocks. He talks with intimate knowledge and controlled passion about the life the prisoners lived there. He *was* one of the prisoners; and every day now he revisits the realities of those years for the benefit of well-paying visitors.

Mandela had been in the most secure part of the encampment: a prison within the prison where two dozen top leaders were kept in tiny individual cells. Mabaso was held in one of the more crowded zones: a large room, now bare, in which seventy men once slept on iron bunk beds and tried to maintain their sense of humanity amid the ever-present brutality of the prison.

Mabaso is a big man with a gruff laugh. He describes himself as "[j]ust a Zulu boy who was a saboteur in the MK." He was arrested after an attack against an electric substation that wounded fifty-four people but killed no one. He talks about three particular security officers who mistreated him badly during his interrogations; and how his father visited him in jail, and disturbed by the signs of torture, later remonstrated with the officers. One of the officers then shot his father.

"Those three went to the TRC—they went to Bishop Tutu—and they got amnesty," Mabaso says. "Now, they are all big businessmen. But my father is still in a wheelchair and blind from the way they treated him."

He judges that, all in all, the country's present situation is better than the old days. He points out, though, that at least when he was in jail the Red Cross provided his diabetes medicine for free. "But now I have to pay for it, and it's very expensive!"

After the tour was over, I stood with Mabaso by the prison walls and asked how he felt about those TRC-granted amnesties. He replied:

When Mandela and the rest of the leadership first told us about the deal at the Truth Commission I was happy—because that way I'd *know* who among the whites did what. I wouldn't be scared and accusing all the white people. We wanted to get the truth.

But the perpetrators didn't tell the truth. They only "confessed" to as much as investigators had already dug up. I saw them there at the Truth Commission. I went to listen to those three, when they had their amnesty hearings. The judge announced a lunch break. And I knew where those three would go, since they were all smokers. So I went up to one of them and introduced myself.

At first they didn't recognize me because I had this big belly. But I said, "Yes it's me, Thulani Mabaso, see this scar on my face." And he just said, "Oh, you? Are you still alive?"

But they never mentioned anything about what they'd done to my father. I went to Desmond Tutu and van Zyl Slabbert and all of them—and I said, "What about that?" And they said the only thing you can do is file a civil case against them. But I can't do that. Those guys have already tried to kill me twice. They'd never let me do that to them.[58]

I asked whether he or his father had filed a victim statement with the TRC. "No, they never gave me the papers for that."

Thulani Mabaso was not the only victim of apartheid who sought to use the opportunity provided by the TRC hearings to "confront" the people who had earlier abused him. (And he was not the only one who found the reaction he received unsatisfactory.) Indeed, at a broader level, one of the most important things that was happening at the TRC was that Blacks (and other non-Whites) sought to use it to initiate a prolonged national conversation in which they *confronted* the architects and implementers of the apartheid system—who were predominantly Afrikaners—with the facts about what apartheid had done to them over the decades, *reproached* them on that account, and *invited them to respond* with some meaningful expression of remorse. Those interactions took place inside and outside the Commission's hearing rooms. Later portions of this chapter will chart some evaluations of the TRC's work subsequently made by, in particular, Afrikaners and Blacks, as well as the TRC's contribution to reconciliation more generally. But first, let us look at some evaluations of the TRC that emerged from a nationwide opinion survey carried out a few years after the TRC had completed the main portion of its work.

The survey was conducted in 2000–2001 by the Cape Town–based Institute for Justice and Reconciliation (IJR). Respondents were first asked for their overall evaluation of the TRC's work. The proportion of each of the four major, apartheid-era population groups that said they *approved either strongly or somewhat of the Commission's work* is shown in Table 3.3. Because of the preponderance of Blacks in the national population, the "nationwide" findings of this survey, like any other survey of national opinion, were far closer to those recorded by the Black respondents than to those of any other group.

Regarding specific aspects of the TRC's performance, Table 3.4 shows the percentages of each group that said the TRC had done an "excellent job" or a "pretty good job" in each sphere. The notable finding here is how *few* Whites said the TRC had done an "excellent

Table 3.3   Truth and Reconciliation Commission Approval Ratings

Group	Approval	Proportion of Total Population
Black Africans	76%	77.6%
Whites	37%	10.3% = 5.5% Afrikaners + 4.8% Anglophones
Coloureds	45%	8.7%
Asian-Origin	61%	2.5%

Source: Data in "Approval" column are from Table 1 in James L.Gibson and Helen Macdonald, *Truth—Yes, Reconciliation—Maybe: South Africans Judge the Truth and Reconciliation Process* (Rondebosch, South Africa: Institute for Justice and Reconciliation, 2001), p.19. Population data are from James L. Gibson, *Overcoming Apartheid: Can Truth Reconcile a Divided Nation?* (New York: Russell Sage Foundation, 2004), pp. 32, 34.

Table 3.4 Truth and Reconciliation Commission Performance Ratings

	African	White	Coloured	Asian origin
Letting families know what happened to their loved ones	55.5/33.2/*88.7*	7.6/55.1/*62.7*	23.0/32.4/*55.4*	22.0/46.4/*68.5*
Providing a true and unbiased account of the country's history	46.2/38.9/*85.1*	3.6/30.9/*34.5*	13.6/34.5/*48.1*	18.8/53.1/*71.9*
Awarding compensation to victims	43.0/30.5/*73.5*	4.5/25.4/*29.9*	10.9/22.8/*33.7*	15.9/40.8/*56.7*
Ensuring that human rights abuses won't happen again	48.6/36.4/*85.0*	6.2/32.1/*38.3*	18.3/28.2/*46.5*	18.9/46.7/*65.6*
Punishing those guilty of atrocities	45.0/30.2/*75.2*	3.9/27.4/*31.3*	16.2/25.9/*42.1*	16.3/44.1/*60.4*

Note: The figures given represent the following response categories: "excellent job"/ "pretty good job"/*total of the two.*

Source: Data from James L. Gibson and Helen Macdonald, *Truth—Yes, Reconciliation— Maybe: South Africans Judge the Truth and Reconciliation Process* (Rondebosch, South Africa: Institute for Justice and Reconciliation, 2001), Table 2, pp. 20–21.

job" in any of the five spheres: The highest number who gave that rating in any sphere was 7.6 percent. Blacks, by contrast, were much more ready to praise the TRC's work to the Institute's investigators: The sphere that drew the *lowest* proportion of "excellent job" ratings from Blacks still won a 43 percent rating. That (perhaps not surprisingly) was the sphere of "awarding compensation to victims." But what remains particularly significant is how *much* support Black South Africans expressed for the TRC—in all those spheres and also for the work of the TRC as a whole.

Afrikaners' Reactions to the TRC

Afrikaner broadcaster and poet Antjie Krog played a unique part in the TRC's years-long "conversation" with the country's Afrikaner community: Hers was the main reportorial voice that introduced the TRC's proceedings to consumers of the SABC's Afrikaans-language radio and television programs. As the TRC's work started to wrap up in late 1997, Krog wrote an intimate, almost real-time memoir of her work there, titled *Country of My Skull: Guilt, Sorrow, and the Limits of Forgiveness in the New South Africa.* In it, she reflected—in English—on the agonies, frustrations, and frequent absurdities of her job at the TRC, as well as on the effects her assignment was having within her own, apparently close-knit, Afrikaner family. Then in 2002, when the TRC published the last two volumes of its Report, the editors used one of Krog's poems as the Preface to Volume 7. The poem starts:

> because of you
> this country no longer lies
> between us but within.... [59]

In her memoir, Krog noted significant details such as the fact that the 1995 parliamentary debates in which the TRC's enabling legislation was hammered out were conducted *in Afrikaans.* Some of the speakers were White Afrikaners affiliated with the NP or groups further to the right; others were Coloured or White Afrikaans speakers affiliated with the ANC. Krog wrote, "Everybody has a story to tell—from members of Parliament whose houses were firebombed, to friends' children whose fingers were put in a coffee grinder.... Most of the speeches were in Afrikaans. *It is with this group, in this language, that they want to wrestle it out.*"[60]

She also remarked on the seeming lack of interest shown by Black journalists in the TRC's early work: "A workshop is organized for journalists who will be covering the Truth Commission.... We are surrounded by German, Dutch, and Chilean journalists especially. More conspicuous even: only two black journalists—one from radio and one from the *Sowetan.* How are we to understand the absence of black journalists at everything related to the Truth Commission?"[61]

Her book—which was published in 1998 and thus did not cover most of the Amnesty Committee's work—contains many vignettes indicating the reactions of her fellow Afrikaners to the TRC. One of the most poignant is a letter she received from an Afrikaner woman using the pen name "Helena," who described herself as "a farm girl from the Free State." She wrote that her husband had worked in the special forces:

As a loved one, I knew no other life than that of worry, sleeplessness, anxiety about his safety.... After about three years with the special forces, our hell began. He became very quiet. Withdrawn. Sometimes he would just press his face into his hands and shake uncontrollably. I realized he was drinking too much.... And the shakes. The terrible convulsions and blood-curdling shrieks of fear and pain from the bottom of his soul. Sometimes he sits motionless, just staring in front of him.

I never understood. I never knew. Never realized what was being shoved down his throat during the "trips."...

Today I know the answers to all my questions and heartache. I know where everything began. The background. The role of "those at the top," the "cliques," and "our vultures," who simply had to carry out their bloody orders. ...

Yes, I have forgiven the freedom fighters for their bombs, mines, and AK-47s that they used so liberally. There were no angels. I finally understood what the struggle was really about the day the Truth Commission had its first hearing. I would have done the same had I been denied everything. If my life, that of my children and my parents, was strangled with legislation ...

I envy and respect the people of the struggle—at least their leaders have the guts to stand by their vultures, to recognize their sacrifices. What do we have?

I wish I had the power to make these poor wasted people whole again. I wish I could wipe the old South Africa out of everyone's past.

I end with a few lines that my wasted vulture said to me one night when I came upon him turning his gun over and over in his lap: "They can give me amnesty a thousand times. Even if God and everyone else forgives me a thousand times—I have to live with this hell. The problem is in my head, my conscience. There is only one way to be free of it. Blow my own brains out. Because that's where my hell is."[62]

Many of the Afrikaners who wrote to Krog were far less appreciative of the Commission's work. Her memoir includes some disturbing samples of the hate mail she received; and the general picture she presented of the immediate reactions of Afrikaners to the TRC was one of great emotional defensiveness. She wrote the following about some of her neighbors in her family's home community in the Free State:

A white woman said to me, "I don't even watch the Truth Commission on television—because all you see there is a sea of hatred." I told her I attend most of the hearings, and that is not true. There is really no hatred....

During that same Free State conversation, a farmer said vehemently, "If these things were done to me, I would hate deeply and passionately, like the Russians. I would have destroyed everything around me: the fact that they didn't just shows you that blacks are not even able to *hate* sufficiently."[63]

Hermann Giliomee is a distinguished Afrikaner historian of his people. In his capstone 2003 work *The Afrikaners: Biography of a People,* he wrote that during the months that followed the 1994 election, "[t]he NP periodically patted itself on the back and told the people that it had abolished apartheid and thus was the coliberator of the country. This euphoria of self-congratulation could not last.... The NP *fell from its position of temporary grace* when the government in December 1995 established a Truth and Reconciliation Commission."[64]

His final judgment on the value of the Commission's work was guarded: "Despite its flaws ... the TRC performed an important therapeutic role in providing victims with the opportunity to tell their story and in acknowledging their suffering. So, too, the hearings exposed the brutality of apartheid and the official web of government lies and deception." But he also identified many flaws he saw in its approach: flaws in the Commission's composition (specifically, that it contained too many pro-ANC people), the fact that the Commissioners were not satisfied with the apology they got from de Klerk, and the role he saw the TRC as playing in the perpetuation of intergroup cleavages within society. "The TRC satisfied none of the main parties, including the ANC," he wrote.[65]

Fanie du Toit is an Afrikaner who grew up in a fairly traditional way, and was even a member of the Junior Broederbond before he became a political liberal. I met him in 2003 at his workplace, the Cape Town headquarters of the IJR. "The hope with the TRC was that the perpetrators would come forward and say they recognized that the acts they'd committed were wrong," he said. "But you can't legislate repentance."

He said he thought there were significant differences of "expressive styles" between most Afrikaners and most Black South Africans that had hindered effective communication and made it harder for the TRC to reach its goal of encouraging former perpetrators to express remorse. "Afrikaners don't know how to express remorse! Also, they would have a fear that if they did so, that might be interpreted as weakness by Blacks. So they played a minimalist game instead. And then, most of them simply weren't sorry." What might have been more appropriate and achievable than expecting Afrikaners to express public remorse, he said, would have been to ask them to carry out quieter, less publicly "expressive" acts such as contributing to a scholarship fund or performing a community service—"things that don't require emotionality."

Concerning the TRC's overall contribution to national reconciliation, du Toit said: "The premise you have to start from is that you cannot repair the damage which has been done.... The TRC was a *symbol*, a national metaphor for the transition. It tried to create a situation in which reconciliation would flourish.... In that respect, it was successful." He admitted that, domestically, the TRC's work had been "very controversial; it positioned itself as a focus point of criticism and pulled criticism out of the society." In that respect, he said, perhaps it had acted as a helpful lightning rod for still-raw emotions that might otherwise have festered and become more intense.

Antjie Krog described the defensive way in which many Afrikaners responded to the TRC. Piet Meiring was an Afrikaner religious affairs professor. Meiring, she wrote,

> often has to contact the ministers of amnesty applicants, and the body language of most *dominees* [Afrikaner ministers] shows that they want nothing to do with the commission. Why? They're afraid of a witch hunt, the professor says; they're afraid the Truth Commission will increase the desire for revenge. ...
>
> No one can escape the process, says Meiring, and the churches ought to be doing much more than anybody else. The Church has a prophetic responsibility. It must admit and confess its guilt.... But the church also has a pastoral responsibility. It must support amnesty applicants; it must support the victims in that area, that town; it must assist the whole community as it wrestles with truth and reconciliation. Meiring says the Afrikaner in particular has been traumatized by the process.... [He] refers to the phases described by the psychologist Elisabeth Kübler-Ross in her work on terminal illness and death.[66]

Krog also cited another experienced observer, forensic psychiatrist Sean Kaliski, as identifying a grieving-like process in the Afrikaner community in response to the TRC's work. In June 1997, regarding the vehemence of the anti-TRC diatribes being expressed within the Afrikaner community, she wrote:

Kaliski says it is a positive development if people feel compelled to deny these things. It is the first step in a process akin to the stages terminally ill patients experience: denial, rage, bargaining, depression—out of which acceptance will eventually surface.

"I think people are too impatient," says Kaliski. "I personally would be very concerned if whites could overnight integrate information that overturns their whole world view. It will take decades, generations, and people will assimilate the truths of this country piece by piece."[67]

Krog's own complex and very intimate reaction to the TRC's work is also significant—even if it was echoed by only a few of her fellow Afrikaners. It was almost exactly the kind of expressive, remorse-filled but ultimately optimistic reaction that Tutu and other Black South Africans had been looking for from Afrikaners. The poem of hers that prefaced Volume 7 of the TRC Report ends like this:

I am changed forever. I want to say:
> forgive me
> forgive me
> forgive me
You whom I have wronged, please
take me
with you.[68]

Reactions from Black and Coloured South Africans

When I talked with Black, church-based social activist Mongezi Goma in Johannesburg in 2003, he described the TRC as "having less to do with perpetrators and victims than with the broader 'Mandela project' of reconciliation." Other elements of this project, he said, included the "sunset clause" that guaranteed job security to the members of the apartheid-era civil service and security forces; the promise that Mandela made before the 1994 elections that, however strongly the ANC won the election, he would form a Government of National Unity thereafter; and conciliatory gestures Mandela made after his inauguration such as his visits to take tea with the spouses and widows of former South African Presidents. "We fail if we look at the TRC as only one event," Goma concluded. "But it definitely helped to wipe away some of the pain."

So, did he feel that the TRC had succeeded in bringing about a recognition by most Afrikaners of the equal humanity of their non-White compatriots? "No, they mostly don't recognize that yet," he said. "The average Afrikaner would still see the transformation of 1994 as a sellout."

Mxolisi ("Ace") Mgxashe, who worked as a researcher for the TRC, had a close-up view of many aspects of its work. We talked in Cape Town, sitting near the building where the TRC had situated its main office. Did he think the TRC had succeeded?

> Yes and no. Yes, because through the hearings we discovered things that we didn't know. Mainly, it came out that it was really a remorseless system! But there are still some very hard-line Afrikaners out there around the country, oh yes.
>
> Reconciliation is not just a symbolic hug. Deep social cleavages still exist here. It's hard to reconcile. Especially since the real culprits—people like P.W. Botha—got off scot-free. They ran this country all that time—and they got off scot-free.

Like many other non-White South Africans I talked to, Mgxashe focused on the economic inequalities that still plagued the country. Some months before we spoke, the Khulamani Victims' Support Group and another nongovernmental group filed a civil suit in New York against 20 multinational corporations, on behalf of 85 named apartheid victims and Khulamani's entire 33,000–strong membership. The suit alleged that through their activities the companies had aided "the commission of crimes of apartheid, forced labor, genocide, extrajudicial killing, torture, sexual assault, unlawful detention and cruel, unusual and degrading treatment."[69] But the South African government had condemned the lawsuit. President Thabo Mbeki argued that many of the companies cited were now aiding the country's development. Mgxashe told me he was disappointed that the government had adopted that stand, and also that it had rejected the idea of any special taxes being levied on corporations to provide reparations to their former victims. "The government is acting out of a passionate desire to appease foreign investors," he said. "But lessening the economic disparities here has to be seen as a major marker of whether the TRC succeeded."

(In the TRC's own 1998 Report, the Commission found that "[b]usiness was central to the economy that sustained the South African state during the apartheid years. Certain businesses, especially the mining industry, were involved in helping to design and implement apartheid policies. Other businesses benefited from cooperating with the security structures of the former state. Most businesses benefited from operating in a racially structured context."[70] The TRC suggested various ways—including a wealth tax and a one-time levy on corporate and private income—in which businesses could contribute to the state's development programs.[71] But as of 2005, the government had not followed any of those suggestions.)

Mgxashe retained many unhappy memories of the rifts that had occurred within the TRC. "The TRC was infiltrated, including by the people who made and supported all those allegations against Dumisa Ntsebesa. There were so many different agendas being pursued inside the TRC—and all in the name of peace and reconciliation!"

Back in the early 1990s, Khoisan X (the former Benny Alexander) played a big role in the peace talks as secretary general of the Pan African Congress (PAC). In 2003, he discussed the TRC's legacy record with me at a coffee shop in Johannesburg. He said:

> Most of my suggestions about how to handle the amnesty issue were not taken. I believe the leaders should have come forward and taken full responsibility for what happened. They didn't. They wanted the foot soldiers to come forward and take responsibility. But this is extremely immoral! The foot soldiers were treated as though they were free-standing individuals who decided to do all those things, but of course that wasn't the case. ...
>
> The weaknesses of the TRC's amnesty project were firstly, that it was based on volunteerism. The masterminds and the political leaders were under no obligation to come forward. And now, no leader will ever be charged in a law court. Secondly, the political leaders didn't guide the process and lead it. Instead, they left it up to one individual: Archbishop Tutu.
>
> I think that confessions and the granting of amnesties should have been addressed separately. There should have been three separate stages. First, a blanket amnesty. Second, confessions. And third, reaching a good agreement on reparations. You can't have reconciliation unless it takes place on the psychological and emotional level. Truth-telling should have been linked to those levels, not to the state and the legal system, which is what happened at the Amnesty Committee.

Khoisan X also described how he thought truth-telling could have been used to contribute to healing: "Churches play an important role in my model. You might sit at home and just nurse your hurt, and as a result develop other complications. What happened to you may have been personal, but still, you need healing in some kind of a communal setting. After you confront the pain of the past, then that helps you to move on." Did the TRC provide that? "Yes, but it was very, very limited."

On reparations, Khoisan X said there should have been a special "reparations tax" imposed on all White South Africans; he suggested a special income tax of 6 percent for three years for that purpose. "You must give white people a *task* to do," he said, echoing Fanie du Toit. "And then, with the money raised that way, I would give no special money to direct victims, but increase the overall level of the state welfare system. I definitely favor community reparations over individual reparations."

The support that Khoisan X expressed for blanket amnesties has been echoed by many other thinkers in the Black and Coloured communities (though it was strongly opposed by others such as Steve Biko's son, Nkosinathi Biko). For example, Letlapa Mphalele, who used to be head of operations for the PAC's military wing, the Azanian People's Liberation Army (APLA), argued in 2001 that South Africa should have (and could still have) a general amnesty for all the violent acts of the apartheid era: "This kind of general amnesty, linked to the handing in of weapons, has become a national priority." He also proposed a list of other things the government could do to deal with the negative legacies of the past, including providing land grants or job training to former freedom fighters; establishing a national fund to care for freedom fighters suffering from HIV or other terminal illnesses; and compiling a list of all activists executed by the liberation movements during the struggle, and giving compensation to their families.[72]

TRC Commissioner Dumisa Ntsebeza also took part in the 2001 conference where Mphalele presented those suggestions. But he expressed a different view on amnesties, arguing that the state should launch some demonstrative prosecutions after the expiration of the TRC Amnesty Committee's work:

At the Nuremberg trials, the purpose was not to punish all the cases but to focus special attention on the horrors of what had happened. The exemplary punishments they meted out served the purpose of restoring the legal order and reassuring the whole community that what they had witnessed for so many years was criminal behaviour. Similarly, in South Africa ... prosecutions will serve to restore the legal order and reassure the South African community that apartheid was a crime against humanity.... Selective prosecution is the only way forward.[73]

In that same discussion, political scientist Zola Sonkosi gave a powerful description of the role amnesty had played in the life of traditional African communities. "During the precolonial era," he noted, "amnesty was part and parcel of the way of life in my rural village [in the Eastern Cape]":

> In a typical African society such as the Xhosa's, amnesty had several important features. It was often granted at the time of trial, specifically after the person had been pronounced guilty and sentenced. Offenders who showed remorse or for whom a cogent presentation was made by a well-respected and prominent elder could be granted amnesty.... [A]mnesty was granted only after broad consultation and if there was a willingness on the part of the community and victim to forgive the offender or offenders.
>
> If successful, persons seeking amnesty were expected to make a symbolic gesture of appreciation—it could be slaughtering a sheep, goat, or cow and offering traditional beer to the panel of arbitrators and other stakeholders from the community. In addition, they were expected to pay material reparations to the victims or victim besides some other form of useful service to the community as a whole.... [T]he gesture was meant to purify the land and society (tainted by the wrongdoing of an offender) and to appease the ancestors and God angered by an offender's misbehavior.[74]

Sonkosi further noted that "amnesty is still largely used in the rural areas where the sense of community still exists" and argued for its use on a much larger scale. Pointing out that traditional amnesty practices were rooted in the communitarian worldview to which most Africans once adhered, he warned that the breakdown of those practices was linked to a breakdown of the broader communitarian outlook. "An attempt to supplant this feature of the African society with individualism, a foreign import, has generated a caricatured African pursuing a false identity, and goals such as conspicuous consumption.... It has distorted people's moral values, the spirit of cooperation, fellowship and support of each other (*ubuntu*), and lost a common affinity to the higher ideals of humanity."[75]

Serving Victims?

The people who designed the TRC's process tried to make it far more victim-centered than any regular criminal court; and many people outside South Africa have written about the nearly cathartic sense of healing they believe was experienced by former victims of apartheid when, as happened with Nomonde Calata, the TRC allowed them to retell their stories in a sympathetic public setting. (There is a widespread view that the HRVC hearings acted as a kind of broad, public therapy session.) What happened during the victim hearings was, however, much more varied than that. Many victims apparently did gain a degree of healing and empowerment from their appearances—though mental health professionals always warned that a single experience like that could not provide all the healing that many victims would likely need. At a broader level, too, the granting of *public, state-backed acknowledgment* of a very harmful state of affairs—even one that had previously been *public knowledge* within the non-White communities—likely helped to restore the dignity of most victims of apartheid, both those who submitted victim statements and those who did not. For some victims, however, participation in the TRC's work proved problematic or even actively harmful. As Piers Pigou, who worked in the TRC's Investigative Unit, has written: "[W]hat had been presented to and accepted by the Commission sometimes proved unacceptable to the victims themselves.... For people like these, the TRC did not provide the balm its authors intended, but actually exacerbated their grief."[76]

Pigou focused his analysis on the experiences of Sylvia Dlomo-Jele, a Black Soweto resident whose teenage son, Sicelo Dlomo, was murdered in 1988. Sicelo had been very involved with pro-ANC organizations; and after his body was found in a field outside Soweto, his mother concluded that the police had assassinated him. She was one of the first to submit a victim statement to the TRC, and to testify at an HRVC public hearing in April 1996. Pigou wrote that, immediately after having done so, "[s]he was ... exhilarated that she had been able to tell everyone how she felt and what she wanted." But over the months that followed she grew increasingly concerned that the TRC's investigation into Sicelo's fate was moving very slowly. Still, Pigou wrote, "[p]ainful as the loss of her son was, Sylvia found some comfort in the knowledge that he was well regarded in the liberation movement as an antiapartheid activist."

Then in early 1997, the TRC's Investigation Unit discovered that, far from having been "martyred" for his nationalist activism by the security forces, Sicelo had actually been killed by four local members of MK.

The MK men submitted amnesty applications for that killing. In early 1998 Dlomo-Jele learned about that. She learned, too, that two of the killers had been among his close boyhood friends, and that they claimed they had discovered Sicelo was a government spy; that was why he had been killed. According to Pigou, Dlomo-Jele was "devastated" to learn these things.

The hearings for these men's amnesty applications were scheduled for February 1999. A few days beforehand, Dlomo-Jele was rushed to the hospital. She still insisted on opposing the men's amnesty applications and had found a lawyer to represent her at the hearings. Shortly after the hearings, she died. Pigou wrote, "Many of her friends and colleagues believe that she had given up the will to live."[77] For Dlomo-Jele, the truth-seeking process had uncovered a picture of the time of violence that completely disrupted the world of (relative) moral certainties that had previously sustained her.

The TRC's Drama of Reconciliation

"Truth, the road to reconciliation" was a slogan the TRC often used: It graced many of the banners that TRC staffers hung in the otherwise undistinguished spaces in which the TRC's committees held their public hearings. However, when I talked with Commissioner Wendy Orr in 2001, she told me quite frankly that when the TRC started work, "[n]o one there had any theory as to how that road was supposed to open."

By 1998, when the TRC published its main Report, Volume Five contained a whole chapter, Chapter 9, in which the commissioners presented their assessments of the degree of reconciliation they felt they had achieved. Most of Chapter 9 deals with reconciliation/healing at an individual or small-group level, though some of it relates to achievements in larger intergroup reconciliation. Taken as a whole, the chapter presents a collection of the different ways in which the commissioners judged that their truth-seeking work had contributed to reconciliation. It has the following subheads:

- Restoring the human dignity of victims
- Restoring the human dignity of perpetrators

- Forgiveness; apologies and acknowledgements; and acts of reconciliation
- Reconciliation without forgiveness
- Restitution or reparation.

The chapter also describes some of the more dramatic reconciliatory acts that took place as a direct result of TRC activities. For instance, there is the oft-cited story of Neville Clarence and Aboobaker Ismail. Clarence had been blinded in an early-1980s ANC bomb attack against the Air Force Headquarters; Ismail was one of the MK commanders who planned the attack. Ismail told one of the TRC committees that he regretted the deaths of civilians that occurred during MK's armed struggle. The Report relates that, in a face-to-face meeting before the start of the hearing, Ismail told Clarence, "This is very difficult, I am sorry about what happened to you"; and that Clarence said he understood and did not hold any grudges. The Report further notes: "Both agreed that they should meet again, and they exchanged telephone numbers. 'Talking about it is the only way to become reconciled,' Ismail said."[78]

Alongside heartwarming stories like that one, however, there are others indicating that reconciliation and forgiveness were hard to achieve and, indeed, were often *not* achieved at the TRC. In the section on "Forgiveness," one unnamed victim at an HRVC hearing is reported as telling Tutu firmly, "I will not be able to forgive anyone until I know who they are. Then I will shake their hands. Otherwise, I will not be able to forgive somebody that I do not know."[79]

In fact, the TRC's rules never *required* victims to forgive or perpetrators to express any apologies or other signs of repentance or remorse. Under the law, all that the Amnesty Committee could require of perpetrators was that they tell all that they knew about gross rights violations committed by themselves or others. In short, they did not have to express any particular personal stand—whether of shame, repugnance, or repudiation—toward the truths thus revealed; and indeed, it sometimes seemed to observers that perpetrators recounted their misdeeds with a quite neutral tone, or even with a distressing degree of smirking or pride.

Nevertheless, many TRC commissioners went beyond the minimalist requirements of the legislation and urged both victims to forgive and perpetrators to express some remorse. Chapter 9 reports a powerful reproach that Commissioner Mapule Ramashala directed to former Defense Minister Roelf Meyer at one hearing:

> May I ask [that] you consider the following comment from the communities, particularly the greater black communities, and I want to quote: "They get amnesty. They get the golden handshake (meaning rewards). They get retirement pensions worth millions. And we get nothing. And on television they smirk or they smile to boot."
>
> As you address that submission, please address the question of the perpetrators on your side ... who, so far, when they apply for amnesty and present themselves, and even say they are sorry. None of them has said: "This is my contribution. I would like to do the following." It stops with, "I am sorry." None of them has said: "As a demonstration, perhaps of how sorry I am, this is what I would like to do." None of them have done that. So ... could you please address that, because that is the more tangible thing that people are asking, and people say that is a revictimisation, that is a dehumanisation and that has caused more pain than you realise. Thank you.[80]

The transcript of the hearing shows that Meyer did not make any immediate response to this plea. At the end of the hearing he merely thanked the chair for "creating this opportunity, allowing us to interact."[81] That nonspecific response seemed unlikely to satisfy Ramashala.

National-Level Reconciliation

National healing and reconciliation are different from the healing of individuals and small groups, though the two sets of processes are evidently related. So, how successful were the TRC and the broader "Mandela project" of reconciliation at building a new, well-reconciled nation in the decade after 1994? At the political level, the election of 1994 was followed by two more national elections, in 1999 and 2004, both deemed by election monitors to be generally "free and fair." Thus, even if serious social and economic cleavages as well as many of the bad legacies of colonialism and apartheid remained, still, the basic concept of a democratic, universal South African citizenship seemed to be taking root.

In each of these elections the ANC increased its representation in the 400-seat parliament while the representation of the NP and Inkatha declined (see Table 3.5). In August 2004, the leader of the "New National Party," Marthinus van Schalkwyk, provided a notable footnote to the history of apartheid when he announced

Table 3.5   Post-Apartheid Elections in South Africa: Number of Seats Held Per Party in Parliament

Election year	ANC	Inkatha	NP	(Other Parties)
1994	252	43	82	23
1999	266	34	28	72
2004	279	28	7	86

Source: Compiled by author from data on the website of the South Africa Independent Electoral Commission, http://www.elections.org.za.

the dissolution of the party that had pioneered that policy—and invited its members to join him in entering the ANC!

Regarding the broad, sociopolitical legitimacy of the elected parliaments, an IJR survey carried out in November 2003 found that 61 percent of South Africans agreed with the proposition that parliament "can usually be trusted to make decisions that are right for the country as a whole." Just over 20 percent of Whites concurred with that statement, as did 70 percent of Blacks.[82] That result, like many others in the survey, indicated that deep differences of opinion continued between the country's major racial groups. (Typically, the results for Coloureds and Indians lay between those for Blacks and Whites.) Of course, stable intergroup reconciliation does not require that members of the different groups should all think alike on all subjects; but still, the number and depth of intergroup differences revealed by the survey could be read as a possible danger signal.

Also, in a country as diverse as South Africa, there are many intergroup cleavages that go beyond the divisions between the four major racial categories identified by the apartheid system—including, for example, the purely "political" division inside the Zulu community between pro-ANC people and pro-Inkatha people. That difference, unlike the differences between Blacks and Whites, continued to generate considerable political violence after 1994, with some 2,000 killings reported as a result of it between 1994 and 2001.[83]

In the IJR poll of 2003, the survey response that showed by far the least interracial difference of opinion came in reaction to the statement: "I want to forget about the past and just get on with my life." Of all the respondents, 79.4 percent said they agreed with the statement—including 78.5 percent of Blacks, 73.9 percent of Whites, and about 85 percent of Coloureds and Indians.[84] That finding was rather hopeful. But perhaps most hopeful of all was the fact that 83 percent of all South Africans—including 67 percent of the country's Whites—agreed that "[i]t is desirable to create one united South African nation out of all the different groups who live in this country."[85]

South Africans offered these expressions of general political satisfaction in 2003 even though the country's economy had stagnated—and, in some areas, deteriorated—since 1994. Huge differences in material standing still divided the major racial groups. Mean per capita incomes in 2000 are reported in Table 3.6.

The UN's *South Africa Human Development Report* reported in 2003 that about 48.5 percent of the South African population fell below the national poverty line, that the gaps between rich and poor had *increased* in the preceding years, and that poverty and inequality "continued to exhibit strong spatial and racial biases." The number of households deprived of access to "good" basic services increased from 5.68 million to 7.24 million between the 1996 and 2001 censuses.[86] And the proportion of the country's children reaching Grade 5 in school declined from 75 percent in 1990 to 65 percent in 2000.[87]

One problem was that the country's GDP per capita remained almost stagnant throughout the 1990s, showing only 0.2 percent annual growth. There was an apparent "peace dividend" associated with ending the conflict over apartheid: Between 1990 and 2003, military spending decreased from 3.8 percent to 1.6 percent of GDP. But little of that dividend was put into increased social spending; indeed, the proportion of GDP spent on education and health, combined, declined a little over that period.[88] Meanwhile, a wave of HIV infections swept the country in the 1990s, badly affecting the active workforce—including professions related to the delivery of education, health, and other social services. By

Table 3.6   South African Per Capita Income, 2000

	Income expressed in Rand	Percentage of Whites' income
Whites	62,360	100.0
Blacks	7,283	11.7
Coloureds	14,126	22.7
Indians	23,938	38.3

Source: Data from K. Lombard, *Opportunities and Obstacles: The State of Reconciliation: Report of the Second Round of the SA Reconciliation Barometer Survey* (Rondebosch, South Africa: Institute for Justice and Reconciliation, May 2004), p. 19.

2003, the prevalence of HIV infection among women aged fifteen to twenty-nine was estimated at around 21.5 percent nationwide.[89]

Black South Africans had been euphoric at the time of the elections in 1994, and expressed high hopes that now, at last, they could start to lead a decent, dignified life. Undoubtedly, the full citizenhood they gained in the elections made a significant contribution to their sense of dignity and well-being. But a person cannot eat citizenhood. The continuation of stark economic disparities between White South Africans and the vast majority of their Black compatriots was mentioned again and again during the TRC hearings, as well as in my interviews, as a factor that maintained anti-White resentments in the Black communities at a high level. Many White South Africans, meanwhile, pointed to the high crime rate throughout the country as showing that intergroup "mixing" was a bad idea, that Black people had "criminal mentalities," and so forth.

In those circumstances it was even more remarkable that people's faith in the basic goals and rules of the country's political system remained so strong. Undoubtedly, a great deal of national reconciliation *had* been achieved, however imperfectly; and the TRC had played a role in that. "The TRC was a healing process," Deputy Environment Minister Rejoice Mabudhafasi said firmly when I talked with her in 2001.

Mabudhafasi's deepest concern, however, continued to be the government's effort to lift up the circumstances of the country's poorest citizens. She was eager to tell me about the challenges of her job as deputy minister; about the waste water treatment projects she was working on throughout the country; and her joy at delivering electricity and basic services to remote villages. She placed the efforts to achieve national reconciliation within that frame. "If we can't have reconciliation, we can't build the country. It does us no good to keep grudges," she said.

I asked how she felt about the perpetrators of apartheid-era violence walking away from the TRC unpunished. "We can never do anything to them as bad as what they did to us," she said. "It's not in our nature. God will deal with them. We leave that to Him."

I also sought assessments of the contribution the TRC had made to reconciliation from two English-speaking White South Africans who are members of the country's post-1994 Constitutional Court: Richard Goldstone, who chaired the key fact-finding commission in the last years of apartheid (and who also had his experience at

ICTR and ICTY to reflect on); and Albie Sachs, one of the ANC's most long-standing White members, who himself had been the target of an apartheid regime assassination attempt. (That attack—in Mozambique, in 1988—blew off Sachs's right arm.)

When I talked with Goldstone in 2001 he gave the TRC "a mixed report, but with the bottom line on the positive side. The greatest value of the TRC is that now we have *one* history of what happened in the apartheid years. That was a great gift to the nation. White South Africans cannot deny what happened." He said he saw truth commissions as "a form of justice—for the perpetrators to come forward in public and give a full account of what they did, that was a form of punishment. And certainly, they are now *out* of any official position."[90] He singled out another valuable way the TRC had contributed to national reconciliation: "The affirmative action efforts we've seen since 1994 have been much easier to enact because of the revelations of the TRC."[91]

Goldstone argued that one factor in South Africa's success in weathering the political transformation of 1994 lay in the fact that "[u]nder apartheid, we had ... all the institutions of democracy in existence here, even though we had the apartheid system and very unjust laws. But the TRC was operating—and the transition in general was happening—*within the context of existing democratic institutions*. That certainly helped."

When I met Albie Sachs, in Cape Town in 2003, he stressed the case management advantages the TRC had over any criminal prosecutions that might have been pursued instead:

> A TRC can deal with many more cases than a due process trial. There is just no way a regular justice system can manage to deal with crime on such a massive scale. And then, with prosecutions, there's the whole difficulty of getting the evidence. ...
>
> Some people put a lot of emphasis on having expressions of remorse and forgiveness at the TRC. I think those were bonuses of the process for many people. In my own case, what mattered was the *conduct* of the person who was responsible for the bombing against me: that he came to TRC and admitted to it. For me, acknowledgement by a person of his past misdeeds is more powerful than an expression of remorse. In making an acknowledgement, a person is accepting responsibility for his actions, acknowledging the gravity of his offense, and "bending the knee" to the rule of law. That is important. Expressing remorse can just be breast-beating, and self-serving.

He also noted the limitations on what the TRC had sought to achieve:

> People burdened the TRC by placing all the pain of South Africa's past on it! But it didn't focus on the whole broad crime of apartheid. It focused only on certain "crimes within the crime." To me, the most poignant feature of the hearings was that at the end the perpetrators would get into their expensive cars and drive back to their lovely homes. Meanwhile, victims and their families might have gotten the benefit of a little more information from the hearing. But they would have to climb into the same overcrowded *combis* [rideshare vans] and go back to their shacks in the former townships. So, inequality continues.... Changing society includes paying attention to redistribution, and including people much more in all the decisions and the planning process.[92]

It seems fitting, perhaps, to give "the last word" on the TRC to the person who suffered the most damaging attacks on his personal integrity as a result of his service to the Commission, Dumisa Ntsebeza. Ntsebeza has written that the TRC hearings revealed "remarkable stories of people [who] showed a willingness to forgive where one would not have expected such forgiveness." He also noted that many victims had not been so forgiving. He concluded:

> [I]t was never the duty of the TRC, contemplated or otherwise, to implement reconciliation. Our duty was to promote reconciliation, as the Act suggests. Secondly ... it is far too early to judge the failures and successes of the reconciliation process. Reconciliation is a process that needs not only the TRC Commissioners, the committee members and the staff to see it through. Each and every member of society in South Africa ... needs to participate in the process, so that the whole nation can be reconciled.
>
> Finally, there will be no reconciliation as long as the division between the "haves" and the "have-nots" exists.[93]

4
Mozambique
Heal and Rebuild

Atrocities, War, and Peace

Two Participants

In the early years of the new century Jacinta Jorge sits—bespectacled, capable, friendly—in an office in Mozambique's bustling capital, Maputo, where she heads an engaging and visionary nongovernmental organization. She talks about how, back in 1975, she was an ambitious teenager from the northern province of Zambézia. That was the year in which, after a lengthy and difficult anticolonial struggle, Mozambique's "Frelimo" nationalist movement won independence from their country's former rulers, the Portuguese.

Back then, Jorge had a clear goal in life. "I wanted to study medicine so I could help my family," she recalled. "I was supposed to be taken to a medical school in Sofala province. But instead, they flew me straight here to Maputo and they told me, 'First you have to do military training, then you can study.' ... That's how I joined the Frelimo armed forces in 1975: I was tricked into it."

The Portuguese colonial administration had invested almost nothing in providing basic infrastructure, schools, or hospitals to the 10 million-plus indigenous people then living in Mozambique. (Located in southeast Africa, Mozambique enjoys a long coastline on the Indian Ocean and long borders with—among other countries—South Africa and Zimbabwe.) Portugal's withdrawal from

Mozambique was extremely abrupt. It had been occasioned by an antifascist coup "back home" in Lisbon, many of whose planners were young Portuguese officers stationed in their country's far-flung colonial empire: Their main desire was to return home to Portugal *as quickly as possible*—to demobilize, and to start living the same kind of easy-going, democratic lifestyle that their age-mates in the rest of Europe already enjoyed. The Portuguese coup-makers did succeed, admirably, in building a robust democracy in their own country. But in Mozambique as in the other overseas lands they departed from in such haste, they left behind a mess of underdevelopment, impoverishment, and extreme vulnerability. (Among the other countries thus afflicted were Angola and East Timor.) After the Portuguese left, independent Mozambique had precisely one Black doctor and one qualified Black agronomist.[1]

The country might well have needed a bright, ambitious young person like Jacinta Jorge to train to be a doctor. But its new rulers faced another big challenge in addition to that of underdevelopment: From almost the beginning of Mozambique's history as an independent state, the Frelimo-run government faced a vicious armed insurgency against its rule. The insurgency was incubated by the White minority rulers in neighboring Rhodesia (as Zimbabwe was then known) who felt threatened by the collapse of White colonial rule in Mozambique and Angola and by the support that Frelimo gave to Black nationalist guerrillas inside Rhodesia. So the infamous Rhodesian secret services worked—with increasing support from their confreres in apartheid South Africa—to strike back against Frelimo inside Mozambique. The civil war thus launched continued, year after year, until 1992. Jacinta Jorge never went to medical school. For the first seventeen years of her adulthood she had to stay in the military.

"After I completed my military training, they decided they wanted to create a special military training center just for women, and they put me through an administration course so I could help to run it," she said. Later, she was given the responsible job of establishing and running training centers in various places around the country for the military. Along the way, she got married and had a child. Her husband was also in the military. He spent a long time at a training course in Cuba, and after he came back to Mozambique he spent most of his time at the front line; so, for many years, Jorge was raising their child nearly on her own. During a posting in Maputo in the 1980s, she was able to put in a few years of night school as she struggled to continue her education.

Nowadays she notes, briskly but without much apparent rancor, that despite all her experience and responsibilities in the military, she was never given an officer's rank—"because I was a woman." In 1992, when the government and the insurgents from the "Renamo" movement decided to make peace, the UN (as noted in Chapter 1) did provide some support to combatants from both sides who joined a demobilization program. But the levels of monetary support distributed under this program *correlated with the pay these people had been receiving prior to that point:* A common soldier got less than one-third the amount given to even the lowliest officer. "Yes, I was classified as a 'soldier,'" Jorge says.

> I was one of 3,777 women who entered the demobilization program.... In addition to the tiny sum of money common soldiers got, everyone in the program was given a set of civilian clothes. But we all got men's clothes, even men's underwear! And the training programs they offered us were pathetic. They said they could give me two weeks training to be a seamstress. But *all* the training programs offered, to men and women, were unsatisfactory. They assumed we were all illiterate, and offered to train us for manual labor. There were no scholarships offered for people like me who wanted to continue their higher studies. There was no education program or counseling offered to excombatants.

Using the considerable organizing skills they had honed in the military, Jorge and some other demobilized fighters founded an association of combat veterans. The association is called Amodeg, and it continues to this day. "At first, it was just an association for excombatants from Frelimo," Jorge explained. "But in 1992, even before the leaders reached the peace accord, we decided we wanted to open it up to excombatants from Renamo, as well. So we took some ex-Renamo people into the organizing committee. One of the main issues we addressed was education, to help all the excombatants to deal with their reintegration into society."

Building on their own experience of reconciling with former opponents, Amodeg's leaders decided—along with the leaders of a group representing disabled veterans—to set up a new organization that would employ mixed (Frelimo-Renamo) teams of excombatants to offer conflict resolution services to other sectors of the national community. That is the organization that Jorge now heads: It is called ProPaz. "We have about 100 peace promoters who work for us," she said. "Nearly all are excombatants. They work in four of our different provinces. They work on many different kinds of issues including community disputes over resources, small arms issues, and now some work with HIV/AIDS."

In war, as in all human endeavors, everyone has his own story. In the early years of Mozambican independence, a young man named Raúl Domingos was working as an industrial designer in the city's main port, in Beira. "One day in 1980 I was traveling by train between Beira and Chimoio," he recalls. "Our train was stopped along the way by guerillas loyal to the Renamo leader Afonso Dhlakama. They convinced me to stay and join them." He offered no further details about that encounter.

When I met him, Raúl Domingos was a settled, prosperous-looking person, a businessman and a two-term member of Mozambique's national parliament. What was it that persuaded him to take up arms against the government in 1980? "I felt I was living under a regime of Marxism and Leninism! I could not get a promotion to a job with a better salary. I was chief of a department there at the port, but I had no privileges. I felt I was being oppressed. The Russians who were my colleagues there had less knowledge than I did, but they had more privileges. And I was told I could not change my job because it would be 'economic sabotage.' So yes, when I got the chance to fight the regime, I took it."

Had he tried to express his grievances nonviolently? "There was no way to fight for my rights without using violence, no." Was it hard to leave his family behind? "It was hard. I was 22. I wrote a letter to my dad telling him of my decision. My family had difficult days because of my decision. When the authorities found out, they sent many soldiers to surround our house there. Fortunately no one was killed, but they questioned my family for days on end."

Domingos rose fairly rapidly inside the Renamo military, ending up as chief of staff for all of Renamo's forces. He lost many friends along the way, and he himself was shot in the leg.

In August 1989, Afonso Dhlakama took four other Renamo leaders along with him to a crucial meeting in Kenya with a team of Mozambican Protestant church leaders who were in touch with the country's president, Joaquim Chissano. Domingos was a member of the delegation. He told me it was easy for the Renamo leaders to agree to enter this negotiation since, "[f]rom the beginning of the war, war was always our response to the lack of a dialogue. We were always appealing for dialogue! When the chance for negotiations came up, we accepted with pleasure."

He recalled what happened in Kenya: "The church leaders brought us a twelve-point proposal from Frelimo. It said that as a precondition for face-to-face talks, Renamo should accept the existing Mozambican Constitution, government, and president. Renamo wouldn't accept that, so for a while we talked with them only through the church leaders. After two rounds, we suggested direct negotiations. But then the issue was where to hold the talks." Several governments in and beyond Africa offered to host this negotiation, but the Mozambique government leaders were very sensitive about the status issues involved. They feared that if their delegation was hosted by another government alongside a delegation from Renamo—an organization that they still routinely denounced as merely a gang of *bandidos armados* (armed criminals)—then that might imply some equivalency in diplomatic status between the two sides.

The deadlock over location continued for several months. Meanwhile, Renamo held its first national political congress, in Gorongosa, in central Mozambique. At the congress, the organization established a political (as opposed to purely military) leadership for the first time ever. Domingos was named its foreign affairs secretary. In early summer 1990, the Renamo and Frelimo leaderships finally agreed that the peace talks could be held in Rome, under the sponsorship not of a government but of a Catholic lay organization called the Sant' Egidio (SE) Community. That formula allowed the parties to finesse the "diplomatic status" issue. When the peace talks opened at SE in early July, Domingos headed the Renamo team.

"The talks themselves were a victory for us because for the first time the government recognized Renamo as a legitimate interlocutor," he told me. "It was also notable that we *started* the negotiations by shaking hands with each other. This is usually done at the end of negotiations—but not on that occasion! After that, we went in to negotiate. The discussion was not easy, but step by step we agreed on the peace agreement."

Was there ever a question inside the negotiations of one side blaming the other for things that had happened?

No, we always tried to avoid that kind of discussion. Peace talks should bring up and privilege those things that unite us over those that divide us. If there are things that divide us, we will leave them for later. This strategy made us see that there are more things that unite than divide us.

We agreed that no one should be prosecuted for what had been done during the war—because if so, then both sides would be prosecuted! *For the benefit of peace and reconstruction we needed to forget those things.* We agreed on that approach at the very end; and all the things that we agreed on in Rome, including the general amnesty, were adopted by the Mozambican parliament.... No, we never discussed the idea of offering amnesty in exchange for truth-telling.

These are things which you can understand in the circumstances. At that moment, after 16 years of war, people were starving. There were water problems and disease. The whole country was at a standstill. This environment encouraged the negotiators to be more flexible. We all said, "Let's end the war!"

Did he feel, in 2003, that the fact of that amnesty had left a lasting legacy of nonaccountability in the country? "I don't think so. Everyone here has a sense that war is always something bad. It is always destruction and killing. People understand that there is one standard for wartime and another standard for peacetime. The people understand this more than the politicians do."

I asked Domingos if, when he was a fighter, he had ever had a desire for revenge. He replied, "At the time when I lost my friends, I did *many things that I could do* in my role. Then, after the peace agreement, I was the first one who wanted to move on. I felt like the peace agreement was my child, and I wanted to watch it grow. Until now, I see it as an example for Africa and the world, and I will never accept for anything to threaten this peace."

In 1994, Domingos was one of the Renamo leaders elected to parliament in Mozambique's first multiparty elections. When he talked with me in the spring of 2003 he was still a member of parliament, but he had broken politically with Dhlakama. Now, he explained, he was working on forming a new party that would be "a constructive and dynamic alternative opposition."

Atrocities and Conflict

During my visits to Mozambique in 2001 and 2003 I met scores of people like Jacinta Jorge and Raúl Domingos who after the end of their country's seventeen-year civil war were able to "move on" from the violence of that era and help to (re)build their country as a peaceful, united, and independent nation. Their ability to do this was all the more remarkable, given the broad extent and extremely atrocious nature of the violence that had accompanied the war, which was every bit as inhumane as that recorded in the better-remembered civil wars of the past twenty years.

For example, the lengthy report on Mozambique that Human Rights Watch/Africa Watch published in July 1992—just four months before the conclusion of the peace accord—noted the following:

> The United Nations estimates that war and war-related hunger and disease have cost a total of 600,000 lives, but this is no more than a gross estimate. Most of the country's economic infrastructure is destroyed or inoperable, and much of the population is dependent on a massive international aid program. Hundreds of thousands of people are refugees in neighboring countries or displaced inside Mozambique. Many rural areas have been reduced to a stone age condition, without trade or modern manufactured goods, education or health services, and suffering from constant insecurity. Mozambique needs to be built almost from scratch.[2]

That report gave a much lower estimate for the number of Mozambicans displaced inside and outside the country than the UN reports at the time. It did, however, note the widespread incidence of mutilation and other forms of direct physical violence against civilians, forced relocation, sexual slavery, forced recruitment, and the creation of famine during the war. Regarding mutilation—which the report described as "one of the most characteristic abuses" of the war—it presented numerous detailed testimonies given by survivors, many of which mention the fact that it was *boys or male teenagers who carried it out under the direct supervision of older commanders.* One such testimony was that given by Rodrigues Laice, forty-two, a resident of Ndlavela, near Maputo. One night in May 1991, Laice and his wife had been at home when a group of about five adults and thirteen young boys, all carrying AK-47 semiautomatic rifles, came to their hut and forced them out of it. The assailants took the couple hostage and forced them to march into the bush with them. Later, the group of hostages grew to ten in number; the soldiers forced them all to porter looted goods to a Renamo-controlled zone some 30 kilometers (20 miles) away. The following day, the soldiers told Laice, his wife, and a third hostage

> to sit on the ground with their hands between their legs. Several boy soldiers, whom Laice said were between eight and nine years old,

opened jack-knives and began severing the victims' ears and slashing their noses. "The commander said we would not return without a sign," Laice said. As the young boys mutilated the three, on-looking rebels clapped and sang.... Laice recalled the commander of the group as saying, "Go and show your president that the guys you call the bandits, the Matsanga, Renamo, did this. Go and show your ears to your president Chissano." Then the three were told to leave, and a young boy soldier ran alongside them shouting "run, run!" The rebels kept five young boys captured in the raid.[3]

The report judged that

> the war in Mozambique has been characterized by a low but relentless level of violence against civilians which has continued without respite.... This has been practiced by both Renamo and FAM [the Mozambique Armed Forces], though Renamo abuses started earlier, have been more systematic and on a larger scale, and have been less subject to internal disciplinary measures than those committed by FAM. Human rights violations have occurred in several contexts. One is indiscriminate violence during military sweeps and raids. A second is exemplary terror, practiced chiefly by Renamo in order to advertise its presence and strength, to humiliate Frelimo and to terrorize civilians. A third is punitive measures against civilians designed to enforce relocation or control, and exaction of produce and labor.[4]

In the late 1980s, the Reagan administration in Washington, DC, became concerned about the level of violence being carried out by Renamo. At an aid donors' conference held in Maputo in 1988, a deputy assistant secretary of state asserted that "[w]hat has emerged in Mozambique is *one of the most brutal holocausts against ordinary human beings since World War II.* ... The supporters of Renamo, wherever they may be, cannot wash the blood from their hands unless all support for the unconscionable violence is halted immediately."[5]

Like the conflict between South Africa's apartheid regime and its opponents (but unlike the 1994 genocide in Rwanda), the civil war in Mozambique was a long-drawn-out, debilitating, and exhausting affair. It was marked by numerous apparent episodes of a kind of "blood-lust" frenzy, though testimonies like that of Rodrigues Laice indicate that much of this inhumane violence was not "spontaneous" but was, indeed, *carefully nurtured in younger fighters by their superiors.* Meanwhile, in Mozambique, as in South Africa, there was an additional, even more pervasive form of violence that—sustained throughout many long years—inflicted the greatest harm on the country's people, in terms of lives prematurely ended or irreparably blighted. In South Africa, most of this "systemic" violence was perpetrated by those who launched and upheld the apartheid system. In Mozambique, we could surmise that the systemic violence that inflicted the greatest human cost was the violence of the "civil war system" itself or, rather, the violence inflicted by those who initiated and perpetuated that war system. Like the apartheid system next door, the Mozambican civil war system forced the large-scale relocation of communities, the severing of vital ties within society, and the destruction of vital infrastructures. In Mozambique, as in South Africa, this very widespread and harmful "systemic" violence was undergirded by frequent enactments of atrocious and direct physical violence.

What was the nature of the intergroup difference that lay at the root of this lengthy and apparently deeply entrenched armed conflict? Was it a difference primarily over "politics," as had been the case in, for example, the civil war in Spain in the 1930s? Or was it also a conflict for power between identifiable religious, ethnic, racial, caste, regional, or other preexisting social groups, as in Rwanda or South Africa? In Mozambique the conflict seems largely *not* to have had the latter characteristic, but to have been overwhelmingly political. As in Spain, the key difference being fought over had to do with conflicting views of how the country's internal politics and external alignments should be organized.

Regarding ethnic and regional differences, Mozambique's indigenous society contains around two dozen different language groups (what in Europe might be called nations or ethnicities). Some of these are fairly small, others much larger and more geographically extensive.[6] After independence, as before it, the country's only official language was Portuguese, a language spoken as the mother tongue by only a tiny sector of the population. (Nearly all the previous Portuguese colonists had fled the country in great haste in 1975. Some went to Portugal. Many stayed closer, in South Africa.) When Frelimo emerged as an anticolonial guerrilla force in the 1960s it had supporters throughout Mozambique, though the first areas it was able to liberate from Portuguese rule were in the north. (Its key training bases had been in Tanzania.) When Renamo started its insurgency in the late 1970s, many of its early commanders were members of the Ndau language group, which resides mainly in the center of Mozambique. That fact was not surprising, given the proximity of Rhodesia/Zimbabwe to the center and the strong role that White Rhodesia played in incubating Renamo's formation and growth.[7]

However, after Swedish researcher Anders Nilsson had made a detailed examination of the regional/ethnic dimension of Renamo's insurgency in the 1980s, he concluded that "the regional or ethnic elements were not developed as a tool of mobilisation."[8] This conclusion was borne out in all the conversations I had with participants in the war.

Regarding religion, probably somewhat fewer than 50 percent of the people had some form of Christian affiliation, and about 10 percent were Muslims. But then as now, nearly all Mozambicans—including many with a formal affiliation as Christians or Muslims—subscribed to one or more of the country's deeply indigenous, animist belief systems. Religious affiliations played some part in sustaining the civil war system. But the civil war did not pit adherents of different religions against each other. Rather, sincere adherents and leaders within many different religions were at times mobilized by Renamo against the secularism long proclaimed by the Frelimo government. And later, as we shall see, religious leaders played a key role in dismantling the war system.

In sum, the civil war looked primarily like a conflict between *parties holding contesting political views* about the direction their whole nation should take, rather than one between religiously, regionally, or ethnically based parties contesting for a bigger share of influence in, or possibly even secession from, the broader nation. In Mozambique, as earlier in Spain, this broad political struggle sometimes did have a regional or ethnic overlay, but it was the broader political struggle regarding the direction of the whole national polity that was the primary issue being fought over. Specifically, in Mozambique, it was fought over whether the country would retain the state socialist, pro-Soviet system bequeathed to it by Frelimo's long-fought battle for national sovereignty and independence or establish the much more "free market" and pro-Western system advocated by Renamo.

One result of the fact that the polarization in Mozambique was primarily political rather than ethnic or regional was that very often indeed—as Nilsson and others have noted—brother ended up fighting against brother, or father against son. (This also happened in Spain.) Based on many interviews, Nilsson concluded that "almost all families in the Mozambican countryside had a relative who was a *matsanga* [Renamo fighter], at the same time that they had one or several relatives who had been killed by the *matsangas*." This fact would have enormous implications for the approach the society took toward dealing with the legacies of the civil war violence. As Nilsson noted, it "*implies a double difficulty in understanding the conditions for the differentiation between victims and perpetrators.*"[9]

During my own conversations in Mozambique a number of people told me they had close childhood friends who had ended up fighting on the "other" side. One was Hermínio Morais, who was head of Renamo's "Special Forces" and, later, head of the military team sent by Renamo to the last phase of the peace talks in Rome. The main person Morais was negotiating with there was Tobias Dai, chief of staff for the government armed forces.[10] "Dai was an old friend of mine, from our schooldays," Morais told me. "I knew who he was though he used the *nom-de-guerre* 'Fidel.' But he didn't have any idea who I was, since I was still only known by the *nom-de-guerre* of 'Bob.' When he saw me, he said, 'Hermínio, it's you!' He couldn't believe I had been 'Bob' for all those years!"

The fact that many fighters from opposing sides had grown up in the same families or communities also perhaps helps explain another phenomenon that Morais described. He (and others whom I interviewed) recalled that in 1992, even before the two delegations had signed off on the multipart General Peace Agreement (GPA) in Rome, many members of the opposing forces present on the various battlefields had started to fraternize openly with their "enemies":

> When I returned from Rome, I got information that there had been contact between my soldiers and Frelimo. This was strange because beforehand they'd been fighting. But then there was a complete change. It was very dangerous for the intermediate commanders because their superior officers might think that if they encouraged the fraternizations, then they must have been Frelimo agents all along. But it actually became something that happened in the whole country.

Hermínio Morais, like everyone else who has reflected on the factors that persuaded the two leaderships to enter serious peace negotiations, mentioned the mounting stress that many years of fighting had imposed on the country's social and economic fabric. "We started to think of negotiations at the time of the famine of 1987–1988," he told me. *"People began to realize the link between famine and war,* and to see the need to slow the war. Soldiers began to desert in large numbers. Most of those on the Frelimo side had joined only because of conscription, so they had no personal reasons to fight. And so we, the leaders, began to meet. We used the church as a bridge."

Conflict Termination

Anglican Archbishop Dinis Sengulane was one of the leaders of the (Protestant) Christian Council of Mozambique (CCM) who went to Kenya to meet with the Renamo leaders in February 1989. I met him in 2003 in his church's charming but dusty headquarters complex in a busy part of Maputo. "The leaders of the churches had been going to visit President Chissano periodically since 1984," he explained.

> We kept saying to him that the way to peace is through dialogue. We kept repeating that. We kept saying to him, "If you speak to the people you call 'bandits' you are not legitimizing their role but you're legitimizing your own role as national leader." At some point, Chissano acquiesced. He said, "Alright, I'm ready to talk to them, but you won't find anyone in Renamo who will talk to us." ...
>
> It wasn't an easy task we had. We had to be discreet, and make our contacts with no publicity. We had to have a *lot* of patience. We had to be impartial. And we were deliberately trying *not* to be an intermediary. We wanted the government to talk to Renamo, not to us!
>
> No doubt, our prayers and our Bible study helped us do our task. Once we had the green light from both sides, we said to the Catholics, "We know you want the same thing," and got them involved too.[11]

Until the point that Chissano agreed to authorize those first, discreet contacts with the Renamo leaders in 1989 he had continued to insist that in addition to being merely *bandidos armados,* and invalid interlocutors for that reason, they were merely "tools" of foreign powers, and that therefore the best way to end their insurgency would be by concluding an agreement with their outside sponsors. In 1984 he did conclude such an agreement, with South Africa. It was called the Nkomati Accord; in it, each side pledged that it would not allow its territory or resources to be used to launch attacks against the other.[12] But the pressures on each side to continue the intervention in the affairs of the other continued to mount, and the Nkomati Accord rapidly broke down.

When Chissano reached out through the CCM to the Renamo leaders in 1988–1989, his decision to do so was still very controversial in most Frelimo circles. In reaching out to Renamo *qua* Renamo, and in holding out the hope of a negotiated political settlement with it, Chissano was according Renamo more stature (i.e., as a legitimately *Mozambican* force that was pursuing a possibly legitimate political agenda within the country) than many Frelimo people were happy with. For example, when I spoke with longtime Frelimo central committee member Marcelino Dos Santos in 2003, he still said, "I will *never* speak about a 'civil war' in Mozambique. It was a war against South Africa. They fought a war against Mozambique through an instrument called Renamo." However, once the majority of Frelimo's leaders had decided they wanted to try to negotiate a peace with Renamo, they realized they would need to ramp down their previous demonization of it as a necessarily illegitimate force and start thinking about Renamo's people as, first and foremost, *fellow countrymen* who were pursuing legitimate, noncriminal goals. Renamo's leaders had to undertake a similar shift: From describing the Frelimo government as an illegitimate, Moscow-imposed "tool" of Soviet imperialism to granting it recognition as being composed of fellow countrymen. The new ideology of "fellow countrymen" required some time to take root; but as it did so, it helped color many other aspects of the negotiations.

The well-informed Mozambican social thinker and sociology professor Brazão Mazula has noted that the mutual decision by the leaders of both fighting parties to *foreswear future criminal prosecutions* played a central role in allowing the peace talks even to start at all:

> Frelimo first asked Renamo to recognize their crimes as a condition to hold peace talks. Renamo responded by saying Frelimo also had to acknowledge their own past crimes. It took five or six very difficult months before this issue could be worked out, with the Church acting as mediator. It was almost impossible to get beyond this issue to get negotiations started. Eventually a policy of "reconciliation" was agreed to, which was understood to mean that there were crimes, that they were forgiven, and that there would be a general pardon.

After this agreement, neither party was obliged to admit their crimes. But it was not easy getting there.[13]

The Catholic church was better connected than the Protestant churches with the Renamo leaders, and two key Catholic church leaders came to play an increasing role in the discreet talk-about-talks. It was they who secured the offer from Sant' Egidio to host the first direct negotiations between the government and Renamo. This arrangement neatly resolved the diplomatic status issue that had caused Frelimo's leaders such great concern.

The chief Catholic prelate in Maputo, Cardinal Alexandre Dos Santos, recalled that an important part of his message during his peacemaking work was to stress the need for a forward-looking rather than backward-looking perspective. "We can't solve anything if you speak about the *reasons* you are fighting," Dos Santos told me in 2003. "You need to just try to find the way to get peace. You want to speak about the way to find a meeting of the minds, not speak about the differences.... I told people, 'We are not here to discuss the reasons, or the past, but the way to get peace!'"

The SE people who took up the peace facilitation role used the same approach. Matteo Zuppi was one of them. He has written that when his colleague Andrea Riccardi opened the first meeting with the Frelimo and Renamo negotiators held in Rome, in July 1990, Riccardi

> recalled the biblical story of Joseph and his brothers who, after years of separation and division, found each other again as members of the same family. Riccardi wanted to express a hope that the same would happen with the Mozambicans.... It was a gamble: peace was possible, even though buried under mountains of distrust and confrontation. *We will look for what unites us, and put aside what divides us.* And the uniting factor was the Mozambican identity, membership of the same family. This was our conviction and our hope. I would also say that this was the working method for the entire negotiations: a method we always defended, even when it seemed simpler and more natural to give way to the things that divided, and there were plenty of those![14]

After that first meeting—the one that began with the famous handshake—Raúl Domingos and his Frelimo counterpart, Armando Guebuza, issued a joint communiqué in which they "acknowledged themselves to be compatriots and members of the great Mozambican family" and stressed their commitment to finding a peaceful settlement. Twenty-seven months later, the two parties concluded the General Peace Agreement that defined the basis on which they would definitively end their lengthy, very harmful conflict. Along the way, the SE people brought in officials from the Italian Foreign Ministry and the United Nations, who underwrote some of the diplomatic aspects of the GPA. Throughout the entire negotiation, the negotiators and their SE facilitators worked according to the forward-looking philosophy that Riccardi had spelled out.

In October 1992 Chissano, Dhlakama, their negotiators, their Sant' Egidio and Italian sponsors, and a gathering of international dignitaries met in Rome to sign the GPA. It consisted of seven detailed Protocols and four appended documents. The first two Articles of Protocol I ("Basic Principles") stated:

1. The Government undertakes to refrain from taking any action that is contrary to the provisions of the Protocols to be concluded and from adopting laws or measures *or applying existing laws* which may be inconsistent with those Protocols.

2. Renamo, for its part, undertakes, beginning on the date of entry into force of the cease-fire, to refrain from armed combat and instead to conduct its political struggle in conformity with the laws in force, within the framework of the existing State institutions.[15]

The three keys to the success of the GPA proved to be, first, that in line with Article 1 above, the government side offered a retrospective, blanket amnesty to all individuals, including those formerly described as *bandidos armados;* second, in line with two of the GPA's other Protocols, both sides pledged to participate in a fair democratic process, and to resolve their remaining differences through that process rather than through violence; and, third, extensive attention was given to the challenge of disarming, demobilizing, and reintegrating former combatants into civilian life (known in common UN jargon as "DDR.") Those three commitments underpinned the successful peacebuilding that followed. Securing the blanket amnesty was the easy part: The Frelimo government simply introduced legislation to this effect into the parliament that it controlled, and won it very rapidly. Undertaking the DDR and electoral components of the peace would take a little longer.

Formal Steps to Build the Peace

Even before October 1992 the United Nations had been playing a large role in Mozambique, where—alongside numerous other aid organizations—it had been trying for many years to relieve the chronic, large-scale suffering that the war had caused. The challenges there included widespread starvation and the displacement of millions of Mozambicans both inside and outside their country.

When the General Peace Agreement was concluded, it assigned to a new UN force yet to be established responsibility for the following:

- monitoring and verifying the ceasefire;
- demobilizing most of the combatants;
- supervising the withdrawal of foreign forces;
- protecting vital national infrastructures;
- providing technical assistance for, and monitoring, the new electoral process; and
- continuing to coordinate and monitor humanitarian relief operations.

In December 1992, the Security Council passed Resolution 797 to establish the new force, which was called the United Nations Operation in Mozambique (UNOMOZ).[16] In early 1993, UNOMOZ's peacekeepers started to deploy within the country. Its military component reached its maximum strength of 6,576 members in November 1993. There was also a civilian police component: Its maximum strength, reached near the end of 1994, was 1,087 officers. By the time UNOMOZ's mission came to an end in December 1994, it had registered significant achievements in all areas of its mandate including, crucially, demobilization of the previously fighting forces and the successful holding of a democratic nationwide election.

Regarding the DDR effort, a study carried out by Iraê Baptista Lundin and a team of Mozambican researchers later reported that the demobilization "did not start until late 1993.... In total, about 92,890 combatants were demobilized, of which 70,910 were Government soldiers and 21,980 Renamo fighters. Of the demobilized combatants 1380 (1.5 per cent) were women. The demobilized had a total of 215,000 dependants."[17] Following demobilization of the fighting units, ONUMOZ, working with other organizations, arranged for the transport of each demobilized soldier to a place of his or her choosing. (In most, but not all, cases this was the soldier's original home.) After arrival there, he or she would receive twenty-four monthly payments, delivered locally, under a "Reintegration Support Scheme." A linked program set up by other UN bodies was supposed to provide vocational and entrepreneurial training to the demobilized fighters. By the time the DDR program was wrapped up in 1997, it had incurred total cash costs of $100.7 million;[18] 89 percent of that came from the international community.

Baptista Lundin and his colleagues noted that significant assistance to the demobilized fighters came not from the formal programs organized by the national government or the United Nations but from the communities to which they returned—communities, as they wrote, that had "little to offer in terms of finance and programmes, but with a commitment to survive and provide a better life for relatives or former strangers." They quoted one traditional chief from Niassa province as saying, "We gave our daughters in marriage to ex-soldiers, so they could settle here with us and help to feed our children. They are our sons now, and are doing good so far."[19]

Under the GPA, a new 30,000-person national army called the Mozambican Armed Defense Force (FADM) was to be formed, made up of equal numbers of former Frelimo and Renamo fighters. However, most former combatants were so weary of military life that only around one-third of the required number opted to join the FADM. Hermínio Morais, who had been Renamo's military negotiator in Rome, headed the commission charged with organizing and training the FADM. He told me that it was particularly hard to find Renamo fighters who could meet the standards required for the new force, and that this caused problems because recruitment was supposed to be on a strictly 50–50 basis.

Baptista Lundin's team wrote that although the bulk of the cost of the DDR effort was met by the international community, the 15 percent of the cost contributed by the Mozambican government represented a burden that just about wiped out from Mozambique's 1996 and 1997 budgets the "peace dividend" that many in government had hoped to reap from the GPA. (The authors note that many in the government had in any case, from the beginning, expressed several reservations about the reintegration payments program, with some officials arguing that there were many extremely needy groups in national society in addition to the former combatants.) Baptista Lundin and his collegues concluded that "[t]here has been a considerable gap between the aspirations and the actual accomplishment thus far. However ... even if the costs of demobilization and reintegration are high, the 'peace dividend' is in fact the *peace* itself—providing an environment for productive and financial dividend-gathering activities."[20]

Regarding the plan to hold democratic elections, in the circumstances of mass hunger, pauperization, large-scale dislocations, and general social neediness that Mozambique faced as it emerged from the war, the infrastructure for planning and holding these elections had to be built up entirely from scratch. In May 1993, the UN Development Program (UNDP) concluded an agreement with the government whereby it provided aid in organizing the elections; but all the important decisions along the way were taken by an all-Mozambican National Elections Commission (CNE), which was established in November 1993 and headed by the widely respected Brazão Mazula, a political independent. Beside Mazula the CNE had twenty members: Ten were from Frelimo, seven from Renamo, and three from the smaller parties. The choice of Mazula as chair turned out to be a wise one. According to UN consultant Richard Synge, "Mazula ensured that all decisions of the CNE were reached by consensus and succeeded in defusing the issues that defied agreement."[21]

Throughout 1994, UNOMOZ supported the election preparations by deploying civilian police units to politically sensitive areas. Meanwhile, between March and May 1994, the CNE recruited and trained more than 12,000 people as voter registration agents, civic education agents, and members of province-level electoral commissions. As part of the registration process, every adult Mozambican was, for the first time ever, issued with a photo ID card.

Voter registration started on June 1. (The demobilization of soldiers was still far from finished, but everyone concerned wanted the elections held before the end of October 1994.) Registration agents were deployed throughout the country in five-member teams. In some places it was hard to find enough people who had had the six years of schooling required for the job. Even ensuring food and lodging for the agents was a tough challenge. Synge wrote, "In all the more remote and war-damaged areas, camping equipment and food had to be provided.... [M]aintaining supplies to the most remote areas was a constant logistical challenge."[22] By the time registration closed on September 2, more than 6.3 million voters had been registered. The CNE ruled that 12 candidates were qualified to run for president and 14 political parties or coalitions were eligible to run for the 250-member parliament.

Even during the hotly contested election campaign that followed, it was notable that the nationwide norm against mentioning the hurts and accusations of the very recent civil war era remained strong. Former Frelimo government minister José Luís Cabaço has recalled that he asked some of the elections experts from (also Portuguese-speaking) Brazil who had come to advise Frelimo's campaign team what strategy they would recommend: "They said they thought the campaign should focus on the abuses Renamo had committed during the war. '*No,* don't do that,' I said immediately. 'That would only create conflict. It would be seen on the ground as trying to bring back conflict into our village, when we've solved it already; [as] bringing back the spirits of evil to the village.'"[23]

Throughout those months of campaigning, Renamo head Dhlakama and some foreign ambassadors started agitating more or less openly for an ex post facto change in the constitutional system spelled out in the GPA from one that allowed for the formation of a government by any single party that could win a parliamentary majority to one that mandated the formation of a national unity government. (This would have been similar to the agreement the ANC had reached with the NP in South Africa prior to the April 1994 vote there.) Many in Mozambique and the international community were worried that if Dhlakama refused to accept the validity of a Frelimo win in the election, he might follow the path that Angola's insurgent leader Jonas Savimbi took in Angola in October 1992 and reignite his insurgency after suffering a loss at the polls. Chissano and his colleagues in Frelimo remained adamant, however, that they wanted to stick with the GPA's existing constitutional formula. Dhlakama was not happy.

The elections were scheduled for October 27–28. On October 25, at Chissano's suggestion, Zimbabwean President Robert Mugabe hosted a summit meeting that brought Dhlakama together with eight African heads of state or government. The summit group presented Dhlakama with a warning that if he contested the election outcome he could not expect any support from outside sources. UN consultant Richard Synge has written that Dhlakama left Zimbabwe for his home city, Beira, feeling "insulted and cheated." He then holed up there; the next day he announced Renamo's withdrawal from the election. Diplomats in Maputo engaged in a flurry of activity to resolve this last-minute crisis. The South African ambassador—whose country had just months earlier survived a series of similarly cliff-hanging threats to its key, transitional election—flew to Beira to confer with Dhlakama.

At 5 A.M. on October 27, the CNE issued a statement saying the elections would start that day as planned. In 7,417 polling places around the country, 52,000 polling officers reported for work. Throughout the day the ambassadors continued to try to reach Dhalakama and persuade him to change his mind. In the small hours of October 28 they finally convinced him to participate in the elections—but only after he extracted their solemn word that they would not publicly certify the elections as "free and fair" before examining all of Renamo's complaints against Frelimo. At 9:30 A.M. on the second election day, the ambassadors signed a commitment to this effect. The CNE then announced it would extend the voting to a third day; and Dhlakama went on Radio Mozambique to announce Renamo's return to the elections. The crisis had been defused.

On November 2, UN Special Representative Aldo Ajello put out a statement saying that the elections had been peaceful, well organized, and free of major irregularities. In the end, the crucial weeks after the election did *not* bring the feared, Angola-style collapse of the whole peace process. Indeed, the security situation actually improved. Though the vote counting and certification process was lengthy, it became increasingly clear that, as everyone expected, Frelimo had won both the presidential and parliamentary races. On November 14, Dhlakama informed the UN secretary general that he would accept the results and was "prepared to cooperate with the government."[24]

Five days later, Mazula announced the final results. The total number of voters was 5.4 million. In the presidential race, Chissano won 53.3 percent of the votes to Dhlakama's 33.7 percent. In the parliamentary race, Frelimo won 44.3 percent; and Renamo, 37.8 percent. UN representative Aldo Ajello certified that the elections had been free and fair. Dhlakama reportedly repeated his accusation that there had been discrimination against Renamo, but he said that Renamo accepted the results "as a basis for it to exercise its democratic rights of opposition."[25]

The new president and parliament were inaugurated on December 8 and 9. ONUMOZ's mandate came to a formal end at midnight on December 9, and by the end of January 1995 the last members of the force had left the country.

Chapter 4

Community-Based Peacebuilding

In 1992, Mozambique's population was estimated at 14.7 million. Military expenditures were 20 percent higher than the combined national spending on health and education. Average daily calorie supply per capita was 1,680—lower than in all other countries that year except Somalia, Afghanistan, and Ethiopia. Of every 1,000 children born, 148 died before their first birthday and a further 186 died before their fifth birthday. Forty-seven percent of children under the age of five were malnourished. There were only three doctors serving every 100,000 Mozambicans.[26]

Much of this human deprivation was the result of damage inflicted during the civil war. But it can also be said that much was the result of earlier centuries of exploitation of the country's people and their natural resources at the hands of the Portuguese colonizers. The same kind of colonial exploitation had also, of course, occurred in South Africa and Rwanda. But in those other countries the colonial powers had at least tried to build some elements of a modern physical and institutional infrastructure. In Mozambique, by contrast, the Portuguese did almost nothing to "develop" the country except in a small number of areas such as the capital, Lourenço Marques (later Maputo), and the strategic port city of Beira.

The near-total failure of the Portuguese to invest in the physical and institutional infrastructure, coupled with the flight of a high proportion of the country's Portuguese settlers immediately after independence, meant that in 1975 Frelimo had to start almost from scratch in building schools, medical clinics, roads, bridges, law courts, and the other institutions of a modern nation. The Frelimo leaders—many of whom had very sketchy educational backgrounds and little experience of managing anything other than guerilla fighting units—set about doing this with much help from their allies in the Soviet Union and Cuba and smaller amounts of help from West European nations. But the institutions they built then became prime targets for Renamo's vicious campaign of destabilization. Brazão Mazula has noted that 59 percent of the primary schools that existed in 1983 had been destroyed by 1992, as had 36 percent of the health posts.[27]

The acute under- and de-development of Mozambique during and after the colonial period contributed significantly to the poverty and deprivation suffered by the population. But it also meant, more fortuitously, that many of the age-old cultural resources developed by the country's people throughout preceding generations had not been wiped out through any "march of modernization." Though the country had few modern-style health institutions such as hospitals, nursing schools, and pathology labs, it boasted many rich strands of traditional knowledge in the fields of physical and psychiatric medicine, as well as a deep philosophical understanding of such matters as the place of the individual in the universe, her relationship with the rest of society, and the nature of violence among humans. Indeed, given that Western-style boundaries between various fields of knowledge such as "medicine," "law," "politics," and "religion" had still not been imposed on the country's knowledge systems, the *curanderos* and *curanderas* (traditional healers) from all the country's different language groups had access to a wealth of accumulated traditional wisdom in all of these fields.

These traditional sets of understandings and their associated practices did a lot to help Mozambicans withstand the tragedies and existential disruptions of the war era, as anthropologist Carolyn Nordstrom and others have chronicled. In addition, as the war wound down they provided a bedrock of understanding of what could help to revive and rebuild a peaceable and productive social order. This understanding informed not only the work of the traditional healers themselves but also that of leaders of many different sectors of society, including activists in social-welfare NGOs, leaders and activists of more institutionalized faith groups, and even many political leaders and activists.

How do thinkers and leaders in Mozambique's indigenous traditions understand the nature of interhuman violence, and how did this affect the way that they and their compatriots responded to the challenge of reintegrating communities torn apart by the atrocious violence of the civil war? In Chapter 1, I noted the description that traditional healer Fernando Manuel Dos Santos Zimba gave of the nature of interhuman violence: "If someone is violent, then that is not a normal state of affairs. It must be a spiritual problem he's suffering from, and this must be dealt with through traditional medicine. Someone who kills another person ... *must have some kind of a wrong spirit with him.*"[28] Nordstrom, who carried out a lot of field research in Mozambique during and at the end of the civil war, has written eloquently about how, throughout the long years of war, the *curandero/as* and other community members continued their work of healing individuals and social groups, and how their exercise of those skills continued almost seamlessly into the period of the peace. She quotes one *curandero* as explaining his efforts thus:

> This war, it teaches people violence. A lot of soldiers come to me. Many of these boys never wanted to fight, they did not know what it meant to fight. Many were hauled into the military, taken far from their homes, and made to fight. It messes them up. You see, if you kill someone, their soul stays with you. The souls of the murdered follow these soldiers back to their homes and their families, back to their communities to cause problems. The soldier's life, his family, his community, begin to disintegrate from the strain of this. But it goes further than this. These soldiers ... have learned to use violence. Their own souls have been corrupted by what they have seen and done ... *We have to take this violence out of these people,* we have to teach them how to live nonviolent lives like they did before. The problem would be serious enough if it were only the soldiers, but it is not. When a woman is kidnapped, raped, and forced to work for soldiers, when a child is exposed to violence in an attack, when people are submitted to assaults and terrible injuries, the violence sticks to them. It is like the soldier carrying the souls of those he has killed back into his normal life, but here, the soul carries the violence.... We can treat this, we have to. We literally take the violence out of the people, we teach them how to relearn healthy ways of thinking and acting.[29]

Many observers of the social healing practices in Mozambique have noted that, as suggested by the *curandero,* "relearning healthy ways" included much attention to healthy acting as well as healthy thinking. In the West, the first of these types of intervention might be described as behavioral therapy, or ergotherapy. In Mozambique it frequently involved—as the Niassa province chief quoted above had indicated—both finding spouses for demobilized fighters and trying to get them reintegrated into the productive life of their communities as rapidly as possible.

Regarding the mechanisms used by the *curanderos* to "take the violence out of the person," they varied somewhat from region to region. But Mozambican social scientist Alcinda Honwana has given us the following description of how this goal was pursued in the case of "Samuel," a former boy soldier who had been abducted by Renamo when he was nine years old and then pressed into service for them for more than two years. After the ceasefire Samuel was reunited with some of his relatives: On his first day with them they took him to the family's *ndumba* (the house of the spirits) where he was presented to the family's ancestral spirits. A few days later the family brought in a traditional healer to help them perform a necessary cleansing ritual for Samuel:

> The practitioner took the boy to the bush, where a small hut covered with dry grass had been built. The boy, dressed in the dirty clothes he brought from the rebel camp, entered the hut and undressed himself. Then the hut was set on fire, and an adult relative helped the boy out. The hut, the clothes, and everything else that the boy brought from the camp had to be burnt. This symbolized the rupture with that past. A chicken was sacrificed for the spirits of the dead, and the blood was spread around the ritual place. The chicken was then cooked and offered to the spirits as a sacrificial meal. The boy had to inhale the smoke of some herbal remedies and bathe himself in water treated with medicine. In this way his body was cleansed both internally and externally. Finally, the spirit medium made some incisions in the boy's body and filled them with a paste made from herbal remedies, a practice called *ku thlavela*. The purpose of this procedure is to give strength to the boy. During this public ritual, relatives and neighbors were present and assisted the practitioner by performing specific roles, or just by observing, singing, and clapping.[30]

The boy was then reintegrated into the life of his home village. This path was pursued even though he might well have been someone who earlier undertook against his fellow villagers acts just as gruesome as the mutilations described above.

Belief in the value of rituals such as these—and in the underlying cosmology of intimate linkages between an individual, his home community, and his ancestors—has remained widespread throughout Mozambique, easily transcending the "boundaries" between the different language groups as well as those between the cities and the extremely underdeveloped countryside.[31] When I met Hermínio Morais in Maputo in 2003, the former Renamo military negotiator (and head of Special Forces) was near the end of his studies for a law degree. Between 1992 and 1994, he headed the Commission for Organization and Training of the new, unified national army. But before doing that, at the end of the war, he, too, took part in a purification ritual. "We slaughtered a goat, and I bathed in the blood," he said, giving no further details. "Yes of course I needed

159

to do it—because during the war I might have stepped over a place where people were killed, or I might have shot someone."[32]

Psychotherapist Lina Luísa Inglês was well aware of the prevalence of this worldview when, after the 1992 peace agreement, she started working with communities seeking to reintegrate members displaced during the war. At that point she was one of only two or three Mozambicans trained in the methods of Western-style psychotherapy. She was working for the Mozambican Association for Public Health, setting up therapeutic services to help the reintegration effort in two very impoverished communities. She knew, as most of the people in those communities also knew, that many of the formerly displaced people who would be returning had been in close contact with acts of extreme atrocity—as perpetrators, victims, or both.

I met Inglês in 2001 in the headquarters of the nongovernmental group Association for Rebuilding Hope, of which she was then executive director. She said that when she started working with residents of Josina Machel Island, one of her target communities, she knew enough not simply to leap straight into the situation, brandishing a panoply of Western-style therapeutic techniques.

> First, I worked with the local leaders there, to find out how they saw their needs, and to tell them what kind of services the Association might be able to offer. I needed to learn what the activity of the population had been, both during and after the war. They were so poor! Their animals had all been killed early on in the war, so the condition of the soil had become really bad, because they needed the animal manure to keep it fertile. Business and trade had shrunk to almost zero.
>
> I needed to find out how the community was planning to receive the returnees, who would include both children, and people who were being demobilized from Renamo. The people on the island, to receive people back from the war, used mainly the rituals of their local church to "take the war out of the people."

The church in question was, she explained, a "Zionist" church—that is, one holding to a strongly Africanized Protestant tradition that had originated in South Africa. Inglês recalled that community leaders on the island used rituals associated with the twelve apostles, combined with some traditional healing rituals, in order to "purify" the returnees. "Yes, and I myself took part in some of these ceremonies—because we wanted to understand how they approach these issues.... We needed to understand the approach used by the local leaders if we hoped to integrate our work with theirs."

In the post-GPA period, it was not just the syncretic churches that worked in consonance with traditional Mozambican understandings regarding the need for deep social healing. The Western-origin churches—Catholic and Protestant—and the Islamic congregations did this, too. Anglican Bishop Dinis Sengulane recalled that once the Sant' Egidio team had taken over sponsorship of the peace talks, he and his colleagues from the Protestant CCM turned their attentions to preparing the ground for the peace, "at home." Boaventura Zita, a CCM staff member, told me in 2001 that "[w]hen the peace was about to be signed in 1992, the CCM's Peace and Reconciliation Committee started seminars throughout the country and amongst the refugee communities outside.... We looked at the question 'How can you build reconciliation between members of the same family?' We did so on the basis of forgiveness—but *without forgetting* what had happened."

In my interviews with Sengulane and Catholic Cardinal Alexandre Dos Santos, both prelates similarly underscored the need *not to forget* what had happened, while also forgiving those who had committed those acts. Sengulane pointed to a light-colored scar on his hand. "I look at that scar and remember the accident that caused it," he said. "The wound no longer hurts at all. But it is important to remember what happened so I don't make the same mistake again." The focus that several Christian leaders put on not forgetting what had happened did not, however, seem very widely shared in Mozambican society. Alcinda Honwana has written about the danger of opening up old psychic wounds if they are redescribed or otherwise actively remembered; and during my interviews in and around Maputo most people expressed the view that it can be very harmful to open up the old social and psychic wounds of the past.

Mozambique, 1992–2005

Mozambique After the Civil War

In the thirteen years that followed Mozambique's peace agreement, its leaders and people never attempted to adopt either of the two main kinds of formal "transitional justice" mechanism generally addressed in discussions on global policy: a war crimes court or a truth commission. What the Mozambicans did instead as they attempted to deal with the needs of victims, perpetrators, and society itself after the war was to continue to focus at the official level on the two main elements of their peace agreement: completion of the DDR program and further institutionalization of the country's fledgling democracy. Meanwhile, with some (occasionally misguided) help from international lenders and donors, the government tried to invest in the country's economy and human resource base. This mix of policies proved remarkably successful at effecting social reconstruction within the country. Indeed, it proved so successful that many participants in the international debates on transitional justice that intensified from the late 1990s on never really thought of Mozambique as a country to which issues of (postconflict) transitional justice were applicable. But during their peace negotiation phase and their immediate post-conflict phase, the country's leaders and people did indeed make concrete choices regarding transitional justice issues. They made a concrete choice to enact the blanket amnesty and thereby abjure the choice of war crimes prosecutions. They also, less formally but with apparently equal determination, made a choice not to "look back" too closely at all the harms and suffering of the war period, and not even to begin to assign formal responsibility for those harms to any individual persons.

So how did the country fare in those post-GPA years? Did its people come to regret the choices they had earlier made not to establish either a war crimes court or a truth commission? In the remainder of this chapter I shall present, first, a quick snapshot of the country's main achievements in the years 1992–2005 and, then, a discursive, people-centered account of what the Mozambicans did to heal their society, including what they say about how and why they believe that their peacebuilding process worked.

During those years Mozambique faced many evident challenges—and not just the ones engendered by the preceding decades of colonialism and civil war. One harmful additional legacy from the conflict era was the widespread presence of antipersonnel landmines, which rendered large tracts of potentially farmable land off-limits to cultivators and herders, considerably complicating the task of resettling the millions of Mozambicans displaced internally or externally during the war. (The mines also, even many years after 1992, continued to kill and maim scores of Mozambicans every month.) In 2000 and again in 2001 Mozambique suffered catastrophic flooding in the broad downstream basins of the Zambesi and Limpopo rivers. In other years, low rainfall in those watersheds contributed to draught in the same areas. HIV/AIDS also swept through the country; by 2001 some 13 percent of all citizens between the ages of fifteen and forty-nine were judged to be living with it.[33] (In the modern era, the rapid spread of HIV/AIDS is one quite predictable result of the social dislocations occasioned by war.) Moreover, throughout the 1990s—while the country was still struggling to (re)build from the privations of the war—the International Monetary Fund was imposing "structural adjustment" onto its economy, a factor that many Mozambicans blamed for the destruction of vital economic sectors.

All these challenges are precisely the kinds of stressors that can be expected to place a heavy burden on any political order, especially in a society where fear, violence, and deep distrust had so recently prevailed. In Mozambique, the political order set in place by the GPA remained generally robust. The national election of 1994 and its aftermath were much more successful than many people had dared to hope. Local elections held in 1998 were less successful: They were not fairly organized and were boycotted by Renamo on those grounds. But in 1999 the country held a successful second national election and, in late 2003, a much more successful round of local elections. (Renamo won four of the thirty-three municipal-level contests, including those in the important port cities of Beira and Nacala; Frelimo won the rest.) In December 2004, Mozambique held its third round of national-level elections. By then, Joaquim Chissano had stepped down as head of Frelimo and had been replaced by former peace negotiator Armando Guebuza. Guebuza won the presidential race as expected, and Frelimo increased its representation in parliament. Renamo, still headed by Dhlakama, was the only other party to win seats in parliament at that time since the other three parties all failed to meet the 5 percent threshold for parliamentary representation. (These included the new party headed by Raúl Domingos.)

There were concerns about the conduct of that last election. The US-based Carter Center monitored it and later issued a statement saying that, while it recognized the overall results, nevertheless "the Center concludes the National Elections Commission (CNE) has not administered a fair and transparent election in all parts of Mozambique.... The overall election results are not in question, as indicated by the wide margin of Frelimo's victory and confirmed by the parallel vote tabulation conducted by domestic observers. However, the problems observed by The Carter Center could have had serious consequences in a closer election."[34] There were some political tensions in the aftermath of the election, though the well-informed analyst Elísio Macamo noted that "at no time was there any hint of violence." By mid-2005 Macamo was writing, "It seems … that the country is now moving towards a sort of entente after the initial postelection turbulence and there is no reason to fear that this trend may be reversed."[35]

Every year, as it has done for many years now, the UN Development Program, which has been deeply involved in Mozambique since 1992, gives all the world's countries a rating called the Human Development Index (HDI), based on per capita income, life expectancy, and provision of schooling. Over the dozen years following the GPA, Mozambique's HDI score went modestly upward: In 1990 it had been 0.317, and by 2003 it was 0.379. But Mozambique remained near the bottom of the list of countries in terms of HDI scores, coming in 168th out of the 177 nations ranked.[36] Between 1990 and 2002–2003 the proportion of the country's primary school-age children who were in school rose from 45 percent to 55 percent, and the literacy rate among youths fifteen to twenty-four rose from 49 percent to 63 percent.[37] In the post-GPA years, the size of the national army decreased to the point where it contained only 11,000 people in 2002. And defense expenditures as a proportion of GDP plummeted from over 10 percent in 1992 to around 2 percent in 2003.[38]

During my visits to Mozambique in 2001 and 2003 I found it to be a country basically at peace with itself but plagued by continuing material poverty, socioeconomic polarization, and significant resulting crime. Vast shantytowns inhabited by displaced people from the war years—and their descendants—still ringed the capital, Maputo. The capital city's colonial-era physical infrastructure was visibly decayed, but there had been some construction of modern high-rises and many of the city's boulevards were frequently clogged with traffic. Most office buildings and private residences in the richer parts of town had armed private security guards standing watch outside, and beggars and street vendors could often be seen. Many people still seemed quite happy to go out at night: Despite the abysmally poor provision of street lighting, the restaurants, bars, and other places of public entertainment were doing a good trade. Nearly everywhere I went outside the central portion of the city, however, material poverty and underdevelopment seemed the norm.

Some Civil Society Voices

When I talked with psychotherapist Lina Luísa Inglês in 2001 I asked if she thought that the use of community-based healing ceremonies, like the ones she witnessed and participated in on Josina Machel Island, had succeeded in "taking the violence out" of the people there; or, conversely, whether there was some residual level of violence in society that perhaps had been deeply repressed along the way, only to reemerge later. Her assessment was: "Because of their beliefs, it works! There is no special violence that has lasted from the war, only the 'normal' levels of violence. But no, no 'cycles of violence' lasting from the war. Also, because the ritual is public, there are many people to help you, and it's very reconciliatory."[39]

She admitted that there was still a lot of domestic violence in some of these communities, but she attributed this to a combination of underemployment and the effects of alcohol rather than to unresolved issues stemming from the war.

How did she feel about the idea of punishing people who had committed violent acts during the war?

> We believe that if you killed someone during the war that was because of the violent spirit. In normal times, we may say that a person should be punished. But in a war, it would be a spiritual crisis, not an issue of individual blame.
>
> Also, children were exposed directly to violence here. Are you going to punish the children for what they did? But the kids are part of the rituals here, and in that way they became reinforced with their family's and community's beliefs.

Another Mozambican I talked with in Maputo that year had a less certain assessment. This man spoke on the condition that he not be named, because of sensitivities connected to his work. He said he felt it was possible that the war-era violence had *not* been fully exorcized but, rather, that "it might be all bottled up, and may come back in another ten years time." He noted that in the national parliament, "when the discussions get tough—people make really tough accusations against each other. So you can see that there is dormant rage there." He also saw a tendency toward rhetorical violence in the responses Mozambicans gave in a recent survey on attitudes about corruption: "People were asked what should be done to corrupt officials. Around 70 percent of the interviewees said something like 'cut off their hands,' 'hang them,' or 'burn them.' ... My conclusion was that there is still a lot of violence inside people."

This man also noted that there had been no attempt to build memorials to those lost in the civil war, "because that would reopen the old wounds." He said there were still noticeable social and political divisions in the north of the country, but attributed that fact mainly to the IMF-forced closing of some big textile factories there: "14,000 people lost their jobs in textiles in one province alone." He estimated that the country's economic woes affected former Renamo supporters disproportionately, since they did not have the same access to government jobs as Frelimo's supporters.

He voiced the following conclusions:

> We may say that what was done in terms of reconciliation was not enough, but it is hard to say what could have been done. Hopefully, if there is more delivery of basic services and the politicians find a way to work together, then maybe after a generation everything would be alright? ...
>
> It is so difficult in societies like Mozambique's to use the same criteria of individual accountability you might use in the west—especially for our child soldiers. So where can you place the responsibility for what happened? I suppose you could externalize the responsibility or cause of the conflict onto evil spirits, or onto the political leadership. Well, at least you can exorcize the evil spirits! But the political leaders are still *there,* and a constant reminder. And if they're not delivering basic services, then that's a problem.

Christian Council of Mozambique activist Boaventura Zita dealt with some of these same issues in the conversation we had in the CCM's rambling headquarters complex, on the site of what was once a Protestant boarding school.[40] Zita recalled that during the war he had worked as a journalist, reporting on many different massacres around the country. He said:

> Now, it's true, we see Chissano and Dhlakama shouting at each other. But still, it's just at the level of talk. ...
>
> Is it good for Mozambique to use what's good for South Africa, like a Truth and Reconciliation Commission? No. We have to find our own way. The biggest need here is for access to resources. We

need reconciliation above all. The country is still in the process of being built! ... Our biggest need is for reconstruction. Since 1960, we have been at war. People are skilled in war fighting. So how can we reintegrate them? The international community has not delivered what it promised to at the signing of the Rome Agreement. ...

We have had to deal with landmines, floods—and the Structural Adjustment Program has been a disaster! The prices for our cotton exports collapsed. ...

We need to be aware of the evils we had here during the war. You can't imagine! *The main thing is not to allow a recurrence of them.* When we are working on grassroots reconciliation projects, maybe sometimes it's not relevant to bring up issues from the past because they can make for divisions.

Former Fighters and Partisans

Boaventura Zita, like many other Mozambicans I talked to, told me firmly that "[I]t was the soldiers who paved the way for reconciliation here, not the politicians." When I returned to Mozambique in 2003, I was particularly interested to gather the views of some of those former soldiers. I was fortunate to work with a local research associate, Salomão Mungoi, a civil war–era soldier who, after the war, had worked with both Amodeg, the (bipartisan) association of civil war veterans, and ProPaz, the conflict resolution organization headed by Jacinta Jorge.

In 1982, when he was fourteen, Mungoi's family had sent him to Cuba to pursue his high school studies there. He stayed six years, finishing high school and some advanced studies in statistics, before returning home to fight on the government (Frelimo) side for the rest of the civil war. (He said he had a good friend who was a high-ranking officer in Renamo.) In addition to his fluency in Portuguese, Spanish, and English, Mungoi speaks three of Mozambique's indigenous languages.

One afternoon Mungoi took me to a meeting with some of Amodeg's leaders. We sat in their dimly lit office in a long-used "temporary" structure thrown up behind a crumbling colonial-era mansion. I asked the Amodeg people to describe what their own main objectives had been immediately after the war. Paciencia, a businesslike woman in a neat blue suit who was Amodeg's general secretary, courteously encouraged her colleagues to speak first. Board member Martin said his main goal had been "psychosocial rehabilitation, both individually and collectively." Marta, an animated woman who was the head of the organization's women's department, said, "rebuilding, both physical and psychosocial." Kefas, a heavy-set fellow who was Amodeg's representative for Maputo province, said it had been "the issue of follow-up: real monitoring of the conditions of excombatants, so they don't end up making problems." Paciencia then echoed the same point, saying that a lot of money had been put into "reintegration" of excombatants, but it was not clear how effectively it had been used. She added: "It was only last year that a Ministry of Veterans' Affairs was set up. But we should have had one since the beginning."

I asked how useful they had found the demobilization help provided by the United Nations. Kefas replied:

> [T]he main gain we felt from the ending of the war was the coming of peace itself. People were so tired of war!
>
> Regarding the UN demobilization projects in general ... Eighteen months of support for reintegration was not enough. The people who returned to the countryside—who were especially the Renamo people—couldn't find training courses. Or the training courses they could find were mainly irrelevant.

Paciencia noted that

> the combat veterans who originally came from cities did at least have some skills. They could speak Portuguese; they could read and write. But the country people, who were mainly from Renamo, didn't have those skills. Some people say the government favored its own side in the reintegration projects. But it wasn't that. It was the difference between the kinds of experience that the combatants on each side had.
>
> After the war, some people were in a worse situation than during the war, because at least during the war they had logistic support—and of course the officers had even had good personal help then. Then after the war, it often turned out they had no suitable skills!

Martin then said that some city-based excombatants had been unable to support their families and had gotten into abuse of alcohol or drugs, "or even killed themselves."

I asked the group whether they would have preferred a system in which, at the end of the war, everyone who had committed war crimes was put on trial. "For our situation it wouldn't make any sense because everyone would end up on trial," Martin said firmly.

"People here follow what has been happening in Rwanda. But there, there seems to be a general agreement that what happened there was a crime, rather than war. That's different."

Paciencia said:

> For me, it is not important to dig back into what happened during the war. It is not important what happened with Dhlakama or Chissano or any other individuals. My sister was taken by Renamo during the war and her face was mutilated by them. What should we do? The person who did it had to leave the area, and that was that.
>
> Digging up what has happened in the past is less important than working to *prevent* it happening again in the future. We remember the war only as an object lesson, in order to avoid its recurrence.

In the dirt yard outside the room where we talked, a group of teens were enjoying a game of soccer, and their exuberant voices flowed in through the open windows. I asked the people inside the room whether and how they talked about their wartime experiences with their children. Martin replied, "Nowadays, some Mozambicans try to talk about the war as a kind of school for life. But we excombatants tend not to talk about it, because it was so bad. We lost so many opportunities that we really don't want to talk about it with our kids."

Mungoi also set up a discussion for me with Evaristu Wanela, the head of Ademimo, the association of disabled excombatants, which claims 14,000 members throughout the country. Wanela came to our meeting in a city-center hotel on crutches, with one pinned-up trouser leg swinging empty between them. He told me he was originally from Nacala, a coastal town in the north. He had been sixteen when he joined the military, and five years later he lost his leg when he stepped on a landmine:

> It was a difficult time. I couldn't run any more. I was young. I had no girlfriend and thought that now I could never get one. It was so hard to come back to my family and try to interact with my friends.
>
> The biggest problem was when my family looked at me. They looked so sad! I felt guilty to be placing such a burden on them. I wondered if I should leave home, or even kill myself. But then I joined a church, a Catholic church, and the people there helped me to see that "this is the way it is," and that I must find a way to live with the way I am now.... My involvement with the church community really helped me.

169

I asked what he thought about the idea of punishing people who had committed war crimes. He replied:

> If you look at the history of Mozambique, there were 500 years of colonialism here. Then, after the Portuguese left, there were interests in powerful countries—both the capitalist countries and the communist countries—that provoked the war. If it was not for the war, Mozambique would not be how it is today. So if you look at that whole history, who would be punished? You would end up punishing everyone in this country and in all those other countries. You would start an unending cycle of punishment! ...
>
> I never consider that any Mozambican is guilty of this war. For example, if I gave money to a girl and then abused her, how would I later find the girl guilty of some immorality that she committed? So here, if I want to say someone is responsible for what happened during the war, I should say it would be the person behind the soldiers, not the soldiers themselves.
>
> There is not a culture of conflict in Mozambique. Most of our neighbors are somehow violent, but we are quiet people. In Mozambique, there is always the mechanism of talking to solve problems.

So how did he explain the violence that happened in Mozambique? Wanela continued to say that it was primarily outsiders who were responsible. "But as soon as we Mozambicans saw we could not benefit from the war, *we* decided we needed peace. Maybe that is why the peace process was so strong."[41]

One other former combatant who talked thoughtfully about the effectiveness of the 1992 peace was Hermínio Morais, the leader of Renamo's Special Forces who had also participated in the peace talks. Morais was another Mozambican who volunteered the judgment that it had been easier for military people to get along with their former opponents than it had been for the political leaders. "At Rome, the political negotiation took four years, but the military negotiation took only four months!" he said, with only slight exaggeration. He said he did not think his time in the Renamo military had been wasted, "because we achieved our objective of a democratic system. And no, there was no other way to achieve the objective." He said he still thought the GPA was a good agreement. "There is mistrust, but now it is all at the political level. And if there were no differences of opinion, there would be no need for political parties or democracy!"

He recalled that throughout the negotiation process in Rome, there was never any discussion of the possibility of anyone being punished for war crimes. "From the very beginning, the decision was to forget the past and look toward the future. That's why we didn't have a war crimes tribunal."

On the Frelimo side, I had a couple of in-depth discussions with the writer and Executive Committee member Marcelino Dos Santos. Talking in his book-lined office in Frelimo's high-rise headquarters, the affable Dos Santos—mocha-skinned, lanky, and bearded—noted that he had been involved in nationalist politics since 1948, the year he first made contact with other nationalist thinkers while he was studying in the Portuguese capital, Lisbon. He had many intriguing stories to tell about Frelimo's struggle for national independence—stories that included a description of how the movement always tried to ensure that its fighters in the field acted according to the norms of international humanitarian law. "If we took prisoners during battles, we would never kill them, but we'd hand them over to the International Red Cross, or the U.N., or to Tanzania," he said. "We did that because we understood there are no antagonistic contradictions between peoples, but only between leaders and governments.[42] . . . So it's *not* true simply to say that 'bad things always happen in war.' They don't have to happen."

He recalled that it had been in 1985–1986 that the Frelimo leadership first recognized that "we would never be able to *win* this war outright," and that therefore they needed to negotiate. Was the peace process worth it? "Naturally! We had to do it. What was difficult was to force the apartheid regime to accept that there had to be peace."

Despite the unequivocal support he expressed for the fact of the peace, there were several aspects of it that Dos Santos still found troubling. One of these was that he still sought from Renamo at least some acknowledgment that their wartime actions had been criminal:

> They need to express this recognition to us so that we can know that they won't do the same thing again. Remember how Willy Brandt went to Poland and knelt at the extermination camp and apologized for what the Germans had done there earlier? The German Catholic Church also came, after 500 years, to apologize for its anti-Semitic teachings and actions. But we haven't seen any apology from the Catholic Church here for the role it played supporting Portuguese colonialism for so many centuries. And we haven't seen any apology from Renamo for what they did to us, either.

I asked Dos Santos, who has longtime friendships with many leaders of South Africa's ANC, whether he thought a TRC-style process in Mozambique might elicit some of the truth-telling and truth-acknowledgment that he sought. He voiced strong opposition to this idea, basing his response mainly on the "even-handed" nature of the TRC—namely, that it had sought to investigate excesses by both the apartheid regime *and* its opponents from the ANC. "No, a TRC would not be useful here!" he said sharply. "No one else should be allowed to judge our revolution. Who has the right to judge the ANC in South Africa except the ANC? Inside Frelimo, we did our own judging. In 1976–1977, we judged people who had been cooperating with the Portuguese authorities. But we gave them a second chance. We sent them to re-education camps."[43]

The View from Belavista

One day, we discussed these issues with a gathering of community activists in Belavista, a small town some 35 miles south of Maputo. Though Belavista was close to the national capital as the crow flies, the challenge of getting there was huge; and the whole trip amply underscored the deficits in physical infrastructure that still plagued this lovely country. We had first to drive across Maputo, through its tiresome early-morning traffic, in order to hire an SUV. (Mungoi judged rightly that his ancient Fiat could never make it to Belavista.) Then, we drove the SUV to a crumbling city-center dock right across from the gleaming, eight-story headquarters of the Ministry of Finance and joined a crowd clambering onto an old, rusty ferry to cross to the far (south) bank of the muddy, quarter-mile-wide Umbuluzi River. The ferry took an hour to load up with six or eight mixed-looking vehicles and a complement of forty passengers. Meanwhile, a number of smaller, passenger-only ferries buzzed in and out of the next spot along the dock. People from the rural areas on the other bank were bringing huge, unwieldy sacks of charcoal and rickety crates of produce into the city to sell. One young woman yanked a reluctant nanny-goat off a small boat onto the dock.

Once our boat had loaded, it took only ten minutes to reach the other side. The hulks of two or three less lucky boats lay rusting by the riverbank. Mungoi said the government had been talking about building a bridge here for a long time—"But who knows when that will happen?"

The contrast between the two banks of the estuary was striking. On the north bank were the high-rises of a big, modern African city. On the south bank, a mere 400 yards away, there was just a dirt road snaking south and east through scrubby bush land, around 50 yards in from the coastline flanking Maputo Bay. Mungoi explained that during the war, this area was very dangerous. "There were some Mozambique army positions here, but there was a lot of Renamo activity too. South Africa is not far away. So the villagers here could not sleep in their villages at night: they would go out to sleep in the bush."

Now, slowly, the area was becoming developed. Parallel with the road, lofty utility poles carried high-tension wires to the south of the country. Mungoi said the lines were completed only a couple of months earlier, and there were still many disputes about the rights of the electric company to sling wire over tracts of land where people had farmed for generations. But despite the promise expressed by the looping electric lines, the area was still very undeveloped. We passed only one other vehicle on the whole one-hour-plus drive to Belavista. Mainly, we saw people walking very long distances along the side of the broad dirt road, carrying heavy loads on their heads or backs. Mungoi explained that seeing these people was, for him, a welcome sign of the general peaceableness. "Back during the war, anyone walking anywhere would melt away from the road to hide in the bush if they heard a vehicle approaching. This is so much better!" he said.

Belavista was once a Portuguese provincial center. Now, it is a sleepy-looking, very rundown small town, and still the administrative center for the surrounding district. Mungoi's friends had arranged a good discussion group for us. Seven Belavistans took part, all of them men; at least three were excombatants. Our host was Jaime Marquez, a local officer for the Mozambican Human Rights League (MHRL). With some difficulty he assembled enough plastic chairs from people in the neighborhood that we could all sit on chairs on the concrete-slab patio outside his one-room office.

I asked our hosts whether Belavista was seeing any continuing legacy of violence attributable to the violence of the civil war. Marquez thought for a moment before he said, "People did, certainly, become violent because of the war." One of the other members of the group was Jorge Moine, a *curandero* and the head of the local chapter of the Mozambican Association of Traditional Healers,

"Ametramo." He said, "We have to blame the war for the issue of violence. After the war, we had to work hard to rebuild bridges between people."

I asked those who were former fighters how they viewed the phenomenon of violence and their experience of participating in it. Amérigo, a member of Amodeg, said that for him the biggest problem had been that he "had to kill people with no clear reason for doing so."

Asked how the Mozambican excombatants had been so apparently successful in putting the violence of war effectively behind them, Moine, the *curandero,* said:

> There was a sense of responsibility to the community—that we are all brothers. So we don't need to *blame* people. It was very hard work because the returning former soldiers had to talk to so many people in order to be reintegrated into their communities—but the talking also helped the reintegration to happen. ...
>
> There was a ritual, in the sense that when a child comes back from war the father has to sit before a holy tree on his property and tell the ancestors that so-and-so is going to return. Then you ask the ancestors for guidance to make it work out.... The ancestors who have the same traditional name as the person returning would have a particular responsibility to give guidance.
>
> Some people would then do ceremonies, either alone or in groups. And the churches might also have a mass on the issue.

Later, he noted that, before the war, many people had still sought out the traditional healers and performed the traditional ceremonies. "But after the war there was a 'church boom,' so people preferred to go to the church to seek help."

I asked the group what they thought about the idea of punishing people who had committed bad acts during a war. Former fighter Amérigo immediately said, "In our case, the whole of Mozambique would be in court!"

Human rights activist Carlos Macuacua said, "The issue here is that this may trigger another war."

"The best decision is forgiving everyone who did bad things," said Amérigo.

Several people very familiar with Mozambique had earlier told me they thought one crucial element in the success of the amnesty-based peace process was that everyone involved felt there had been a "clean break" between the era and norms of war, on the one hand, and those of the peace that followed it, on the other. I asked the group in Belavista whether they felt such a "clean break" had indeed happened.

"The first thing to remember is that here, everyone was tired," said Amérigo. "Therefore, soon after the peace talks began, people were hopeful. Then, after it was signed, people took a long breath. But people had stopped shooting even before the peace accords!"

So, was it important to remember what had happened during the war, and if so, how should it be remembered? Amérigo again: "If we want to remember it, we should put it firmly into the *museum of things that are past!*"

I asked how many of these people had lost family members or others who were close to them during the war, and whether they had experienced any desire for revenge. Excombatant Paul Assuate said he had lost a close relative—"But there is no way I could think of seeking revenge for him. War is war. My relative was a victim of war, that's all." Our host Jaime Marquez had also lost a cousin in the war. He said: "I cannot accuse anyone of killing him because the circumstances were so unclear. Policies were different then than now. People did not have time to think about such things."

Religion-Based Leaders

Afiado Zunguza heads a Methodist-linked organization called Justapaz that provides social-service and leadership programs in various places around the country. In one discussion we held in Justapaz's neat, well-organized offices in Maputo, Zunguza talked a little about his youth. He grew up during the civil war in the northern port city of Beira. There was a lot of Renamo activity around the city then, he said, and twice he was the target of Renamo kidnapping raids. "But both times I managed to fool them by pretending I had a broken arm!" He recalled that though the city's hinterland was very unsafe, the city itself was much safer because it was protected by Zimbabwean forces. "We had so many refugees and displaced people who poured into the city," he said. "And at one point, we had no electricity for a whole year. But it was better than many other places."

Did he think that perpetrators of civil war–era violence should have been put on trial, and might that have provided something of value to their victims?

"You would have to punish everyone!" he said. "You see, the country itself was a victim of the war. In this war, there were not 'victims' and 'perpetrators.' There is no clear line you can use to sustain your idea of a 'victim.'"

How about the idea of reparations to former victims?

> Officially, no, that has never been mentioned. People's entire lives and lands were destroyed. Frelimo had described the war as an aggression from outside, so there would be no reparations unless there were an international agreement for that. The foreign governments concerned would have to agree to accept responsibility for what they did here. For example, South Africa: historically, South Africa *has* destabilized Mozambique. But in order for South Africa to pay reparations to us, it would be quite a process.

Zunguza noted that regarding Namibia, where South Africa's apartheid regime maintained an illegal military occupation for forty-five years after World War II, the post-1994 government in Pretoria had agreed to pay some reparations, in recognition of the harm caused by the apartheid rulers. "But our situation is completely different. It's hard to see that the ANC would inherit any kind of legal battles with Mozambique from their predecessors! In addition, one prerequisite of the whole peace negotiation was that Frelimo accepted that Renamo was a legitimate, Mozambican force, 'fighting for democracy.' When they accepted that, they essentially let all the foreign interests off the hook." He made no mention of the idea that Renamo or any other domestic party should be asked to provide any reparations for the war damage.

I asked if he thought there would have been some value in establishing a South Africa–style Truth Commission, so that at least the facts about some of the atrocities committed during the war could be revealed and acknowledged. "We do try to get to the truth," he said, "but in our own way, by understanding it from the community's point of view. For us, reconciliation is based on what would work well for the community, not the individual. That was the approach my father always used."

He recalled that one foreign writer had told him he was impressed "by the way that Mozambicans can laugh at their own distress, at their own misery. So maybe our joking is a way of speaking about things that make us uncomfortable?"

He talked about the historic role that some Protestant churches had played in helping to educate and incubate the country's nationalist movement. "Most black Africans from Mozambique who managed to get a higher education in the days of colonialism did so by going abroad with scholarships from the Methodist or Presbyterian churches. Eduardo Mondlane [the founder of Frelimo] went to the U.S. with help from them. At that time, the law here was to educate black Africans *only up to the fourth grade:* to teach them to serve, but not to give them any intelligence."[44]

Zunguza talked, too, about the syncretic nature of many Mozambicans' belief systems, and how this affected many areas of life. He said there was still a lively debate over whether and how recourse to traditional justice mechanisms should still be actively encouraged and supported by the government.

> The government has been trying to get assistance in getting a western-style court system here.... But it also still encourages communities to establish traditional-style "community courts," with some innovations, and there has been some capacity building in that area. You'll find a lot of people who will go to a western-style court, and go through the whole process there, and then they'll say after the judge's decision, "Okay, now we will have to find another way really to resolve this." Our customs are much more in favor of restorative rather than retributive justice.
>
> And then, people will often go to the *curanderos,* kind of covertly. Even, many churchgoers do that. Our culture is really a balance here! Often people will go to "mainstream" churches in the morning, and then to the Pentecostal churches in the evening. You have to cultivate a tolerance and a sense of pluralism!

To get another perspective on this cultural pluralism, Mungoi, my research assistant Leila Rached, and I drove one day to the heart of Xipamanene, a shantytown housing scores of thousands of families who had come here as internally displaced persons (IDPs) during the years of war—and then stayed on. Most of the tiny, tightly packed homes here were one-room, cinder-block huts roofed with either corrugated metal sheets or long palm fronds. The streets between them were winding, very badly rutted alleys. Children dodged between the cars, clutching schoolbooks as they ran to or from classes that were scheduled on a double-shift basis in the badly overcrowded schools. Other kids stood chatting in line at the public spigots placed every 50 yards or so, carrying the jerry-cans that they would then haul back for all their family's needs. In the heart of Xipamanene is a large structure, more robust than the shacks around it, that once was a food warehouse. It was the national headquarters of Ametramo, the Association of Traditional Healers of Mozambique. The straitened financial circumstances of the association were evident from the fact that very little had been done to renovate or even furnish this empty and dusty structure.

I had first visited this place in 2001, and on that occasion I had a short but interesting talk with association head Dr. Fernando Manuel Dos Santos Zimba, as described in Chapter 1. When I returned in 2003, Dr. Zimba once again greeted me. But he had also assembled a dozen other *curanderos* and *curanderas* to talk with us. Some wore regular civilian clothes, but around half wore Ametramo's Western-style uniform of blue slacks or skirt and a white shirt with blue epaulettes bearing the logo of the association. They greeted us warmly and sat with us at a long, red-clothed table; after I made a small offering to them they agreed to discuss the question of violence with me.

The main spokesperson this time was a middle-aged *curandero* called Morais, who carried a cell phone in one hand and a short, carved divining stick in the other. This Morais (apparently no relation to Hermínio Morais) noted that a number of sub-Saharan African countries had seen a lot of violence, but he argued that it was not necessarily the desire of the local leaders concerned to promote war:

> There are other interests at work, too! When a country is poor, it is easy for foreign interests to influence them and use them for their own purpose. In the case of Mozambique, we have problems of illiteracy and poverty, so it was easy for outsiders to use and manipulate Mozambicans. But the war was not a Mozambican idea. ...
>
> Democracy is a good thing. But making war for democracy is not a good thing, at all. Any form of government or democracy must be indigenous. Just as a peace process must be indigenous, too.
>
> A nationalist conscience is very important! How can we "use" foreign help to serve our own purposes and not let it use us, instead?

I asked him what a *curandero* actually does to deal with someone who has violence in his or her heart. He replied:

That is an easy issue. If someone goes to war, when he comes back his father will realize that he may have been exposed to bad things. (When people have guns, they are not thinking one hundred percent in the right way, anyway!) So the father will go to the healer, and the healer will go to the bush and "cook" the person, in order to take out the bad behavior.[45] As fathers, we all have to look for traditional healers to help our children.... There is really no difference of views on this matter, so long as you are a black person here.

Sometimes, people become crazy because, for example, they shoot people *whom they can see;* and then that person's spirit will come back to haunt them. It is not so bad if you shoot someone whom you can't see.

I asked if the treatments undertaken by the healers seemed to be successful in exorcizing the bad spirits under such circumstances. "There is always enough knowledge to remove the problems," he said firmly.

Did he see a meeting place between the views of the traditional healers and those of the country's Christian churches? "Our views are all the same," he replied. "At the bottom of it, peace is just the respect between me and you."

Anglican Bishop Dinis Sengulane echoed some but not all of the same views when he told me,

[A] punitive approach is totally foreign to Mozambique. One can describe the Mozambican position by saying that we recognized a long time ago that it's not in our interest to look at the past, but let's look together at the future.

This relates, of course, to the Christian concept of forgiveness: not to *forget* what happened in the past but to look at the past and forgive.

Sengulane's embrace of the idea of remembering the violence of the civil war was different from the attitude I heard expressed by most of my other Mozambican interlocutors. But still, the kind of memorialization that he sought was one focused in a general way on the ugliness of war:

My position has been, "Let's have some kind of a monument reminding us of the ugly past." For example, there are a number of mass graves around the country from that time. We could make them into monuments. We could make them dignified. We could write a plaque on them that says something like this: "This person was killed by war. He was unknown to the local people but known and precious to God. Never again, war! War: no! Peace: yes!" This would remind people that war is ugly and yet the future can be beautiful. *We* are the ones who can avoid the ugliness of the past!

And while we're about it, when we're looking for heroes, let's not just look at military heroes. We want to make sure our shaping of the future is much wider than that: heroes should also be those who have a vision of a much more beautiful future.

I asked Sengulane whether he wished that people who had committed or organized atrocities during the civil war had been tried in some kind of a war crimes court. He replied, "I'm not sure whether Mozambique has the kind of a legal system that would enable a war crimes court to be set up. In addition, there were so many situations where *you didn't know who did what.*"

Later, I asked whether and how he thought the processes the Mozambicans had gone through after the war had enabled them to defuse any desire for revenge that might still have remained in the hearts of the country's people. I asked him also, more broadly, to account for the durability of the peace. He replied:

> I have no answer for that, except to say that in our situation God, the author of this peace, has acted in a special way in the hearts of Mozambicans.
>
> You know, it has now been eleven years since the peace agreement. At the time of the signing, it all still seemed so doubtful. Renamo had promised that within 24 hours their people would cease all firing. Who could believe that? But this actually happened, which is remarkable! This showed that the people in the field were very much in contact with their leaders. So that was one good factor.
>
> Secondly, the peacemaking was a process organic to Mozambique. It didn't come from outsiders. This might have helped in making it acceptable to the people. Thirdly, we from the churches went to the places where the war had happened and we talked with the people there about making our hearts into "peace factories." At the present, I am very hopeful of the peace continuing to be a reality in our midst.

Remembering

The conversation I had with Sengulane about the possibility of memorializing those killed during the civil war was part of a broader inquiry on memorialization of atrocity-laden conflicts that I pursued while I was in Mozambique—as also in Rwanda and South Africa. In Rwanda I visited the large public memorial that the government was building at Gikosi, a steep, hilly portion of the capital where the remains of many genocide victims had been found. And in South Africa I visited memorials to the sufferings under apartheid created and maintained by the government (Robben Island), by community groups (in Soweto and Cape Town's District Six), and by a private entrepreneur (in Johannesburg). But in Mozambique I noted that there did not seem to be any public memorials to the million or so people who died in the civil war—though there are several very esthetically striking memorials to those who died in the war of national liberation against the Portuguese.

Salomão Mungoi told me that he knew of no public memorials to the civil war dead—though he knew of two places in the country where there were what he described as "sort of informal memorials, that is, places where local people do the traditional ceremonies for people who died in massacres."[46] One of these informal memorials was only 25 miles from Maputo, at a slightly remote place called Chi-boene. Mungoi said he had visited it once, a couple of years earlier: It was a memorial/mass grave for "around 40" militiamen who had been massacred there "sometime during the civil war." He contacted Afiado Zunguza and a couple of days later Mungoi, Leila Rached, and I all piled into Zunguza's 4x4 vehicle and headed to Chiboene.

We drove 12 miles north out of Maputo along a tarmac road and then took a twisting, much-forked dirt track that for 35 minutes took us ever deeper into the dry, thorn-tree-studded bush. Finally, as we approached a cluster of huts, Mungoi called to a young man and asked if someone could escort us to the mass graves. A group of three local women soon joined us. One of them fetched a jerry-can of water and a dipper, and they all came in the car with us to the graves, which were not far away.

There were two mass graves, each sited under the spreading boughs of a mature cashew tree. One was "marked" by a 10-inch-high platform of crumbling cement about 20 feet by 10 feet. The other was unmarked. Both grave areas were studded with numerous sprigs of a tough-looking form of flowering impatiens that grew straight out of the dun-colored earth.

The women—Priscina, Antonietta Jeremias, and Ana-Paula— picked sprigs from some of the impatiens plants and handed them to each of us four visitors. At each gravesite the women first kicked off their sandals and walked into the grave area, bending from the waist to clear it of dead leaves and twigs. After doing so they stood back, sang a couple of hymns in their language, Shangana, and said a prayer. Then each in turn took a dipper of water from the can, sprinkled the water onto a portion of the grave, and planted the impatiens sprig that she had earlier reserved for herself in a crack on top of the crumbling cement, firming the sprig upright into the crack with a handful of wetted earth. The dipper was passed around for all of us to do the same.

Afterward, we talked a little with the women. Priscina told us that each grave held the remains of twenty-two men who had been slaughtered during the massacre. Most of the victims had not been local people: They were men from different places who had come here for basic training with the progovernment militia. They had been killed either while asleep or shortly after waking up, at a time when they were unarmed. The women said they felt responsible for doing the same graveside rituals for these men that they did at the graves of their own ancestors. Antonietta Jeremias told us her father had been with the militiamen who were training here, but he was one of the lucky few who escaped alive. The women dated the massacre as having occurred "somewhere in the mid-1980s." They said they had been living in a communal village not far away and had heard the screams of the men being slaughtered, and the guns with which many of them had been killed.

As Mungoi interpreted I asked the women how they felt about those acts of violence, and whether they still blamed the people who had committed them. They said they found it difficult to feel blame. It had been such a hard time altogether during those years, they said, that it was hard to keep strict accounts of who was to blame for what, and when. "Sometimes, we even had to smother our own babies in the bush, if their crying would give away our hiding place," one said. "That's how hard the times were then."

"But now, the violence is finished, and we just pray that we don't have it again," Priscina summed up at the end of our visit. As we walked back to the car the women said they would like to upgrade the gravesites a little, perhaps with new concrete edgings and a concrete platform. They said they had some connection with the Anglican church, and Mungoi said he would pass on their request to Bishop Sengulane. No one, however, talked about getting any government help for this.

5
Comparing Postconflict Justice in Rwanda, South Africa, and Mozambique

Rwanda, South Africa, and Mozambique all went through markedly different experiences as they moved to and through their periods of hoped-for conflict termination in 1992–1994. This means that making direct comparisons among these experiences and drawing out general lessons from the comparisons are tasks that need to be done with great care. Nevertheless, the fact of these differences need not in itself deter us from undertaking these tasks; and indeed, many of the differences among the experiences of these three countries can helpfully suggest which kinds of postviolence policies—as well as which means of conflict termination—can be expected to make the most constructive contribution to long-term peacebuilding and thus to the general well-being of citizens of countries wracked by atrocious violence.

Comparing the Burdens of Conflict and Atrocity

It is worth restating here that the kinds of mass atrocities with which this study (and, indeed, the whole emerging body of "international atrocities law") is concerned are acts that are always associated with significant political conflict. The present study has traced and sought to understand the political context of atrocity perpetration in the countries researched, as well as the nature of the atrocities themselves.

In both these dimensions of their experience, the three countries differed significantly from each other. Let us first consider the *political context of atrocity commission*. In Rwanda, the conflict between Hutu power extremists and those Tutsis and Hutus who challenged their views had continued to some degree for more than thirty years (and the Hutu-Tutsi cleavage had been exploited and exacerbated by the Belgian colonial regime prior to 1959 as well). The atrocities of 1994 occurred in the more immediate political context of the war waged in northwestern Rwanda since 1990 between the Hutu-dominated government and the returning, armed exiles of the Rwandan Patriotic Front (mainly Tutsis). There was little direct involvement by outsiders in the war, though Rwanda remained vulnerable to many strong indirect influences from Uganda, France, and other outside actors.

In South Africa, the conflict between African nationalists and the country's White colonial regime had lasted 350 years and taken many forms, though by the second half of the twentieth century most of the internal opposition to the minority regime was not armed. In 1976–1977 and again from 1985 on, there were serious upturns in the pro-ANC, antiapartheid movement inside the country and in the repressive measures that the government used against it. From the late 1980s on, the apartheid regime also successfully enrolled the Zulu party Inkatha in fighting against the ANC. There was very little involvement by non–South Africans in this conflict.

In Mozambique, the armed conflict between the Frelimo government and the Renamo insurgents started in the late 1970s and was almost purely political. It had some regional and ethnic dimensions, but these were relatively insignificant. There was significant involvement by White Rhodesia and then South Africa in launching and sustaining Renamo's antigovernment insurgency.

Regarding the *profiles of the atrocities committed during these conflicts*, the three countries' experiences were also divergent. In Rwanda, both sides had (however asymmetrically) committed war crimes during the forty-two-month civil war that preceded April 1994. Then, starting early that month, the paroxysm of genocidal violence perpetrated by the Hutu extremist militias against Tutsis and pro-coexistence Hutus lasted for only 100 days—though the experiences of those atrocity-laden days were such as to rupture the known world for all who survived them. The organizers of the genocide had aimed for and won a high level of popular participation in this violence in many Hutu communities. There was also some retaliatory violence against Hutus during the genocide and especially at and after the point when it was ended.

In South Africa, the regime used massive administrative violence and significant direct physical violence against its opponents for 350 years, and the levels of this violence were ratcheted up in the years after the "Soweto Uprising" of 1976. The regime's African nationalist challengers pursued their goals mainly by using tactics of mass organizing (which included some violent coercion of fellow Blacks viewed as collaborators); they also undertook some small armed operations against regime-linked targets, some of which killed or harmed noncombatants.

In Mozambique, Renamo used a large amount of extremely atrocious violence over a period of fifteen years, in an attempt to terrorize communities into cooperation or acquiescence. For its part, the Frelimo government generally tried to abide by the laws of war, but it also committed some excesses including the use of villagization programs and other coercive methods that uprooted a large number of communities of food and restricted their access to food and other vital needs.

Finally, at the time that the three countries attempted to end these conflicts in the 1992–1994 period, they faced widely varying *situations of basic demography and socioeconomics*. Of these differences, the most distinctive was that between South Africa's relatively high per capita GDP at the time of conflict termination and the much lower figures registered by both Rwanda and Mozambique—though in South Africa, the raw per capita figure for GDP masked extremely serious inequalities between the incomes and wealth enjoyed by the country's White and non-White (especially Black) communities. Table 5.1 lists some of the basic facts about the three countries at the time of conflict termination.

Ending the Conflicts

The *ways in which the three countries' conflicts were terminated* diverged markedly. The most evident difference was that in Rwanda, the conflict that ravaged the country in spring and summer 1994 was ended through the military victory won by the RPF; in both South Africa and Mozambique, by contrast, the conflicts were terminated through lengthy negotiations among the previously contesting

Table 5.1 Basic Country Data at Time of Conflict Termination, 1992–1994

	Rwanda	South Africa	Mozambique
Real GDP per capita (PPP$)	352 (1994)[a]	4,291 (1994)	380 (1992)[b]
Population size, 1992[c]	7.4 million	38.8 million	14.7 million
Estimated population mix	Around 85% Hutus, 14% Tutsis, 1% Twa	Around 78% Black in twelve or so language groups; 10% White in two language groups; 11% "Coloured" and Asian/Indian[d]	Nearly all Black Africans in approximately twenty-four language groups
Basic strategic geography	A small, landlocked country in a region dominated by the chronic instability of neighboring behemoth Zaire (DRC)	A large country able to dominate or influence many neighboring states	A large country sprawling along the Indian Ocean that has always faced much pressure from South Africa and other neighbors

[a]This and the South Africa figure are taken from *Human Development Report 1997* (New York: UN Development Program, 1997), Table 1, pp. 147–148.

[b]This figure is taken from *Human Development Report 1995* (New York: UN Development Program, 1995), Table 2, p. 159.

[c]All of the population-size data in this row are taken from *Human Development Report 1995* (New York: UN Development Program, 1995), Table 16, pp. 186–187.

[d]These were roughly the proportions existing in 2001.

Source: Compiled by author.

parties. In the latter two cases, the negotiations lasted three to four years. In the course of these negotiations, the relationship between the contesting parties moved from one of extreme distrust marked by the frequent voicing of charges that the other party was "not even a legitimate interlocutor," through a phase of wary intention testing, to a situation of conditional cooperation marked by agreement on at least the ground rules for further mutual engagement on nonviolent, purely political terms. In South Africa, these negotiations were conducted purely among the concerned national-level parties; but several world powers and the United Nations urged the parties to enter, then stick with, the negotiations and provided other incentives for the negotiators. In Mozambique, outsiders played a larger role, though the original mediation effort was undertaken by national-level church leaders who only subsequently brought in mediators from elsewhere (Sant' Egidio), and these mediators in turn brought in the Italian government and the United Nations. Finally, as the Mozambique peace talks neared their conclusion, the UN role in underpinning the peace agreement became quite significant. In Rwanda, meanwhile, outside actors played almost no direct role in the RPF's attainment of its military victory in June/ July 1994. But as the RPF's government struggled to rebuild the country after the genocide, the role of outside aid donors became very large indeed.

Regarding the *state of each country's national infrastructure* at the time of conflict termination, there were clear and significant differences among the three countries. In 1994, South Africa had a relatively highly developed physical infrastructure that had been little dented by the conflict except in some parts of KwaZulu-Natal. The country's sociopolitical infrastructure, which included many of the institutions of a functioning (though until 1994, strictly segregated) democracy including a well-developed judicial system, likewise remained largely in place. One consequence of this was that the new South African government could express a "threat" to prosecute perpetrators of earlier atrocities that had some degree of credibility with those individuals—though not, as it turned out, very much.

In Rwanda, the country had had a fairly well-developed physical infrastructure prior to the genocide. (That fact had greatly aided the *génocidaires* in carrying out their grisly project rapidly, and on a nationwide basis.) Rwanda's physical infrastructure was badly damaged by the violence of the spring and summer of 1994; but its sociopolitical infrastructure suffered even more from that violence. Its cadres of experienced administrators and professionals were shattered first by the genocide and then by the mass exodus of Hutus that followed. Equally important, basic social trust among Rwandans had also been shattered, and this affected all the country's institutions without exception.

In Mozambique the physical infrastructure, which had already been very underdeveloped at the time of national independence in 1975, received further blows during the years of civil strife and almost did not exist by late 1992. Many millions of Mozambicans had been displaced by the fighting and were near starvation; millions of acres of arable land were contaminated with landmines; a large proportion of the country's already meager stock of schoolhouses, health clinics, and courthouses had been destroyed. But Mozambique's sociopolitical infrastructure proved much more resilient than its physical infrastructure. Some of the key precolonial underpinnings of its multifaceted national society had managed to survive the decades of liberation war and civil war more or less intact.

The *"content" of the peace* varied greatly among the three countries, depending mainly on the means that had been used to end the conflict. Since conflict termination was not the subject of any negotiation at all in Rwanda, the government that took power in July 1994 was under no contractual obligation to anyone to take the kinds of peacebuilding steps—holding elections, offering amnesties, demobilizing former fighters—to which the postconflict governments of South Africa and Mozambique were, by contrast, obligated (see Table 5.2).

The Postconflict Era

It was within the context of those broader peacebuilding efforts that the postconflict governments in these countries chose *policies to deal with the legacies of the conflict-era atrocities.* At that point, it was Mozambique whose path was most markedly different from those, followed by the other two. The post-GPA government in Maputo had already enacted a blanket amnesty for all civil war–era political violence; that amnesty resonated widely in a national culture that placed a lot of emphasis on forgiveness, social reintegration, and "not dwelling on the hurts of the past." Additionally, there were many evident infrastructural constraints on the country's ability to undertake any form of "accountability" project that would require the processing of individual cases in any significant numbers. Therefore, the government made no attempt at all to enact any kind of an "individual accountability" project; and nor did it undertake any memorialization efforts with respect to the civil war–era atrocities. It received wide public support for those decisions at the time (and apparently also since then, as discussed below.)

By contrast, both Rwanda and South Africa tried to pursue policies based on the concept of "individual accountability" and the processing of the cases of individual suspects in significant numbers, though this approach took very different forms in the two countries. (Both governments also undertook nontrivial memorialization projects.) In Rwanda, the initial stress at both the national and international levels was on prosecuting all suspected *génocidaires* in regular-style criminal courts. At the national level—though not the international level—the counterproductive nature of that approach became clear within a few years, and by 1998–1999 the RPF-dominated government started moving (slowly) to establish the community-based *gacaca* courts to handle the vast majority of its genocide-related cases. The process of establishing the *gacaca* courts ran into many problems: They finally went into full operation in March 2005, almost eleven years after the genocide, and the prospects were that their work would last for several years thereafter. Regarding memorialization, the Rwandan government made a strong commitment to preserving and refurbishing the sites of several large genocide-era massacres, and to maintaining them as prominent public memorials. It also started sponsoring a month of nationwide genocide commemoration in April of each year.

For its part, ICTR was scheduled to finish its processing of some sixty top-level cases in 2008, fourteen years after the genocide.

In South Africa, the TRC was established primarily to operationalize the processing of the previously promised amnesties, but its procedures were designed in a way that sought also to provide a public voice and valuable public acknowledgment to victims. The various different parts of the TRC's process were designed with the goal of establishing a full historical record of the "gross human rights violations" (as per the TRC definition) of the apartheid era. The work of the TRC proved noticeably speedier than the mechanisms used by, and with respect to, Rwanda. It started this work in late 1995; the main part of it was finished in October 1998, though the Amnesty Committee continued through August 2002—just over eight years after the country's major "transition event," its landmark 1994 elections. Only a handful of TRC-related cases still dangled after 2002. Regarding memorialization, the government made some half-hearted efforts in this regard, but it saw its main priority in the cultural sphere as being the implementation of a series of much broader language, renaming, and re-education projects that would entirely transform the cultural content of what it meant to be a "South African."

The *costs and direct achievements of these postatrocity policies* differed widely. In Rwanda, the total number of genocide suspects, each of

Table 5.2 Content of the Peace

	Rwanda	South Africa	Mozambique
Elections	The RPF was under no obligation to hold elections.	Full democratization and the holding of elections formed a central pillar of the peace agreement.	Democratization and holding free elections were mandated by the General Peace Agreement.
Amnesties	The RPF regime was under no obligation to amnesty anyone.	The new regime was obligated by the Interim Constitution to offer an amnesty to those who committed politically motivated violence during apartheid.	As one of its commitments under the GPA, the Frelimo-dominated government and parliament enacted a blanket amnesty for all civil war–era violence.
Demobilization/ reintegration efforts; cost of these; and who paid	The RPF regime was not obligated to demobilize, and did not. Nor did the Hutu extremists disarm: Their military regrouped in refugee camps around Rwanda. The government pursued the Hutu militias into Zaire/DRC and resumed its conflict there.	As part of the transition agreements, c. 35,000 freedom fighters and c. 101,000 members of the apartheid-era military were integrated into a new national army. Later, c. 7,200 freedom fighters, and c. 12,500 former SADF members were demobilized. The government invested 168 million Rand (c. $21 million) in these programs.[a]	The GPA mandated a broad demobilization of former fighters from both sides and their reintegration into civilian life. Fighters not demobilized were integrated into a new national army. Some 93,000 former fighters were demobilized at a cost of c. $100 million. Of that cost, 11% came from the government and the rest from international donors.[b]

Table 5.2 *(continued)*

	Rwanda	South Africa	Mozambique
Other significant efforts at peacebuilding or social transformation	• The government ordered nationals to self-identify only as "Rwandans" and to erase the concepts of "Hutu," "Tutsi," and "Twa." • Relatively large amounts of external aid flowed into Rwanda after 1994. • By the early 2000s some faith groups were undertaking grassroots reconciliation projects with some apparent success.	• The cultural content of "South Africanness" was transformed to reflect the ANC's nonracial multicultural view of the country. This was reflected in language policies, the new Constitution, etc. • Some attempts were made by the ANC governments to redistribute land and other forms of wealth in a noncoercive way and to equalize opportunity for all citizens.	• Opinion leaders such as the *curanderos/as*, other cultural figures, and religious leaders worked hard to implement grassroots community rebuilding and social healing efforts. • Relatively large amounts of external aid flowed to the country in the decade after the GPA.

[a]Peter Batchelor, Jacklyn Cock, and Penny Mackenzie, *Conversion in South Africa in the 1980s: Defence Downsizing and Human Development Challenges* (Bonn, Germany: Bonn International Center for Conversion, n.d.), pp. 43, 44; available online at http://www.bicc.de/publications/briefs/brief18/brief18.pdf.

[b]Iraê Baptista Lundin et al., "Reducing costs through an expensive exercise': The impact of demobilization in Mozambique," in Kees Kingma, ed., *Demobilization in Sub-Saharan Africa: The Development and Security Impacts* (New York: St. Martin's Press/Basingstoke, UK: Macmillan, 2000), pp. 186, 187.

Source: Compiled by author.

whose cases had to be considered individually, rose swiftly in the mid-1990s to more than 140,000. By 2004, the regular national court system had completed the processing of some 1,000 of these cases. By then, many of those suspected of "lower-level" crimes related to the genocide were being released and their cases transferred to the *gacaca* courts. Early reports from the *gacaca* courts indicated they were having some success in resolving cases. But their operation also greatly exacerbated intergroup sensitivities in the country. Moreover, the confessions submitted during the process caused a huge ballooning of the potential caseload both for the *gacaca* courts themselves and for the regular courts, so by early 2006 it was hard to imagine how all these potential cases could ever be resolved on an individual basis. Regarding the budget for the *gacaca* courts, one September 2003 report estimated that the whole, multiyear project would cost around $75.5 million, with nearly all of this sum expected to be met by foreign donors.[1] (An expenditure of this amount to resolve the 130,000 cases originally sent to *gacaca* would result in a per-case processing cost of $581—but huge uncertainties in the eventual scope and cost of the process evidently remained.)

The major UN contribution to helping Rwanda deal with suspected genocide perpetrators was, of course, ICTR: In its first eleven years of operation, the court had completed the first-instance trials of *only 26 suspects* (and the appeals in several of these cases were still outstanding). ICTR's budgets are hard to figure out accurately because some foreign governments gave a lot of support to it in the form of "special" supplementary aid and in-kind aid. By the end of 2005, however, ICTR had evidently consumed more than $1.1 billion of international funds, yielding a per-case processing cost of *more than $42.3 million*. In South Africa, meanwhile, throughout the total, seven-year life of both the main TRC and its Amnesty Committee (1995–2002), the TRC accepted 21,000 victim statements, processed 7,116 amnesty applications, and produced a seminal seven-volume report of the gross rights violations of the apartheid era. Its main budget for the years 1995–2000 totaled 244 million Rand (about $30.5 million).[2] This was all met from the national budget, though some foreign donors contributed small amounts of in-kind aid for supplemental programs. It is hard to give a good picture of the proportions of TRC spending that went into each of its major areas of activity. But if we were to say that the whole of that $30.5 million of TRC spending went *only* into processing the cases of suspected rights abusers (which, after all, comprised the most lawyer-heavy and therefore most expensive portion of its budget), then we could say that the per-case processing cost for each of those cases came to around $4,290—that is, roughly one ten-thousandth part of what ICTR's per-case processing cost amounted to. (Of course, if we say—quite realistically—that only a portion of the TRC's budget was used to process the cases of perpetrators of violence, then the estimated per-case processing cost would be correspondingly lower.)

Outcomes

Some dozen years after the ending of these atrocity-laden conflicts, it becomes possible to assess the *broad sociopolitical outcomes attained by these societies* as a result of the mix of policies—including the atrocity response policies—pursued by their governments in the postconflict era. Regarding the situation in Rwanda, longtime Rwanda affairs analyst René Lemarchand noted at the end of 2004 that the country enjoyed a high level of general stability. But he added: "[W]hat lies at the heart of the country's stability [is] the ever present threat of repression. The Tutsi-dominated state has successfully eliminated all forms of organized political opposition." Regarding conflict and cooperation inside the country, he wrote: "[C]ooperation is essentially between the government and the Tutsi minority, while conflict, with few exceptions, sets Hutu against Tutsi."[3] In late 2003, Rwanda held its first multiparty elections since 1993. They were widely judged to be neither free nor fair.

At the international level, meanwhile, Rwanda's RPF government had continued to pursue a highly militarized and often escalatory policy inside neighboring DRC. In December 2004 it launched a new and very destructive military incursion there that blatantly flouted commitments it had made at preceding international gatherings.[4]

In South Africa, democratic elections that were judged to be free and fair were held at both the national and the provincial level in 1994, 1999, and 2004. In November 2003, the Cape Town–based Institute for Justice and Reconciliation reported that 83 percent of all South Africans—including 67 percent of the country's Whites—agreed that "[i]t is desirable to create one united South African nation out of all the different groups who live in this country."[5] In stark contrast to the record of the country's apartheid-era governments, South Africa's democratic governments launched no military expeditions against any other countries.

In Mozambique, national elections that were judged generally (but not totally) free and fair were held in 1994, 1999, and 2004. A first round of local-level elections held in 1998 had many problems, but local elections held in 2003 were judged free and fair. Like democratic South Africa, post-GPA Mozambique had launched no military expeditions against any of its neighbors.

Other aspects of the sociopolitical outcomes in these three countries, ten to twelve years after their conflict termination attempts, are summarized in Table 5.3.

What, finally, do we know about the *satisfaction of the primary stakeholders* regarding the policies adopted by their respective national governments (and, in Rwanda's case only, that adopted by the United Nations) in order to deal specifically with the legacies of the conflict-era atrocities? In South Africa, in late 2000, 68.2 percent of all citizens, including 76 percent of Black South Africans, said they approved strongly or somewhat of the TRC's performance.[6] In Rwanda, a February 2002 attitudes survey found that only 29.2 percent of the Rwandan respondents expressed any degree of approval of ICTR's record, while 56.5 percent expressed some approval of the work of the national-level courts.[7] Regarding the *gacaca* courts, it was still far too early in the initial months of 2006 to measure Rwandans' "satisfaction" with their work, but low rates of participation in many of the earlier pilot *gacacas* had indicated a low popular investment in the project's general success and/or low expectations in its projected level of achievement. In Mozambique, meanwhile, though there were no survey data to rely on, I was able to observe clearly during research trips in 2001 and 2003 that there was still a very high level of general satisfaction in the "forgive, heal, and rebuild" policy that the government adopted in 1992.

Conclusion

An examination of the data above clearly indicates that South Africa and Mozambique, whose conflicts were ended in the 1992–1994 period as a result of negotiations that involved offers of amnesty to former rights abusers, experienced a considerably better general outcome than did Rwanda, where the conflict was ended through a military victory that left the victors quite free of any obligation either to provide amnesties to former rights abusers or to address the country's remaining political differences using democratic rather than violent means. This is a bold conclusion that challenges much of the currently "mainstream" wisdom in the international community—including the international human rights movement—about the necessity of prosecuting all perpetrators of gross rights abuses. Reaching the conclusion expressed here also raises broader philosophical challenges. Crucially, it forces us to ask whether, and under what circumstances, it can ever be valid to apply a consequentialist, outcomes-based analysis to developments that are usually thought of as engaging issues of absolute, deontological "right and wrong." My belief is that it can be—and I base this belief primarily on the judgments made by those people who are, after all, the primary stakeholders in the outcomes of these decisions: the women and men who are citizens of the countries concerned. In the chapter that follows I shall identify, record, and start to analyze the views of these primary stakeholders regarding the weighty considerations and tradeoffs involved when societies affected by the recent, widespread commission of atrocities start to craft and enact policies to deal with the legacies of that violence.

Table 5.3 Broad Sociopolitical Outcomes as of 2004–2005

	Rwanda	South Africa	Mozambique
Democracy well-institutionalized?	No.	Yes.	Fairly well.
Movement on Freedom House indicators, 1994-2006[a]	1994: 6; 5 2006: 6; 5 Total positive movement: 0	1994: 5; 4 2006: 1; 2 Total positive movement: 6	1994: 6; 5 2006: 3; 4 Total positive movement: 4
Human Development Index ratings, 1990–2003[b]	HDI figures for 1990: 0.340 1995: 0.335 2000: 0.435 2003: 0.450	HDI figures for 1990: 0.735 1995: 0.742 2000: 0.696 2003: 0.658	HDI figures for 1990: 0.311 1995: 0.328 2000: 0.360 2003: 0.379
Movement on size of military forces, 1993–2005[c]	Size of military forces: c. 5.2K–51K Soldiers per 10,000 population: c. 6.5–60.4	Size of military forces: c. 67.5K–55.75K. Soldiers per 10,000 population: 17.5–12.5	Size of military forces: 50K–11.2K Soldiers per 10,000 population: 29.1–4.5
Status of political and other violence, end of 2005	Rwanda-linked political violence continued in 2005, inside and (mainly) outside the country.	Political violence persisted at a high rate after 1994 in KwaZulu-Natal, but not elsewhere; it abated in KZN in the late 1990s. A high rate of nonpolitical crime persisted nationwide, including a 2000 murder rate of 51 murders per 100,000 people.	Levels of political violence were low but not zero after the conclusion of the GPA. Levels of violent crime were fairly high in the early 2000s, but not nearly as high as in South Africa.

Table 5.3 *(continued)*

	Rwanda	South Africa	Mozambique
Other factors	• An estimated 5.1% of people aged 15–49 were living with HIV in 2003.[d] • Rwanda continued to entangle itself in regional wars. • It received relatively generous international aid through 2003.	• An estimated 21.5% of people aged 15–49 were living with HIV in 2003. • South Africa had one of the highest levels of economic inequality in the world. • The country received relatively small amounts of international aid.	• An estimated 12.2% of people aged 15–49 were living with HIV in 2003. • Two very serious floods along with externally imposed economic adjustment impeded development. • The country received relatively generous international aid (although in varying amounts) through 2003.

[a]Freedom House country ratings are available online at http://www.freedomhouse.org/ratings/index.htm. (1 represents "most free," 7 represents "least free." The rating for "political rights" is given first; that for "civil liberties" is given second.)

[b]The Human Development Index (HDI) is an index of human well-being developed by the UN Development Program. It is compiled on a scale of 0 to 1.000 from weighted components derived from national figures for GDP per capita, life expectancy, and educational levels. In 2003, the country with the highest HDI score was Norway, at 0.963. The figures presented here are taken from *Human Development Report 2005* (New York: UN Development Program, 2005), Table 2.

[c]Force-size figures are taken from International Institute for Strategic Studies, *The Military Balance 1993-94* (London: IISS, 1993) and International Institute for Strategic Studies, *The Military Balance 2005-2006* (London: Routledge, 2005).

[d]The figures for HIV infection rates are taken from *Human Development Report 2005* (New York: UN Development Program, 2005), Table 9.

Source: Compiled by author.

6
Restoring Peacemaking, Revaluing History

Restoring Peacemaking

In the first half of the 1990s the three countries studied in the present work all made significant attempts to escape from grave intergroup conflict. Mozambique did so with the General Peace Agreement of October 1992; South Africa, with the holding of the democratic elections of April 1994; and Rwanda, at the time of the RPF's victory over its adversaries in July 1994. The twenty-one-month period spanning those events was significant in international politics because it saw the establishment of the first international criminal court since the International Military Tribunals for Germany and Japan had completed their work, 45 years earlier. The Security Council's creation of the International Criminal Tribunal for Yugoslavia (ICTY) in May 1993 was the significant first achievement of a campaign maintained by influential, Western-based human rights advocacy groups around an agenda that stressed what American legal scholar Diane Orentlicher has called the "duty to prosecute" the perpetrators of atrocities.[1] As noted previously, when the Security Council established ICTR in November 1994, it built directly onto the institutional and jurisprudential framework already established at ICTY.

Orentlicher, British attorney Geoffrey Robertson, and other legal thinkers working in prosperous and settled Western countries have contested the notion that offering amnesties during peace negotiations may bring something of value to men and women seeking to escape from a climate of atrocity. These scholars have argued that the risk that such amnesties will foster a "climate of impunity" and thus allow the continued commission of atrocities, or their resumption after a brief hiatus, is so great that no peace that is won through the granting of amnesties can be considered valuable—or, indeed, secure.

The evidence presented in this book challenges those arguments. In particular, the experiences of South Africa and Mozambique in the dozen years after their conflict termination events of the early 1990s show clearly that an amnesty-reliant peace agreement does not always foster (or more accurately, prolong) a "climate of impunity." On the contrary, such a peace agreement can, if well crafted, *mark a clear turning point* between the conflict-riven and impunity-plagued climate of the past and a new, much more peaceable social climate in which human rights that have long been trampled on can finally start to be ensured and the basic norms of the rule of law—including the end of impunity for all persons, however powerful—can start to be respected. It is worth noting very forcefully here that in situations of classic warfare or other grave intergroup conflict, none of the human rights of civilians in the territories affected, including rights as basic as those to life or the physical integrity of persons, can ever be ensured. Indeed, in conflict zones the entire panoply of human rights articulated in the Universal Declaration on Human Rights and its two attendant Covenants are under constant assault. This simple truth about warfare and other forms of grave conflict seems to have escaped the attention of too many Western-based rights activists in recent years.

Meanwhile, the experience of Rwanda since 1994 stands in stark contrast to those of Mozambique and South Africa. It indicates that pursuing a rigorously interpreted "duty to prosecute" can all too easily perpetuate deep-seated social and political cleavages, keeping in place a situation in which fundamental human rights continue to be denied and threatened on a massive scale.

Traveling in Mozambique in 2001 and 2003 I heard over and over, from people in all ranks of society, expressions of great satisfaction with the peace agreement their political leaders had concluded in 1992, and horror at the thought that anything might happen in the country to reignite the violence and turmoil of the war years. To them, the post-1992 peace most evidently was its own dividend; and though their country was still plagued with many problems—including many stemming from its generations-long impoverishment—I found no Mozambicans who thought that their situation had been at all better during the war. They all seemed to highly value the fact that the continuing disagreements between their politicians could now be mediated through parliamentary mechanisms rather than through armed conflict (though I did hear from some Mozambicans the same kind of criticisms of the pretensions and alleged corruptibility of their politicians that one hears from citizens in many other democracies). The concept of the rule of law seemed to be broadly respected and generally implemented in Mozambique. One example: In November 2000 a noted journalist, Carlos Cardoso, was murdered while researching a story about fraud at a state-run bank; but in 2003 two businessmen and a former manager of the bank were convicted of having contracted the killing, along with three other men for having carried it out; all received lengthy prison terms.[2] The major problem that groups such as Amnesty International and Penal Reform International noted with respect to rights observance in Mozambique in the early years of the new century had to do much more with the general impoverishment of society, and the accompanying lack in government institutions such as prisons of even the most basic tools or amenities needed to do an acceptable job, than with the existence of a "climate of impunity" or the absence of the rule of law.

Visiting South Africa, also in 2001 and 2003, I found a similarly palpable (though slightly less universal) sense of relief that the long-running conflict over political equality within the country had finally been resolved at the political level in 1993–1994—though in South Africa, too, many other important parts of the human rights agenda, particularly in the economic sphere, still needed considerable attention. In South Africa, more evidently than in Mozambique, there had been some citizens who in the period after their "transition event" of the early 1990s felt they had lost out under its terms. These were primarily members of the White community who, even if not perpetrators of the atrocious violence on which the apartheid system had been built, had nevertheless been well-rewarded beneficiaries of the system. After 1994, the country's White citizens retained the economic and educational capital they had accrued over preceding generations, but from then on they lost access to all the special, preferential benefits they had hitherto enjoyed simply by virtue of their racial classification. Indeed, after 1994 they found themselves exposed to demands for "affirmative action" rectifications in several spheres of national life. But very few of even those Whites who felt disgruntled with the post-1994 order ever seriously proposed restoring the blatant inequalities of the past and thus risking a reignition of the violence of the apartheid years. A far more common reaction of disgruntled Whites was to (re)emigrate to other countries where they hoped not to be exposed to the same demands for affirmative action that they faced in South Africa.[3] Most White South Africans, meanwhile, continued to do fine (some even experienced new opportunities for prosperity in their newly democratic country), although, like all the country's citizens, they were affected by the postdemocratization crime wave and a small number of White South Africans found themselves experiencing a level of poverty previously unknown in their community for a couple of generations. (During the same period, a much larger proportion of the country's non-White citizens continued to find themselves trapped in the same deep, structural poverty and crime-ridden communities in which their forebears had lived for several generations past.)

In South Africa, as in Mozambique, a number of important rights protection issues evidently remained to be worked on ten years after the transition. These issues had particularly to do with ensuring the basic economic and social rights of all citizens, but also with preventing police brutality. Human Rights Watch reported with respect to South Africa that "[f]rom April 2003 to March 2004 ... a statutory oversight body received reports of 383 deaths in police custody."[4] Meanwhile, as noted in Chapter 5 (Table 5.3), the records kept by Freedom House (FH) showed that in South Africa, as in Mozambique, the aggregated ratings of the country's political rights and civil liberties had registered a significant improvement between 1994 and 2006: by a total of six points (out of a possible seven) in the case of South Africa, and by four points (out of a possible nine) in Mozambique. In Rwanda, meanwhile, the FH ratings showed *no change at all* between 1994 and 2006. They remained mired near the bottom of the FH charts and earned the organization's summary judgment that the country was still "not free."

When I visited Rwanda in 2002, the Rwandans whom I met were unanimous in expressing relief that their country was no longer living in the horrific maelstrom of violence that had beset it in 1994. But many Rwandans still seemed extremely fearful—either of a recurrence of violence broadly similar to that which erupted in 1994, or of the eruption of some other form of atrocity-laden mayhem.[5] Meanwhile, inasmuch as President Kagame had significantly consolidated the RPF's hold over all of the country's institutions, the norms of the rule of law were not even on their way to being respected. In early 2005, Human Rights Watch noted:

> In 2004, the RPF further reinforced its control by attacking civil society organizations, churches, and schools for supposedly disseminating "genocidal ideology." Authorities arrested dozens of persons accused of this crime.
>
> Judicial authorities carried out a sham trial of a former president and seven others, but few other trials. Tens of thousands of persons remained jailed on accusations of genocide, some of them detained more than ten years. ...
>
> In the course of reforming the judicial system, authorities obliged judges and judicial personnel, more than five hundred of them, to resign. Fewer than one hundred were reappointed to positions in the new system. During [2004] nearly half the 106 mayors were also obliged to resign.[6]

With Kagame's RPF still able to manipulate, undermine, and control all the country's national institutions at will, the climate of impunity reigned supreme.

In short, an insistence on prosecutions, such as was actively pursued for a number of years in postgenocide Rwanda but had been consciously eschewed by both South Africa and Mozambique, seemed *not* to have helped Rwanda to escape from impunity and establish a general respect for the rule of law. On the contrary, the two countries that had used amnesties ended up with many more significant improvements in their assurance of and general respect for the rule of law![7] Clearly the paradigm posited by Orentlicher, Robertson, and others, whereby allowing amnesties necessarily leads to fostering a climate of impunity and thus to a failure to establish the rule of law, needs considerable reexamination. I submit that what is wrong with this model is that it is fundamentally apolitical. Specifically, by focusing on such purely technical legal aspects of these situations as a "duty to prosecute," it neglects the broader political context within which decisions to prosecute or not to prosecute are always taken; and this broader context is particularly crucial in countries experiencing the kinds of grave intergroup conflict in which, in the modern age, a very high proportion of atrocities—including all those described and discussed in this book—have actually been committed. Above all, it ignores the need for an intentional and successful politics of peacemaking.

Negotiations Versus the Temptations of Victory

In the late 1990s, after the generally acknowledged success of South Africa's amnesty-reliant TRC had posed a first significant challenge to those who advocated the "duty to prosecute," there were many earnest discussions among (primarily) liberals and rights activists in Western-cultured countries over how the possibly competing interests of "truth" and "justice" could somehow be reconciled.[8] (Justice, in this context, was nearly always understood to denote only the narrow procedural issue of the pursuit of criminal prosecutions rather than anything broader such as, for example, distributive justice or the assurance of fundamental human rights and liberties.) What nearly all of those discussions failed to pay much heed to, however, were the interests of "peace"—that is, the interests of both peace*making* and longer-term peace*building*—in situations of atrocity-wracked intergroup conflict. Indeed, the present work has amply illustrated the fact that the commission of all the kinds of atrocities that are recognized in current international law (war crimes, crimes against humanity, and genocide) *always takes place in circumstances of deeply rooted and violent intergroup conflict,* whether at the international or intrastate level. Any strategy, therefore, that seeks to put in place a situation in which women and men can have credible assurance that atrocities will no longer be committed should be based on successful strategies for ending the desire of the parties to these conflicts to continue to pursue them through violent means. This requires success both in peacemaking and in longer-term peace-building. By peacemaking I mean a policy that seeks explicitly to resolve the deep political differences that lie at the root of the conflict in question and puts in place a sustainable and fundamentally egalitarian political order in which those political differences that will inevitably remain, or will emerge over time, can be resolved through nonviolent, noncoercive means. By peacebuilding I mean a set of policies in different spheres that aim at transforming public attitudes and social and economic relationships in ways that will sustain the noncoercive, postconflict political order.

In both Mozambique and South Africa, the requirements of peacemaking were identified, clarified, negotiated, and then agreed upon during the course of the four-year peace talks that brought about those countries' signal "conflict termination events": in Mozambique, the October 1992 conclusion of the General Peace Agreement (GPA), and in South Africa, the holding of the April 1994 elections. Beyond peacemaking, each of those negotiations also gave the leaders of the conflicting parties a good opportunity to address many key items in the longer-term peacebuilding agenda. Crucially, it gave the negotiators themselves—who were high-ranking representatives of the contending parties—the opportunity to experience for themselves and then model for (and explain to) their respective home constituencies the kinds of transformations in attitudes toward "the other" that could help to reframe the relationships among the relevant social groups on a much more respectful and constructive basis. It also, equally crucially, allowed the negotiators and the leaders and broader social movements to whom they reported the time they needed to work through the two processes of (1) envisioning how a new social-political order based on political equality might be fashioned in practice and (2) understanding what kinds of accommodations their own party would need to make if it wanted to allow such an order to be built. In the process of these negotiations, therefore, not only were the fundamental political terms of conflict termination agreed upon, but considerable work was also done in preparing the social and psychological ground for the cooperative (or at least nonantagonistic) relationships of the postconflict era.

The parties did not reach agreement on absolutely everything in the course of these pretransition negotiations. For example, in South Africa, they agreed to defer until later the fashioning of the full, final version of the country's democratic Constitution (as well as the exact procedure whereby the promised amnesties for apartheid-era rights abusers would be granted). They also agreed to defer resolution of some of the thorniest issues having to do with the long-standing claims of non-Whites to land and other resources that had been expropriated from them over the preceding centuries. But in South Africa, as in Mozambique, in the course of the pretransition negotiations each of the conflicting parties certainly did give up a lot of its previous claims, arguments, and strong social and political predispositions—*in the interests of allowing the peace process to succeed.* In a real sense, therefore, we might say now (though it may not have felt like that to many of the stakeholders at the time) that the South Africans and Mozambicans ended up being relatively lucky that the conflicts that had burdened their countries for so long were *not* resolved through the outright victory of one side over the other, since it was precisely the years-long period of negotiations that allowed the parties to these conflicts to work together to craft a shared vision of a form of egalitarian citizenship with which both (or all) of the previously contending parties felt they could live throughout the decades to come.

The people of Rwanda were not so "lucky." From this point of view, the outright military victory that the RPF won in July 1994 could even be seen as something of a burden for their country, since any party that wins such a victory faces the huge temptation of thereafter being able to impose a vindictive form of "victors' justice" on its former foes; and the RPF was no exception to that rule. It takes a high degree of political vision, self-discipline, and basic self-confidence to intentionally stand aside from pursuing such a policy. The widely varying records of the victorious Allies at the close of the two World Wars of the twentieth century are instructive in this regard. After World War I, the Allies imposed a harshly punitive settlement on the defeated Germans—and the outcome of that, in Europe, was the emergence of Nazism from the bosom of the humiliated and embittered German citizenry. Then, less than thirty years later, Allied statesmen for whom the whole record of the Treaty of Versailles and its tragic consequences was still a vivid object lesson took a markedly different path. Instead of seeking once again to impose broad punishment on all the German people, the leaders of the Western Allies (if not their counterparts in Moscow) pursued a policy that aimed broadly at rehabilitating Germany while radically refashioning it as a country committed to the norms of tolerance and democracy. It was in that broader political context of *strategic restraint* toward Germany that the Allies organized the Nuremberg Trials, which were an exercise designed, in the words of Chief Prosecutor Robert Jackson, to "stay" the hand of vengeance much more than to extend it.

It has been noted at various points throughout this book how strongly those who made some of the crucial decisions described herein—particularly those involved with ICTR and, in a different way, those in South Africa's TRC—tended to look to the record of the Nuremberg Trials as providing the key, groundbreaking precedent whose work (or key aspects of it) they were seeking to emulate and build on. The record of those trials has stood as an icon for many Western liberals and human rights activists since 1945, and especially since the end of the Cold War in 1991. However, the aspect of the Nuremberg Trials that most of these people have focused on has been their proactive "breaking of new ground" in the practice and jurisprudence of international criminal law—that is, by using a fairly narrow, technical legal lens through which to view them rather than by locating them within the broader political approach to the governance of occupied Germany of which they were a part, which (as noted above) was an approach marked primarily by strategic self-restraint. Historian Bradley F. Smith has provided a clear description of how, during the key weeks in the late summer and fall of 1944 when the Roosevelt administration was trying to decide how to govern Germany after the increasingly imminent victory in Europe, Secretary of the Treasury Henry Morgenthau, Jr.—who favored an extremely punitive policy toward Germany—lost the battle of influence to Secretary of War Henry Stimson, whose basic approach was one of self-restraint aimed at the later rebuilding of Germany along democratic lines.[9]

As secretary of war, Stimson had direct governmental responsibility for the administration of all foreign territories over which the U.S. forces came to exercise military occupation; and after Roosevelt's death in April 1945 he continued to exercise that responsibility under President Harry S. Truman. It was lawyers working in Stimson's War Department who drew up the London Charter for the Nuremberg Trials. Stimson picked the two American judges on the court (Francis Biddle and John Parker) as well as its chief prosecutor (Jackson). And the US military, which reported to Truman through Stimson, then made all the administrative arrangements for the court's work. Writing in 1977, historian Smith concluded his detailed description of the court's achievements by focusing not on the "groundbreaking" advances in international jurisprudence that it achieved but on the "caution" and "moderation" that marked the work of its judges.[10]

The geopolitical context within which the Nuremburg court was operating cannot be stressed too heavily. Because of the devastation that all the U.S. European allies had suffered during the war, Washington was clearly the commanding actor in determining the policies of the first few years of the occupation of Germany. Moreover, in Europe—unlike in East Asia—the victorious Allies never had to negotiate a surrender from their defeated foes, since the national command authorities in Germany collapsed nearly completely under the weight of the Allies' final advance. As a result, Stimson and the administration he represented were in a position to enact victors' justice in the portions of Germany they controlled in just about any way they chose.[11] And as noted above, the way they chose to deal with their defeated foes was marked at the broad political level, as well as in the specifics of the work of the Nuremberg judges, by "caution" and "moderation."

In Rwanda, forty-nine years later, the victorious party in the war there also won an outright military victory over its foes that involved no formal surrender and no element at all of negotiation. Like Presidents Roosevelt and Truman, President Kagame was in a position to enact almost any form of victors' justice that he might choose in the country that came under his undiluted control. He and his well-disciplined RPF forces evidently chose not to engage in wide orgies of retributive killings inside Rwanda. But they showed far less restraint in neighboring DRC. Meanwhile, inside Rwanda, Kagame—cheered on by the Western liberals with their cries about the "duty" to prosecute—put in place a prosecutorial and mass detentions policy that was far less restrained and less forward-looking than the policies that Stimson's War Department had pursued in Germany a half-century earlier. Indeed, Kagame's policies of broad collective punishment of the Rwandan Hutus seemed to have much more in common with the Allies' approach to the conquered community after World War I than with that pursued by Henry Stimson's War Department in and after 1945.

Prosecutions, Opportunity Costs, and Peacebuilding

How does the issue of launching (or refraining from launching) criminal prosecutions of alleged perpetrators of atrocities affect the processes of peacemaking and peacebuilding? It can do so in a number of ways. First, the offering of amnesties is often, as in Mozambique or South Africa, the *only* way that a negotiated transition out of a deep-seated conflict can be effected. This price is often—in many countries around the world today as in Abraham Lincoln's United States—seen as one that is worth paying in the broader interests of conflict termination. Second, at a wider level, amnesties can frequently be part of a process of broadening political inclusion. The language of criminalization (*bandidos armados,* etc.) is most often the language of political exclusion; and the policies that flow from implementing such language tend to be policies of political exclusion, divisiveness, and polarization, rather than of inclusion. By deliberately foreswearing both the language and practice of political exclusion, amnesties can make a huge contribution to the interests of long-term peacebuilding.

It is true that there may be some circumstances in which using the language of criminalization might perhaps help "prod" reluctant parties toward a political settlement. For example, did the UN stigmatization of South Africa's practice of apartheid as "a crime against humanity" help persuade the country's White rulers to reach the judgment they eventually made that they needed to enter serious negotiations with their non-White countrymen? Or, did it make them feel they were being "forced into a corner" and thus lead them to stiffen their resistance to democratization? In 2005–2006, will the ICC's pursuit of cases in Darfur or Northern Uganda help persuade the parties to these conflicts to negotiate?[12] Much more research is needed on such essentially political/diplomatic issues. However, any explicit use of criminalizing language in a situation of potential conflict-ending negotiations should surely be extremely judicious, in order to avoid stiffening the resistance of the targeted parties against the idea of entering or continuing in the negotiations. Care should also always be taken to apply such language and any attendant threats in a politically quite even-handed way, in order to strengthen long-term support for the norms of the rule of law.

One final, very important point with regard to the decision to use or to foreswear the option of criminal prosecutions in postatrocity situations: Everyone needs to be aware that undertaking criminal prosecutions, if it is to be done in a legalistically and more broadly politically credible way, is *an incredibly expensive project,* and that there are very high opportunity costs to doing this. These costs affect not just finances but the peacebuilding agenda itself.

Based on the figures given in Chapter 5, the "per-case" processing cost for adopting various different kinds of policy toward suspected or actual former perpetrators of violence can be roughly calculated as shown in Table 6.1. This listing reveals the stunning disparity of per-case costs between those incurred by ICTR and those incurred by all the other programs mentioned. Nor was it just the *per-case* cost at ICTR that seemed wildly disproportionate; the global cost of establishing and running the court—over $1.1 billion by the end of 2005—was a sum that, had it been differently used, could have made a substantial difference to the long-term economic and social well-being of Rwanda or any of a number of other very vulnerable, very low-income countries. For example, the entire amount of overseas aid invested in Rwanda's 8.8 million people in 2003 was $331.6 million, and the amount invested in Burundi's 3.7 million people was $224.2 million. How much more stabilization and how much less human misery might the citizens of Rwanda and Burundi have known if ICTR's budgets for the preceding years had been spent, instead, on supporting economic and social stabilization programs in one or both of those countries? But the very high financial opportunity costs involved in, in effect, taking $1.1 billion out of the available international aid budget and pouring it into sustaining an extremely high-cost and low-efficiency war crimes court in Arusha have seldom been mentioned in all the flood of articles in Western publications about the court's "jurisprudential breakthroughs."[13]

Meanwhile, study after study of the needs and preferences of people living in postconflict, postatrocity societies show that economic and social stabilization has been their main priority. In Rwanda, an opinion survey conducted in June 2000 indicated that 81.9 percent of respondents identified "Poverty/economic hardships" as a major social problem. (The next most frequently named problem was specified by only 20.8 percent of respondents. It was "insecurity.")[14] Eric Stover and Harvey M. Weinstein summarized the results of the detailed survey research they organized in Rwanda, Bosnia, and Croatia in 2000–2002 by noting: "Our informants told us that jobs, food, adequate and secure housing, good schooling for

Table 6.1   Cost Comparisons Among Cases

Each case completed at ICTR	$42,300,000
Each amnesty application at TRC	$4,290
Each case in Rwanda's *gacaca* courts (projected)	$581
Mozambique: each former fighter demobilized/reintegrated	$1,075
South Africa: each former fighter demobilized/reintegrated	$1,066

Source: Compiled by author from data presented in Chapter 5.

their children, and peace and security were their major priorities."[15] My own respondents in Rwanda, South Africa, and Mozambique all stressed the absolute centrality of economic stabilization to the success of the postconflict peacebuilding project.

In this regard, too, there is a strong resonance with the record of peacebuilding efforts in twentieth-century Europe. The post–World War I settlement there, pursued under the general rubric of "punishing" Germany for its role in the just-finished war, intentionally kept Germany trapped in deep poverty for a number of years, thereby inadvertently contributing to the rise of Nazism. By contrast, the years after 1945 in West Germany (but not East Germany) saw a large-scale infusion of U.S. aid and investment under the Marshall Plan, and then the establishment by France and West Germany of the European Coal and Steel Community, which formed the core of the later European Union. Both those steps helped to rebuild Germany as a stable economic powerhouse, and by the late 1950s a reemergence of war between those two centuries-long antagonists, France and Germany, had come to seem unimaginable. It still does.[16]

Meanwhile, it is clear in the early years of the third millennium that a high proportion of the atrocities still being committed in different parts of the world are occurring in the context of conflicts being pursued *in some of the world's most deeply impoverished nations.* In many of those countries, including those referred to in cavalier fashion as "failed states," there is an apparent vicious circle at work in which grave conflict wrecks the social and physical infrastructure needed to sustain livelihoods, and the dashing of the expectations of many people—especially young people—that they might be able to find a sustainable livelihood in the civilian world then continues to fuel the conflict and all its attendant lawlessness and violence.

Given, then, the absolute centrality of economic stabilization to postconflict peacebuilding, it seems clear that we cannot neglect the opportunity costs incurred at the financial level by the pursuit of a very expensive project like that of launching extensive programs of criminal prosecutions. There are other, more purely political, opportunity costs at stake, too. The chapters in the present work that describe the postconflict period in Rwanda show clearly that the pursuit—by both ICTR and the Rwandan government—of criminal justice proceedings had a strong effect in keeping the Tutsi-Hutu cleavage alive and wide, and thus in perpetuating political tensions within the country (and in the DRC). Was this a function solely of the "one-sided" nature of all these proceedings? Probably not. The Nuremberg trials, after all, had been extremely one-sided—but in their case the tightly limited number of those charged, and the fact that the trials were embedded in a broader project of the social and political rehabilitation of Germany, mitigated, and eventually overrode, any longer-term effect they might have had on fueling anti-Allied feeling among Germans.

In addition, more recently, we have seen the contrasting example of a court where "multisided" prosecutions have been undertaken in a (problematically) postconflict context. This is ICTY, whose caseload has included prosecutions against Serbs, Croats, and Bosniaks. But even there, the "multisided" nature of the caseload has apparently not enabled the court to make any significant contribution to intergroup reconciliation in former Yugoslavia. Reporting on a late-2003 visit to Serbia, Croatia, and Bosnia, the veteran Balkan affairs analyst Tim Judah wrote, "In Serbia, Croatia, and Bosnia ... I met virtually no one who believed that the tribunal was helping to reconcile people."[17] Harvey Weinstein and his colleagues, who researched attitudes among Croats, Bosniaks, and Serbs in three different locations in 2000 and 2001, found that only among the Bosniaks did the level of "acceptance" of ICTY run any higher than the midpoint.[18] Assessing the effects that both the ad hoc tribunals—ICTY and ICTR—as well as Rwanda's national-level pursuit of both regular prosecutions and *gacaca* courts had on national reconciliation in the countries concerned, Weinstein and his colleague Eric Stover concluded that "our studies suggest that there is no direct link between criminal trials (international, national, and local/traditional) and reconciliation, although it is possible this could change over time. In fact, we found criminal trials—and especially those of local perpetrators—often divided multiethnic communities by causing further suspicion and fear. Survivors rarely, if ever, connected retributive justice with reconciliation."[19] The aspiration that the Security Council had expressed when it established ICTR (and ICTY) a decade earlier—that these courts would somehow "contribute to national reconciliation"—was sorely disappointed.

Notions of Accountability and Punishment

In addition to challenging many widely held Western assumptions about the value of criminal trials in the aftermath of atrocity, the records of South Africa and (especially) Mozambique challenge some deeply held Western notions about the "accountability" of individual persons for all their actions, under all circumstances. By and large, the worldview that dominates the thinking of nearly all Westerners holds that under nearly all circumstances individuals are able to make considered, autonomous choices about all their actions, and that they can and should be held accountable on a strictly individual basis for those actions. These assumptions undergird the view that prescribes criminal prosecutions as the best policy response to the commission of atrocities, as well as that underlying the work of most postatrocity truth commissions. Although this worldview is specifically Western in its origin, having its roots in the ontology of philosophers of the Western Enlightenment such as Thomas Hobbes and John Locke, many Westerners claim that these assumptions about the strict accountability of individuals somehow represent universal truths about the human condition and are therefore seamlessly applicable to all the peoples of the world. When faced with evidence of, or reports about, the commission of violent acts, advocates of this view often place their greatest stress not on trying to comfort the bereaved, succor the injured, or repair broken relationships but, rather, on trying to determine—and preferably on a strictly individualized basis—exactly how the responsibility for the commission of the acts should most appropriately be divided among the alleged suspects and, then, how to hold these individuals strictly accountable for their actions.

In any event, the form of accountability demanded of even a convicted *génocidaire* within a criminal justice proceeding is, in a number of respects, very thin and formulaic. For example, at no point throughout a criminal proceeding are defendants, even if convicted, required to do any of the following:

1. give any acknowledgment of the factual truth of the findings the court has made on the matter, including on their own role in the commission of the criminal acts in question;
2. give any acknowledgment of their personal responsibility for having committed those crimes;
3. express any attitude of repugnance or repudiation toward such acts in general;
4. express any recognition that those of their own acts for which they were found guilty (or any other acts) caused real harm to other members of society;

5. express any remorse or regret for having undertaken those acts and inflicted those harms;
6. ask for the forgiveness of the victims or society in general for their role in committing those acts;
7. offer to undertake some form of reparative action, or
8. promise not to undertake any similar actions, or any other actions that harm others, in the future.

Thus, like any other convicted criminal, even a convicted *génocidaire* can emerge from an entire criminal proceeding while still denying the factual basis of the court's findings, while expressing a general attitude that says that—whether he committed the crimes in question or not—there is nothing wrong with such actions, and indeed while still also exhibiting an attitude of strong disdain to the court, to the political order that it represents, and to all the victims of his act. (At ICTY, Slobodan Milosevic's performance exhibited all these traits. Saddam Hussein also exhibited many of them during his trial in postinvasion Baghdad.) It is true that during the sentencing phase of a criminal proceeding a public expression of attitudes of disdain may cost the convicted criminal dearly, while expressions of remorse about his action and of a desire to repair the harms he has caused may (or may not) help somewhat in mitigating the severity of his sentence. True, too, that the maneuver of "plea bargaining" as used in U.S. courts requires that the defendant admit to his or her guilt for having committed some of the crimes as charged, while also admitting that these actions were in fact criminally illegal. But participation in any form of plea-bargaining arrangement remains quite optional, as does the voicing of any attitudes of contrition or remorse in the sentencing phase. The broader fact remains that the criminal's attitude toward such facts as are revealed during the criminal proceeding, or toward the people he has harmed through his actions, is not central in any way to the technical "success" of the trial's conduct. Indeed, real moral engagement with the perpetrators of violent acts is just about as peripheral to the main concern of a criminal proceeding as is the rehabilitation of their victims.

Nonetheless, many in the Western-based rights movement continue to judge that criminal proceedings are the best way of holding perpetrators of atrocities "accountable." The kind of accountability they seek is, perhaps, a more abstract form of accountability: an accountability to the broad sweep of the historical record, such as was achieved (if only imperfectly) at Nuremberg, rather than an accountability to the *existing* members of the society in which the perpetrators live, to the institutions of this society (including, centrally, its criminal courts), and to the victims of their past acts.

Or perhaps what these rights activists are really pursuing is the *punishment* of perpetrators that is attendant on their being found guilty. However, even in this regard, the form of accountability can seem very thin. International criminal courts have become notably more focused on due process and more squeamish about punishment since the days of Nuremberg. There, after a single joint trial that involved twenty-two defendants and lasted just over ten months, twelve of the defendants were sentenced to death, and their hangings were carried out (in, reportedly, a fairly inhumane way) just a few weeks after their sentencing.[20] At ICTY and ICTR, the death penalty is no longer on the books. It can seem a little bizarre to imagine the judges at these courts sitting around during the sentencing phase to determine whether for each convicted person's particular combination of proven crimes of mass murder, rape, or mutilation under the rubrics of war crimes, crimes against humanity, and genocide he deserves to spend five years in jail, twenty-five years, thirty-five years, or life. Here, too, the form of accountability being won—if the accountability of these individuals in the form of punishments appropriate to their crimes is what is sought—can seem thin, formulaic, and generally unsatisfactory.

And what, anyway, is the goal of all these punishments? Western thought traditionally distinguishes between theories of punishment that hold that to mete out punishment is somehow to give the perpetrators what they "deserve" and those that seek more concrete and utilitarian social goods. Regarding the matter of "deserving," South African government minister Rejoice Mabudhafasi was surely voicing the thoughts of many other people when she said of the apartheid system's abusers and torturers, "We can never do anything to them as bad as what they did to us. It's not in our nature. God will deal with them. We leave that to Him." I heard a very similar sentiment expressed by the evangelical social program head Michel Kayetaba, in Rwanda.

If it is impossible, then, for mere mortals to give to former abusers the treatment that they "deserve" to have, then what more down-to-earth social goals might punishment seek to attain? One might be the deterring of other would-be abusers. But in the circumstances of social breakdown and massive political violence in which most atrocities occur, it is hard to imagine that the rational calculations so vital to the successful operation of any deterrence strategy could reliably be expected to occur; and anyway, the existence of the UN ad hoc tribunals for over a decade and of the ICC since 2002 seems to have done precious little, if anything, to deter the continued commission of atrocities in various places around the world. Another social goal that might plausibly be attainable through punishment would be the *incapacitation* of the criminals and their networks.[21] This is, without doubt, an extremely valuable goal, one that is essential to the rehabilitation of any violence-torn society. However, as we learned from Mozambique and South Africa, the winning of convictions in a criminal court is not the only (and quite frequently, not even the best) way to bring about this end. Especially in the aftermath of grave intergroup conflict, an emphasis on rebuilding society on a sustainable basis of political equality while working proactively to reintegrate into society all those caught up in the earlier violence, whether as perpetrators or victims (or both), can indeed "drain the swamp" of political conflict within which the commission of atrocities previously festered; and the commission of atrocities has often throughout history been ended in precisely that way. As Abraham Lincoln famously said following the atrocity-laden Civil War inside the United States, "The best way to destroy an enemy is to make him a friend."

In today's world, the best way to incapacitate a network of *génocidaires* or war criminals may well still be to turn them—if not into "friends"—then at least into recognized and valued partners in the creation and maintenance of the emerging political order. That was what happened in South Africa with the Nationalist Party leadership and the leaders of their apartheid-era security forces; and in Mozambique, with the military and political leadership of Renamo. In both those cases, integration into the political leadership of the new, postatrocity order incapacitated the formerly existing and highly organized and violent networks of atrocity perpetrators far more effectively than a prosecutorial "victory" over them in a courtroom could ever have done.

Regarding the TRC, while it did not—by design—hand out any punishments to the perpetrators who came before it, it was nonetheless firmly based on the notion that individuals could and should be held strictly accountable for all their actions. Indeed, the form of accountability that the TRC required of perpetrators of atrocities was at one level significantly thicker than that required by a criminal court, since it required that amnesty applicants satisfy the Amnesty Committee that they had "told the whole truth" about their own roles (as well as those of others) with regard to the commission of grave human rights violations. That requirement corresponded, roughly, with requiring applicants to carry out the first two of the eight kinds of possible "personal accountability" tasks listed above. But even at the TRC, none of the third through eighth tasks on that list were ever required from former perpetrators, despite all the public pleadings of Archbishop Tutu, other commissioners, and other TRC staff members that accused wrongdoers such as Winnie Mandela or the NP leaders at least express some remorse or contrition for their actions. At the TRC, a truculent, quite nonrepentant former perpetrator could completely satisfy the demands of the Commission and win a total amnesty simply by telling "the truth" about all of her or his own actions, without having to express in public any attitude at all toward the moral quality of the facts she or he had thus related or toward the individuals harmed by those acts. However, the availability of amnesties at the TRC meant that if accountability is to be equated with punishment, then the accountability demanded by the TRC was notably thinner that that demanded by a criminal court.[22]

Accountability, Individualism, and Manichaeism

Despite its ability to grant amnesties for past misdeeds, the TRC, like nearly all criminal courts, continued to base most of its work on the notion of the strict accountability of individual persons. However, in addition, it quite consciously set out to emulate the approach the Nuremberg court had used when it tried to pinpoint the role that "leading institutions of society" had also played in sustaining the broad climate of violence within which the individual acts of atrocious violence were committed. At Nuremberg, the twenty-two defendants were chosen specifically to "represent" certain leading sectors of Nazi society rather than according to the prosecutors' prior ranking of their supposed degrees of culpability as individuals. In addition, the Pentagon lawyers who designed the Nuremberg charge sheet specifically inserted "criminal organizations" charges into the charge sheet with the goal of later being able to use convictions on those charges as the basis for the broad, and quite nonindividualized, application of administrative sanctions against former members of the organizations named. At the TRC, the "institutional" hearings were held with the more purely heuristic goal of being able to demonstrate the role that broad social sectors had played in undergirding the apartheid system, rather than with the goal of proscribing any particular organizations (and the work of its centrally important Amnesty Committee was organized entirely on the basis of the cases of the individual amnesty applicants, and of a strict assumption of the accountability of individuals for all their actions). At the TRC, in addition, the view of victims as having been harmed mainly as individuals rather than as members of a much more broadly oppressed group also prevailed—though, as we have seen, this view was widely criticized within the wider South African society, including by many members of the new, ANC-led political elite.

To most of the people I talked to in Mozambique—and to some of my interlocutors in Rwanda and in the Black communities of South Africa—the whole notion of the strict accountability of individuals for actions undertaken during a time of atrocious mass violence made little sense at all. (Nor, in their view, did the idea that during or after such violence, society could be strictly divided into discrete groups like perpetrators, victims, and bystanders.) In the Mozambican provincial town of Belavista, the whole group of seven civil society leaders with whom I talked in 2003 completely dismissed the notion that people who had committed violent acts during a war could, or should, be punished for those actions. That group included, notably, two men on the staff of a nationwide human rights organization. "In civil wars, terrible things happen" was the general view expressed by these men.

I heard exactly the same sentiments expressed by just about all the Mozambicans I interviewed. In 2003, I talked with Afiado Zunguza, the executive director of the church-related organization Justapaz, about Martha Minow's list of the eight "meta-tasks" that a society recovering from recent mass violence needs to address. Zunguza subjected the second of these goals ("Obtain the facts in an account as full as possible in order to meet victims' need to know, to build a record for history, and to ensure minimal accountability and visibility of perpetrators") to a particularly strong critique. He said that in traditional Mozambican society the reaction of respected elders to this would be to say: "Pointing fingers won't help. Perpetrators are a part of us. We believe they didn't want to go to war. They are our sons, and we want them back. To accuse them would mean that they would continue to be bandits."

In Rwanda a year earlier, Attorney General Gerald Gahima mused openly about whether, in times of mass violence, the "normal" rules about the strict accountability of individual persons for their actions could be held to apply. As recounted in Chapter 2 of the present book, Gahima told me how hard he had found it to make judgments about the actual responsibility of one individual (a priest) for a sequence of actions undertaken during the harsh and coercion-pervaded circumstances of the genocide. At a conference in New York in 2005, Gahima—who by then had resigned from Rwandan government service—gave additional examples of such dilemmas. One involved the challenge of determining the criminal responsibility of a Hutu woman who during the genocide had "denounced" her beloved Tutsi husband and children to the *génocidaires* in her neighborhood—who happened to be her own brothers. Gahima's reaction to the many cases of this nature with which he had wrestled as attorney general: He concluded that what was really needed was to work much harder on preventing the outbreak or recurrence of the kind of mass violence within which such wrenching dilemmas would always be found.

This phenomenon—whereby in the midst of extremely grave, antihumane violence, moral truths that in normal times seem easily discernible can suddenly become quite indecipherable—is not a new one. Primo Levi's *The Drowned and the Saved* is a sustained reflection on the experiences Levi had suffered during his time in Auschwitz as a youth. He wrote a whole chapter there on the moral "Gray Zone" in Auschwitz that was inhabited not only by the "trusty" Jewish and Ukrainian subofficials who kept much of the order within the Nazi extermination camps through their own exercise of extreme violence and terror, but by just about all the other prisoners in the Lager (the camp system) as well. Levi wrote:

> Before discussing separately the motives that impelled some prisoners to collaborate to some extent with the Lager authorities ... it is necessary to declare the imprudence of issuing hasty moral judgments on such human cases. Certainly, the greatest responsibility lies with the system, the very structure of the totalitarian state; the concurrent guilt on the part of individual big and small collaborators (never likable, never transparent!) is always difficult to evaluate. It is

a judgment that we would like to entrust only to those who found themselves in similar circumstances and had the opportunity to test for themselves what it means to act in a state of coercion.... The condition of the offended does not exclude culpability, which is often objectively serious, but I know of no human tribunal to which one could delegate the judgment.[23]

The moral truths that Levi was expressing there were, first, that during any situation of very grave intergroup violence, many people who commit atrocious acts do so because of coercion or because of extreme mental stresses and fears caused by the maelstrom of violence all around them; and, second, that many people who are the immediate victims of atrocious acts—perhaps even fatally so—are not in fact themselves perfectly "innocent."[24] Most survivors of the atrocious violence in Mozambique, and probably elsewhere, would agree heartily with those judgments. But for its part, the Western-originated legal system finds such moral cloudiness very unsatisfactory and hard, if not impossible, to deal with.

Rama Mani, in her fine work *Beyond Retribution: Seeking Justice in the Shadows of War,* urged policymakers at all levels who are assessing the challenges societies face as they try to escape from grave violence to move beyond the simple, dyadic division of people caught up in atrocious violence into quite separate and discrete groups of "victims" and "perpetrators" and to consider instead that all these men and women are in fact "survivors" of the violence:

[A]n exclusive focus on individual accountability, and on the individual identification of perpetrators and victims, is not helpful ... as it denies both the guilt and the victimization of the vast majority of society [in situations of grave violence]. Moreover, it ignores what all citizens in society share in common: that they are all survivors, whatever their past role, and that they now have a common stake in building a future together.

[Martha] Minow observed the need to define the entire society as one of victims. While this is an advance as it acknowledges the real impact of conflict on an entire society rather than a targeted few, to do so would only entrench the notion of victimhood, and concomitant helplessness. Rather, it is more useful to recognize that in such circumstances, to emerge alive, regardless of one's role and affiliation during conflict, is to be a survivor. More useful than Minow's notion of collective victimhood is a redefinition of the entire society as *survivors....*

Adopting this common identification that embraces all members of society may render more feasible the task of (re-)building a new political community that overcomes divisiveness between perceived perpetrators and victims.[25]

Mani based these conclusions on a consideration of justice issues in a large number of countries that in the post–Cold War era were struggling to escape from grave intergroup conflict. My study here has focused on only three countries, but in more historical and anthropological detail than Mani used. Based on all the evidence I have collected and considered in the present book, I believe she was quite right to advocate this move of considering all members of societies struggling to emerge from war and conflict as "survivors" rather than as "perpetrators" or "victims." (She was equally right in stressing the urgent need to address issues of distributive justice in the aftermath of conflict, if a strong basis is to be provided for a stable and sustainable postwar order.)

In the national discourse of Mozambique, there has been almost no reference to either the "perpetrators" or the "victims" of the country's civil war–era atrocities. Instead, all those who came into close contact with the violence are referred to in that discourse simply as the *affetados* or *affetadas* ("those affected by it"). This might be a nice term to adopt more broadly in the global discourse except that it carries some of the more passive connotation that Mani—rightly, in my view—rejects with regard to Minow's suggested broader use of the term "victim." Indeed, Mani stresses the fact that the term "survivor" carries with it the sense of a person who has lived through something, and surmounted obstacles while doing so.

Already, in some crevices of Western culture, there is a recognition that engagement in acts of grave violence as a perpetrator can also, in itself, be damaging to the perpetrating individual, and that perpetrators should therefore often be considered along with the immediate victims of their acts to be traumatized survivors of that climate of violence who may need some healing, rather than simply as "perpetrators" who should be judged and held strictly accountable for each and every act of violence that they have committed. For example, this view is widely held in the Western medical community, which has largely embraced the view that their own countries' warriors who return from wars in which they may well have perpetrated acts of grave violence as well as seen their own comrades suffer from violent acts are very frequently in need of psychosocial healing to help them escape from what has been described, medically, as "posttraumatic stress disorder" and, before that, "neurasthenia" or "shell shock." There is also, among the former combatants themselves, a broad recognition that the general moral and existential climate in the midst of warfare is very different from that in settled civilian society. However, the kind of allowances that many Western rights activists have been prepared to make for their own compatriots and friends who may have been involved in armed conflicts elsewhere have too rarely been extended in an equally generous way to former combatants from other, far more impoverished and war-damaged lands.

Remorse, Culture, Memory, and Peacebuilding

In the earlier chapters on Rwanda and South Africa, I made a number of mentions of the contribution that expressions of remorse from perpetrators of atrocious acts can make to the process of rebuilding interpersonal (and possibly also intergroup) ties in the aftermath of atrocity-laden conflict. In Chapter 3 I wrote that one of the most important things going on at South Africa's TRC was that "Blacks (and other non-Whites) sought to use it to initiate a prolonged national conversation in which they *confronted* the architects and implementers of the apartheid system—who were predominantly Afrikaners—with the facts about what apartheid had done to them over the decades, *reproached* them on that account, and *invited them to respond* with some meaningful expression of remorse."

The TRC, as we have seen, strove to give a significantly weightier role than is given in most criminal proceedings to the victims/survivors of the former violence; and many of the victims used their time in this public space not just to retell the stories of their grief and suffering but also to add their own reproaches to those being voiced by the commissioners toward the perpetrators of the earlier violence. On a number of occasions, too, the victims added their voices to the appeals the commissioners made to the perpetrators to express remorse and thus, in essence, to "rejoin the human family."

TRC staff psychologist Pumla Gobodo-Madikizela has written with great wisdom about the contribution that remorse and its credible public expression can make to bringing about social healing:

> When perpetrators feel remorse, they are recognizing something they failed to see when they violated the victim, which is that the victims

feel and bleed just like others with whom they, the perpetrators, identify. Remorse therefore transforms the image of victim as object to victim as human. ... [26]

When perpetrators express remorse, when they finally acknowledge that they can see what they previously could not see, or did not want to, they are revalidating the victim's pain—in a sense, giving his or her humanity back. Empowered and revalidated, many victims at this point find it natural to extend and deepen the healing process by going a step further: turning round and conferring forgiveness on their torturer.[27]

Some of the stories of the personal interactions among former antagonists that occurred as a result of the TRC's giving so much voice to the survivors of violence were very moving indeed. Gobodo-Madikizela wrote at length about the personal journey undertaken by Eugene de Kock, a noted organizer and perpetrator of apartheid-era atrocities, after one of his appearances at the TRC's Human Rights Violation Committee. He had testified there about his role in organizing the killing of three Black policemen on the grounds that they knew too much about the security forces' earlier involvement in many, very atrocious "dirty tricks." After that appearance, de Kock asked to meet the widows of the three murdered officers—and two of the women acceded to his request. Gobodo-Madikizela met with these two, Pearl Faku and Doreen Mgoduka, shortly after their meeting with de Kock and described their reactions to their encounter with the man who had killed their husbands:

> "I was profoundly touched by him," Mrs. Faku said.... Both women felt that de Kock had communicated to them something he felt deeply and had acknowledged their pain. [Mrs. Faku said,] "I couldn't control my tears. I could hear him, but I was overwhelmed by emotion, and I was just nodding, as a way of saying yes, I forgive you. I hope that when he sees our tears, he knows that they are not only tears for our husbands, but tears for him as well.... I would like to hold him by the hand, and show him that there is a future, and that he can still change."[28]

When one party expresses a reproach to another party, the reproacher is urging the reproachee to undergo precisely this kind of change of view, to "recognize something they failed to see when they violated the victim"—that is, to rethink the moral content of the act he had previously committed. At the TRC, these reproaches were being launched both between individual persons and at a broader societal level, in that the TRC as a whole, and the newly emerging democratic society in whose name it spoke, was inviting members of "the community from which the worst perpetrators had sprung"—that is, the White community, and especially the Afrikaner wing of it—to completely rethink their former view of their non-White compatriots. At this level, the TRC can be seen as part of the broad post-1994 effort to re-educate or resocialize the country's Whites. Inasmuch as Nuremberg in its day, or ICTR or the national-level efforts in Rwanda more recently, all had a heuristic goal, they too were aiming at a similar re-education of members of the formerly perpetrating communities. In the case of Nuremberg, that re-educative effort was largely successful over time—but not immediately. Historians of modern Germany note that it was not until the early 1960s—some seventeen or eighteen years after 1945—that most Germans were ready even to start critically examining their country's actions in the Nazi era.[29] In the case of the postconflict efforts in both South Africa and Rwanda, it is probably still too early yet to tell how successful these two re-educative efforts have been, though for now the project seems to have been markedly less successful in Rwanda than in South Africa.

This "reproach-rethinking-remorse" paradigm of attempting social healing seems roughly parallel to the "accusation-confession" paradigm that is familiar in Western culture from a combination of the general popular understanding of Western criminal law ("accusation") and the general understanding of Christian religion ("confession"). However, launching a *reproach* against another person is significantly different from launching an accusation against him. A reproach, to be effective, is always best offered in a spirit of friendship and concern for the well-being of the person reproached. By contrast, it is hard to voice an accusation against someone in anything approaching a spirit of friendship, and the situation is even more polarizing when it is the institutions of a state launching the accusation (or "criminal charge") against him.

Expressing remorse for one's past actions is also significantly different—and, as suggested above, morally much "thicker"—than merely confessing to having committed them. Indeed, if remorse is sincerely experienced, and not merely expressed in a superficial way, it should naturally lead to a desire to *repair* what has been harmed, as much as possible, and thus to the provision of some form of material or symbolic *reparation*. In the accusation-confession model, meanwhile, whether or not there has been a confession, the accusation against a perpetrator will, if proven in a criminal court, necessarily lead to a punishment. (The analogue of that in the religious system of at least the Catholic portion of the West is that a confession of sins to a priest will lead to the imposition of some symbolic form of penalty such as saying a certain number of "Hail Mary's.")

We have, then, at least two broad paradigms for how peoples and cultures have thought that social healing can be effected in the aftermath of acts of interpersonal violence: the reproach-rethinking-remorse-reparation (RRRR) paradigm and the accusation-(optional) confession-punishment (ACP) paradigm. The evidence presented in this book strongly indicates that the RRRR paradigm, which was the one most broadly followed in the postconflict years in South Africa, was considerably more successful in building a sustainably peaceful postconflict order than the ACP paradigm, which has been pursued in a number of different ways in and for Rwanda.

For their part, the Mozambicans pursued an entirely different paradigm. Both the RRRR paradigm and the ACP paradigm rely on *explicitly verbalized forms of interaction*. But in Mozambique, as noted in Chapter 4, the kinds of healing rituals practiced and sustained by the country's traditional healers over the generations have all been strongly performative rather than verbal—this, in line with the Mozambicans' broadly held belief that, as described by Alcinda Honwana (who is also cited in Chapter 1), "[r]ecounting and re-membering the traumatic experience would be like opening a door for the harmful spirits to penetrate the communities."[30] Mozambicans are, indeed, far from the only people in the world who have such a large regard for the generative power of the spoken word or other representations of things. The phenomenon of retrau-matization of former victims of violence when, for example, they are required to testify verbally in a court proceeding about what happened to them is well known throughout the world. For that matter, the entire global industry of pornography would collapse if representations—including verbal representations—of things did not have such generative power.

In another publication, Honwana has written that the objective of the kind of postconflict cleansing ceremonies held in traditional Mo-zambican culture "is not to ignore past trauma, but to acknowledge it symbolically before firmly locking it away and facing the future."[31] Her colleague João Paulo Borges Coelho has contrasted these nonverbal traditional ways of enacting and marking the transition from military to civilian life with the noticeably different rituals of transition that Frelimo used back in the early days of national independence, to try to reintegrate into national society those thousands of Mozambicans who had worked with the former colonial regime. On that earlier occasion, Coelho wrote, Frelimo insisted that as a condition for reintegration into postindependence society the former "collaborators" should publicly reveal their whole records of service for the Portuguese. "However, the effect of coming clean was often humiliation. 'Collaborators' were persecuted for their past and saw their careers and attempts to rebuild their lives blocked. As a result, many fled the country, with some subsequently offering their services when Renamo was formed by the Rhodesians in 1977." Coelho noted that in 1992, by contrast, the General Peace Agreement "avoided a 'winner-takes-all' scenario.... A fortunate combination of local circumstances also ensured that the principle of 'purification' adopted by Frelimo following the colonial war would be replaced by a more conciliatory stance towards Renamo."[32] Frelimo, like the Allies in Europe in 1945, seemed to be showing that it had learned from its past errors of judgment.

The fortunate combination of circumstances cited by Coelho had indeed been achieved, at both the national and international levels. Frelimo, as noted above, was forced to end its conflict with Renamo through negotiations rather than through an outright victory. The Mozambican people already had a strong cultural preference for using well-respected and generally successful performative rituals to mark the ends of conflicts. And finally, in 1992 there was still no general expectation—much less any requirement—in the international community that all major perpetrators of atrocious violence should be held "accountable" in a criminal court for their actions. Taken together, these circumstances led to the nearly nationwide use and broad public acceptance of performative rather than verbalized ways of reintegrating the national society. As a result, in Mozambique there was no systematic attempt at all to compile a complete "historical" record of who exactly had done what to whom, and how, in the long, dark years of the civil war.

Patricia Hayner visited Mozambique in late 1996 to research Mozambicans' attitudes toward the idea of establishing a truth-telling mechanism. She summed up what she heard from her interlocutors there in these terms: "No, we do not want to reenter into this morass of conflict, hatred, and pain. We want to focus on the future. For now, the past is too much part of the present for us to examine its details. For now, we prefer silence over confrontation, over renewed pain. While we cannot forget, we would like to pretend that we can."[33]

When I was in Mozambique in 2001 and 2003, the same kind of views still seemed overwhelmingly dominant. In addition, by then it appeared that many of the people I talked to really had forgotten many of the details of what had happened during the civil war. Thus, while in 2003 and 2004 thousands of survivors of the Rwandan genocide were still continually being pressed by officials at ICTR and in Rwanda's own justice system to remember and recount the most intricate details of who had committed precisely what gruesome act against whom back in 1994, in several conversations I had in Mozambique in that period a Mozambican colleague would fail to recall even fairly large and significant facts like which side—Renamo or Frelimo—a particular friend or colleague might have fought on during the civil war. It was not that the Mozambicans had altogether forgotten about the violence of the war years. Rather, they had chosen and carefully framed exactly *what it was about the war* that they wanted to remember and discuss. They remembered mainly, as Zunguza told me, the many ways in which the civil war had been a disaster for the whole national community, rather than the details of what had happened during it to individuals within the community.

These culturally based attitudes toward explicit and detailed representations of past traumas had a big effect on whether and how leaders and citizens of these three countries chose, in the years after their respective conflict termination attempts, to memorialize the victims of the conflicts. In Mozambique, the country's political leaders decided not to establish any public memorials to the dead of the civil war years, though there were many public memorials to those who had died in the liberation war that preceded it. In Mozambique, too, there seemed to be no, or almost no, attempts by nongovernmental bodies to establish public memorials to the civil war's victims. (It is hard to decide whether the carefully tended mass graves in Chiboene should be considered public memorials.)

In South Africa, many of the country's Black citizens and members of the new ANC political leadership had a complex reaction to suggestions from White liberals that it would be a good idea to erect memorials to the sufferings of the non-White communities under apartheid. In Johannesburg, a vast and expensive "Apartheid Museum" built by White developers as part of an obligation to the City Council stood almost completely empty the day I visited it in 2003. However, the Hector Pieterson Museum in Soweto, the District Six Museum in Cape Town, and the Robben Island memorial near Cape Town are all sites that memorialize the same era; and when I visited them in 2003 they all seemed to have considerably greater support from South Africans than the grandiosely overdesigned Apartheid Museum. But still, eight and nine years after democratization, most of the country's citizens seemed to be placing much more emphasis on the continuing campaign to rename places with non-European names, to change national curricula, and to implement other parts of their broad cultural transformation agenda than they did on establishing memorials to specific aspects of the recent past.

In Rwanda, meanwhile, the government continued its policy of establishing and maintaining numerous very high-profile sites around the country to memorialize the human suffering of the genocide (but not that inflicted through the RPF's own war crimes). Most of these memorials centered on displays of skeletal parts or other human remains that were publicly presented in ways that some Rwandans and non-Rwandans found very disturbing—not least because to many Rwandans these displays flagrantly violated their norms of how the mortal remains of loved ones should be treated.

The contribution that memorials like these make to long-term peacebuilding can be problematic and hard to gauge. In many places around the world they have greatly facilitated public understanding of the suffering caused by atrocity and war. But elsewhere—for example, in Northern Ireland, Saddam Hussein's Iraq, and Franco's Spain—the building of grandiose memorials and the enactment of regular commemorative rituals have done more to perpetuate divisiveness and conflict than to help ease them. Certainly the heuristic content of any memorial to victims of past violence should always be open to interrogation. At the Robben Island memorial, and in the District Six Museum and the Hector Pieterson Museum, the "message" about the suffering and evil of the apartheid system has been intelligently complemented by other messages about the value of a cultural diversity that includes White people, and about the contributions that a number of White people made to the struggle against apartheid. The genocide memorial museum that I visited in Kigali was still unfinished and its eventual heuristic content still unclear; but I found the careful arrangements it presented of hundreds of skulls, other human bones, and small personal possessions recovered from the dead to be starkly shocking.

Peacebuilding as a Process over Time

Peacebuilding is a process that takes place over time and requires a continuing commitment to the principles of political fairness, socioeconomic justice, and nonviolent resolution of conflicts that undergird it. Obviously, not all the tasks of building a stable long-term peace can be accomplished in one fell swoop. It might seem as though that came close to being the case in Mozambique, with the conclusion of the GPA in 1992. But even there (as noted above), much of the basis for successful peacebuilding had been established through the four-year period of negotiation that preceded that event, and many very important parts of the peacebuilding agenda remained to be implemented throughout the three to five years that followed October 1992. In South Africa, too, though the holding of the landmark democratic election of 1994 marked a clearly identifiable transition out of conflict and into a new era, the years after 1994 saw the country's people continuing to wrestle with many extremely important peacebuilding tasks in the economic, political, and cultural spheres. In both those countries, the busy years that immediately followed the main conflict termination "event" evidently formed a crucial period of incubation for the infant peace agreement; and it is hardly surprising that, for example, many influential people in the new South Africa said they were "too busy" attending to the forward-looking tasks of national governance to pay much attention to the workings of the TRC. In Mozambique, meanwhile, since there was no project at all that sought to untangle the complex issues of the accountability of individuals for the atrocities of the past, the leaders and members of the society could use the post–October 1992 incubation period to focus even more determinedly on the urgent tasks of the present and future.

In Rwanda, the RPF's battlefield victory of July 1994 constituted a clear conflict termination *opportunity* for the victors, and the RPF did thereafter try to bring an end to their long-running conflict with the large "Hutu Power" networks. But they did so on their own determinedly punitive terms. It was quite understandable from a psychological perspective that representatives of a demographic minority like the Tutsis, who were emerging from a period of their own extreme traumatization, would have a strong inclination to act punitively toward the demographic majority in order to gain some assurance of their own survival as a group. In post–World War II Europe, after all, the three Allied governments whose people had suffered the worst from the crimes of the Nazi years all originally sought to inflict harshly retributive policies on the conquered Germans, at all levels. It was perhaps only the relative distance and insulation of the American people from the privations of the pre-1945 years that allowed Washington to conceive of, and push hard for, the policy of relative restraint that was ultimately (though not immediately) also adopted within occupied Germany by France and Britain. Meanwhile, it was the massive U.S. material superiority over all the other Allies in 1944–1945 that allowed Washington's (specifically, Stimson's) views on how to deal with the former Nazis to prevail. In Rwanda in 1994, by contrast, the punitive inclinations of the regime so recently instituted by those who claimed to represent the former victims were considerably *strengthened* by the pressures that came from outside, since much of the "international community" was strongly urging the RPF government to institute a system of strict accountability for all those suspected of participation in the genocide. (To his immense credit, Archbishop Tutu was one of the few outsiders who made a big effort to go to Rwanda to urge a policy of restraint and relative generosity. But when he arrived there, in 1995, the RPF rulers were not ready to hear his message.)

In any event, Rwanda's postgenocide government failed to take the best advantage it could of the conflict termination opportunity it had access to in the summer of 1994. The RPF's conflict with the Hutu Power networks was never definitively terminated. The conflict was tamped down (or repressed) to a considerable extent within Rwanda itself; but at the same time, from 1996 on, it was largely displaced to the much more extensive areas of eastern DRC, where it took on much more lethal and damaging forms. It is hard to gauge the degree to which the continued pursuit of criminal prosecutions—by both the RPF government and the United Nations—contributed to the perpetuation of intergroup hatreds and suspicions in those years. But the fact of those prosecutions and of the Kigali government's associated campaigns of widespread detentions and "re-education camps" undoubtedly did have such an effect, and it was probably all the larger since in both ICTR and the Rwandan courts the prosecutorial strategy was, and was seen as, *so markedly one-sided.*[34] But beyond the fact of that one-sidedness, individual Rwandans, more or less continuously after July 1994 and even a decade or more after the end of the genocide, were still being forced by ICTR and by the regular and *gacaca* courts inside Rwanda to continually revisit, retell, remember, and revisit the events of the genocide in great detail. This continued to have a very bad effect on intergroup relations in communities throughout the country.

In South Africa, the truth-establishment exercise of the TRC was, as noted in Chapter 5, substantially completed in August 2002, eight years after the country's main conflict termination event. (Government prosecutors continued to pursue just a handful of cases after that; and some nongovernmental groups continued to pursue civil cases against their former oppressors, primarily through the U.S. courts.) For Rwandans, ICTR promised that its work would continue until 2008 or 2010—that is, fourteen or sixteen years after the end of the genocide. At the national level, Rwandan officials estimated that the *gacaca* courts, which were their main "truth establishment" exercise and which did not even start work until 2005, would wrap up their efforts within three to five years—or even, according to one official—ten years. That is, Rwanda's national-level efforts at "truth establishment," which had already run continuously since 1994, could end up continuing throughout a twenty-one-year period following the end of the genocide!

Societies exiting from periods of grave and atrocity-laden intergroup conflict are very vulnerable indeed. This circumstance has at least two implications on policy. First, it means that developments of any kind that tend to stunt the process of peacebuilding can be particularly damaging in those early years and that those damages, once inflicted, may take further years (or even generations) to repair. Second, it means that such societies are extremely vulnerable in those years to influences from external forces, especially those that are politically stronger or much better resourced than they are; so aid donors and other outsiders need to be very aware of their capacity for inflicting unintended harm on these societies.

If we look at the process of repair and building (or rebuilding) of healthy societies in the aftermath of conflict as an organic process that has its own rhythms and takes place over a number of years, we should be led, as well-meaning outsiders, to adopt a much more humble pose of focusing on supporting that process of social repair rather than rushing in with our own prescriptions of what else might need to be done. For example, Martha Minow's listed meta-task "Establish a clear historical record of the harms that have been done" may seem like an urgent priority to many Westerners in such circumstances—as it was (or more precisely, as it became over time) for many Jewish survivors of the Holocaust in Europe and for survivors of repressive regimes in Chile or Argentina. But other groups throughout the world, including in Western society, have not placed such a high temporal (and financial) priority on this task. Such groups include, for example, the Roma (Gypsy) survivors of the Holocaust and the Spanish survivors of the Francoist era that lasted until the late 1970s. Regarding Roma views on seeking public memorialization of the 500,000 of their people who were killed in the Holocaust, historian Isabel Fonseca has written, "The Second World War and its traumas are certainly within memory; but there is no tradition of commemoration, or even of discussion. Some thought that such talk might actually be dangerous: "Why give them ideas?" a young Hungarian Rom asked, fifty years after the event."[35] Regarding the attitudes of Spaniards to the civil war of the 1930s and to the long decades of Francoist repression that followed, Andrew Rigby has written that, once democracy started to reemerge in the late 1970s, "[a]ll those parties and groupings that sought to see Spain transformed into a political democracy agreed on a pact to forget the most painful elements of the past and engage in a form of selective amnesia."[36]

Of course, matters are not really quite so clear-cut as that, since the views of survivor communities can also shift significantly over time, in a dynamic process propelled by the debates that take place inside them over this issue. Many Jewish survivors of the Holocaust were, for some decades after 1945, reticent about talking about their experiences under Nazi rule: They had a lot of personal healing and rehabilitation to do before they felt confident enough to take on that task. (And as previously noted, most Germans did not seem ready to grapple with the moral challenges of the Holocaust until the 1960s. In 1945, and for several years after that, their main imperatives were bare human survival, the absorption of 8 million ethnic German refugees from the East, and the rebuilding of national institutions shattered by twelve years of Nazism and war.) Similarly, it was not until the early 2000s that some—but not all—descendants of the Spanish Republicans finally started to feel that the time had come to seek their own answers about what had happened to their forebears. In all these cases, the desire to discover and establish a detailed historical record of past harms is deferred, or suppressed, or reemerges according to a rhythm that seems largely internal to the community concerned.[37]

It is almost certainly much harder, ten or twenty or a hundred years after the event, to go back and recreate a satisfactorily full historical record of past harms done. On the other hand, for many societies emerging from periods of atrocious conflict, the survival of the national or subnational community may itself still be felt to be at stake, and members of that community may be quite justified in judging that ensuring the survival of their community by avoiding the reeruption of violence and trauma should take priority over the establishment of a painstakingly full historical record. (This is probably true of the still very hard-pressed Roma.) World history is, tragically, far too full of the—necessarily sketchy—records of national groups of different sizes in North America, Africa, and elsewhere that have, indeed, completely ceased to exist.

Revaluing the Role of Religion

The physical damage suffered by communities struggling to emerge from grave conflict, and by the women and men who make up these communities, is often horrendous in its nature and extent. But the damage inflicted on the conceptual worlds of these individuals is also often enormous. Many of the key institutions of these societies, including educational and religious institutions and even families, may have betrayed the trust that people placed in them. Since these institutions are important bearers and transmitters of spiritual and conceptual meaning in people's lives, the entire conceptual universe in which the survivors live may lie as shattered as the physical infrastructure around them. A large number of survivors may have lost their capacity to trust their fellow men or women. The religious faith of many—the faith that had previously given meaning, rhythm, and purpose to their lives—may lie in tatters. Communities emerging from atrocious conflict have many needs in the psychosocial realm, including in the spiritual portion of that realm.

Indeed, in many of these societies the disciplinary boundaries that in Western society establish separate zones of responsibility for "law," "medicine," "politics," or "religion" have no meaning. Religion, with its associated arts of healing, law, and governance, may have a much larger and determinative role in these people's lives than it does in many Western nations. When the institutions of religion themselves become infected with violence, as happened to many of the churches in 1994 Rwanda, the damage to the believers' conceptual and spiritual worlds is correspondingly grave. By contrast, when the institutions of religion retain their integrity and their capacity to provide healing and regenerative services to the people—as happened in Mozambique throughout the lengthy civil war—they can help the people to withstand even the most terrifying assaults on their lives and their communities, and to emerge from this violence with their psychosocial and spiritual well-being remarkably intact.

In South Africa, the various institutions of the Christian religion played a distinctive and complex role in the centuries-long struggle for human equality. The colonial project of the Afrikaners, and its associated expropriation of most of the best land in the region, had been motivated to a great degree by their own view of themselves as furthering a Bible-based "redemption" of the land of South Africa for their own version of Protestant Christianity. Along the way, the Afrikaners and the country's English-speaking White settlers also converted many of the country's indigenous and mixed-race people to various forms of Protestant Christianity, very often using incentives or even coercion. Then, during the twentieth century, some of the country's non-White thinkers and leaders started to take the teachings of the Christian Bible about human equality quite seriously—in part, as a means of buttressing the reproach and the claims they voiced against their country's colonial rulers. And these rulers were, crucially, people who proclaimed *the same holy scriptures.* (In Mozambique and elsewhere in colonial Africa, many Black nationalist leaders similarly used Bible teachings to buttress their claims against professedly "Christian" colonial powers.) In the struggle of South Africa's people for human equality, the teachings of Christianity, Islam, Hinduism, and the country's remaining indigenous traditions all made distinctive contributions;

and the institutions maintained by these religions certainly helped buttress the survival of the beleaguered non-White communities. The support that European and North American churches gave to their struggling coreligionists in South Africa was often—as in Rejoice Mabudhafasi's case—very direct. And when, finally, the leading institutions of the Afrikaner community did start to rethink their view of the ontological status of their non-White compatriots and to move toward accepting one-person-one-vote elections, stirrings of conscience among some Afrikaner church leaders contributed somewhat to this rethinking (though the "re-education" of many of these church leaders still seemed worryingly incomplete even some years after 1994). Then, as we have seen, when the TRC enacted its nationwide dramas of reproach in 1995–1998, the symbolisms of Christianity played a prominent role in helping to frame those dramas.

Because of the extreme and multifaceted vulnerabilities experienced by societies trying to escape from atrocious violence, religion—meaning religious ideas, understandings, and experiences, as well as the institutions that embody and transmit them—has an almost unique capacity to help or hinder the process of peacebuilding. In Rwanda, the tainting of most of the country's existing religious institutions on account of the complicity of many of their leaders with the genocidal networks left the country's people after July 1994 particularly bereft—and also particularly vulnerable to ideas of all sorts coming from outside. Those ideas included notions about a rigid and highly individualized version of accountability, and the need for extensive prosecutions and detentions. Few and far between in postgenocide Rwanda (as in post–Nazi Germany) were church leaders, or leaders of other religions, who during the era of mass violence stood up and enacted any kind of a personal witness against it and thereby retained their credibility as moral leaders in the postviolence era—though in both situations, small numbers of such people did indeed exist. In Rwanda, given the deep moral collapse of the Catholic church and many of the Protestant denominations during the genocide, prophetic, values-based religious leadership took some time to reemerge after July 1994. But by the time I visited the country in 2002 it did seem to be reemerging within some of the country's Protestant (and Muslim) institutions.

Most rights activists and liberal governments in the West pay little heed to the role that religious concepts and religious institutions can play in helping societies as well as individuals to reconstitute themselves in the aftermath of atrocious violence. Many rights activists in the West are concerned about keeping religious institutions out of intervention in the politics of their own countries. Many live lives in which the role of personal religious belief and affiliation is minimal or absent, so they have a poor understanding of the value of such affiliation to others of their fellow humans and correspondingly little curiosity about the religious and cosmological beliefs of others. For their part, liberal governments and the officials who staff them are generally (and quite understandably) wary of becoming involved with religion-based institutions at home or abroad, and intergovernmental bodies like the UN agencies have almost no capacity at all to address and harness the potential of such institutions. Yet throughout the present study, we have seen the strongly positive role that religious ideas, practices, and institutions played in helping individuals and communities to survive during periods of mass atrocity, and then to recover and rebuild their societies once the atrocities ended. We saw how religious beliefs and institutions helped sustain Rejoice Mabudhafasi in South Africa, Agnès in Rwanda, and Evaristu Wanela in Mozambique throughout their days of trial and sorrow. We saw how religious concepts and institutions helped make and build the peace in Mozambique; how they informed the work of the TRC in South Africa; and how in recent years they have started to put some Rwandans back on a path toward personal recovery and socioeconomic reconstruction. Yes, it is true that religious ideas have often—everywhere around the world, including in these three countries—been harnessed to divisive, heinous, and violent ends. But still, they are extremely powerful ideas that speak to the core of what many people believe makes them human. To ignore the role that religions and their understandings of the world can play in helping societies recover from atrocious conflict is therefore to make a dangerous mistake. And when religions do play that role, they also necessarily speak to core issues of justice.

Lessons from Mozambique

Given the remarkable success of Mozambique's transition out of the atrocious violence of its civil war years, it is important to pull together here the main lessons of how the country's people and leaders actually achieved that transition. It is true that several aspects of what the Mozambicans did seemed to be highly dependent on the healing-focused nature of their culture and belief system and on the high degree of popular "buy-in" enjoyed by these beliefs within the national community. But still, similar or parallel kinds of cultural resources that can support successful escapes from the climate of violence do still exist in many other cultures around the world. So if we can clearly identify what it was in Mozambican culture that supported the Mozambicans' successful transition from war to peace, then perhaps we can all be more aware that these kinds of belief systems are indeed cultural resources of continuing value and, therefore, that it is worth trying to identify similar kinds of cultural resources in other places around the world and working to preserve and strengthen them rather than allowing them to be drowned in a rising global tide of Western-style prosecutorialism.[38]

As best I understand it, what enabled the Mozambican model of conflict-transcendence to work in the post-1992 years were the following six aspects of what the country's people and leaders did. First, during the pre-GPA negotiations and during the crucial transition period of 1992–1994, Mozambicans made a strong commitment to giving the demands of the future priority over any desire to reexamine the past. Cardinal Dos Santos recalled that during the negotiations, his prime message was "We can't solve anything if you speak about the *reasons* you are fighting. You need to just try to find the way to get peace. You want to speak about the way to find a meeting of the minds, not speak about the differences." Sant' Egidio's Andrea Riccardi described in very similar terms the approach he used as he facilitated the peace talks. It was fortunate that these moral leaders were able to find resonance in this from the political leaders of both Frelimo and Renamo—a factor that allowed the negotiations to progress toward success. Their emphasis on the need to prioritize the future over the past also resonated with the broad masses of the country's people.

Second, the rituals used at all levels, from the national to the personal, all signaled the existence of *a clear temporal and existential transition from war to peace.* Several people have noted that the much-publicized handshake between Chissano and Dhlakama in October 1992 was the key transformational act at the national level. And at the local and personal levels, the reintegrative ceremonies undertaken by nearly everyone who had come into direct contact with the war's violence made the experience of that transition out of the era of war and into the era of peace very present in people's lives. Thereafter, it was on the basis of people's clear and direct experience of the fact of this transition that the argument that "there was one set of rules for those times of war, and another completely different set for the present time of peace" could be sustained. The near-universal acceptance of this argument was essential for the postwar implantation of the norms of the rule of law.

Third, like the "peace accord" between the apartheid regime and the ANC in South Africa, the GPA centrally included an agreement on establishing an egalitarian and fundamentally democratic political system from then on out—and, moreover, this system took root and proved sustainable.

Fourth, no attempt at all was made to draw distinctions among those who had had close encounters with the violence of the civil war. All were viewed alike as simply *affetados,* and they were generally not further identified as "victims" or "perpetrators." In addition, because of the need to sustain the strength of the ontological break between the time of violence and the time of peace and normalcy, any attempts to revisit or reexamine the violence of the war years in detail were viewed with great trepidation, and generally rejected. There remained a lively concern about the risks of retraumatization and bringing the violent gestalt of the past back to life.

Fifth, because no Mozambican participants in the war's violence were ever publicly identified as "perpetrators," there was no need to adopt any special programs to deal with them. Like everybody else who had been "affected" by the wartime violence, they were expected by society, now that the war was over, to participate responsibly in the building of the new peaceful order. The same expectation was expressed toward those who had been "victims" of the violence. For example, Carolyn Nordstrom described a ritual for a woman previously used as a sex slave in which the woman was reminded through the symbolism of the ritual that she, too, now had the responsibility to let go of the hurt of the past and not to pass it on to others. This seems a mature and constructive way to address people victimized by earlier violence. Certainly it avoids infantilizing these individuals by conveying to them and others that they need not take any responsibility for their behavior going forward.

Sixth, during the community-level rituals of reintegration of the *affetados,* all the cultural resources of the society were brought to bear in the attempt to make this reintegration successful. These resources included the relationships of survivors of violence with the spirits of the ancestors, the sacred home, and the extended family and broader community. They also, crucially, included the economic resources of the local (and global) community, building on the view that the best way to ensure the long-term rehabilitation of war-scarred individuals is to make sure they have the best chance possible to attain a decent livelihood, a stable family life, and a supportive, regenerative community.

Peacebuilding and Atrocity Prevention in the Twenty-First Century

The 1990s were a period in which the United States and its Western allies enjoyed unrivaled power in international affairs. Important participants in the political elites in those countries sought, usually from the best of motives, to use Western power in the world to further the implementation of their own views regarding the best way to bring an end to the commission of atrocities and the impunity of high-placed perpetrators, and to expand to all portions of the globe respect for the basic principles of the rule of law. The views of most of these people had been strongly influenced by a slightly mythologized, deeply depoliticized, and often aridly legal-technical view of what had been accomplished during the Nuremberg Trials of 1945–1946. For many Westerners the Nuremberg Trials had come to stand as a foundational beacon in the campaign to end respect for the much-chafed-against norm of the sovereign immunity of national leaders, and to put even the highest officials of various countries' governments on notice that they, too, could be held responsible for atrocities carried out by subordinates acting under their command. The establishment of ICTY in 1993 and ICTR in 1994 was seen as building directly on the legal and political precedents of Nuremberg. And the momentum gained by the pro–war crimes court movement then led to the establishment of the permanent International Criminal Court (ICC) in 2002.

The research presented in this book, however, suggests that a different, much more political and more deeply historical view of the nature of atrocities as events in human affairs can be more useful than a simple, unidimensional reliance on prosecutorialism in suggesting ways to bring the commission of atrocities to an end, and to start to instill the rule of law (and, therefore, the ending of impunity) in places where the rule of law has hitherto been most flagrantly disregarded. The differing trajectories that Rwanda, South Africa, and Mozambique followed in the dozen years after their key conflict termination events/opportunities of the early 1990s have shown that the provision of amnesties did indeed allow atrocity-laden conflicts in the latter two countries to be ended on a stable and sustainable basis, and the rule of law to be considerably strengthened in both places, while a reliance on prosecutions in Rwanda failed to bring about respect for the rule of law there.

A focus on the *politics of conflict termination,* such as is strongly advocated here, requires close attention to the politics of both peacemaking and peacebuilding. I have suggested above that antagonists who are able to achieve peacemaking through negotiation can get a good head start, through that negotiating process, on some of the basics of longer-term peacebuilding, too—though even those antagonists who succeed in negotiating a peace are by no means guaranteed success in the peacebuilding task. Meanwhile, the record of the victorious (Western) Allies at the end of World War II shows that even those parties that achieve a formal "peace" through outright military victory can succeed at the subsequent tasks of long-term peacebuilding—provided they pay enough attention to the planning and implementation of the vital postconflict phase and that they adopt a wise and restrained approach to governance.[39]

In my conversations about building a sustainable, postatrocity political order in Rwanda, South Africa, and Mozambique, people from those countries spoke again and again about the need to have their still-pressing economic needs met, and a stable, reliable socioeconomic order built (or rebuilt) if their societies were to avoid falling back into additional rounds of atrocity-laden war. In Rama Mani's fine study of postwar justice issues, she gave as much weight to the need for distributive (i.e., economic) justice in postwar situations as to the need for legal justice (i.e., restoring the rule of law) and rectificatory justice.[40] And Roland Paris, in his study on building peace after civil conflict, identified the adoption of conflict-reducing economic policies as one of the six key tasks to be addressed in any successful peacebuilding effort.[41] Indeed, many or most members of societies reeling from recent conflict, when asked to define the kind of justice they would most like to see, speak about burning matters of economic justice before they say anything about seeking prosecutions, trials, or punishments of wrongdoers. In this sense, perhaps, the concept of "justice" that is held by many people living in Western societies that enjoy a high degree of economic well-being has become stunted, shorn of some of the richer dimensions of justice that are still held by communities living on the brink. For most members of those latter communities, the idea that "justice" could be equated with the technical feat of conducting an orderly criminal trial would seem strange indeed. Yet that, for many in the rich West, is the first remedy they think of when confronted with unsettling facts about the perpetration of atrocities.

In this regard as in so many others, any consideration of peace-building immediately brings us to the important political question of *who it should be* who makes the key decisions for societies as they start to emerge from periods of grave conflict. Should it be the fourteen members of the Security Council, sitting in their offices in New York City? Should it be a consortium of nations that, egged on by rights activists from Western countries with blessedly little recent experience of war, have created a permanent International Criminal Court that may act to proscribe or limit the offering of amnesties even when amnesties could help to secure a much-needed peace agreement? Or should it be the community leaders, political leaders, and negotiators from the war-plagued communities them-selves? My own strong preference is to give by far the greatest voice in making such decisions to those who have the greatest stake in their outcome—those who will have most of the responsibility for implementing them on the ground and whose families will be living for generations to come with the consequences, whatever they might be. If well-wishers in the international community seek to influ-ence these decisions and the climate in which they are made, they can probably have the most impact for the good if they lay strong and continuous stress on the need to *end conflicts,* most preferably through negotiations, and on the basis of sustainable political equal-ity, the strengthening of democratic institutions, and due attention to tasks of socioeconomic construction, rather than by laying down strict and quite acontextual prohibitions from outside on the offer-ing of amnesties in the context of peace negotiations.

Finally, I want to come back to the list that Martha Minow compiled (and that I introduced in Chapter 1) of meta-tasks that members of societies emerging from periods of mass violence ur-gently need to address. After my many discussions with colleagues in Mozambique, South Africa, Rwanda, and elsewhere, and my reflections on these experiences as outlined above, I now offer my own modified list of meta-tasks for such societies, grouped into two ranks by their urgency as follows:

Top rank (all of equal urgency):
1. Establish rigorous mechanisms to guard against any relapse into conflict and violence.
2. Actively promote reconciliation across all intergroup divisions.
3. Build an equality-based domestic democratic order that allows for nonviolent resolution of internal differences and that respects and enforces human rights.
4. Restore the moral systems appropriate to an era of peace.
5. Reintegrate former combatants from all the previously fighting parties into the new society.
6. Start restoring and upgrading the community's physical and institutional infrastructure.
7. Start righting the distributional injustices of the past.

Second rank (of somewhat less urgency):
8. Promote psychological healing for all those affected by the violence and the atrocities, restoring dignity to them. (The top-rank tasks, if addressed, will do much to achieve this psychological healing; but it will probably need continuing attention.)
9. Establish such records of the facts as are needed to meet victims' needs (death certificates, identification of burial sites, etc.) and to start to build a record for history.

Several of these goals are mentioned by Minow in her listing. The most stark difference is over what each of us advocates with regard to former "offenders." Whereas Minow advocates the "punishment, exclusion, shaming, and diminishment" of offenders, the evidence strongly indicates to me—and I hope to my readers, as well—that a well-crafted policy of amnestying, reconciliation, and reintegration of offenders will serve the long-term interests of many of these very vulnerable societies very much better.

As they consider this issue in the future, decisionmakers and rights advocates throughout the world would do well to keep in mind the relatively well-known story of how amnesties enabled a breathtakingly successful political transformation within South Africa—and also, the stories of Raúl Domingos, Hermínio Morais, and their beloved homeland, Mozambique. I started this book with some very poignant testimonies from victim/survivors of atrocities such as Agnès, Nomonde Calata, and Rejoice Mabudhafasi, and I hope those stories and others like them will stay with readers. But as we look to the challenges of making and building sturdy peace agreements in troubled lands, the possibilities for the real transformation of perpetrators should also, certainly, be kept in mind.

During the Mozambican civil war Domingos, Morais, and the networks of individuals they commanded organized and perpetrated some of the worst kinds of atrocities human society has ever known. But after the war Domingos—formerly Renamo's chief of staff—moved on to become a parliamentarian, business executive, and social thinker. Morais, the former head of Renamo's Special Forces, became a key leader and organizer of the country's new united military, and then entered law school. These two men, the people they had commanded, and the people against whom they had fought for fifteen long years all worked together to rescue their country from the abuses and intense suffering of the war. They succeeded in that, and they also did an admirable job of starting to build a new social and political order based on the rule of law. As the world community faces the many "justice" challenges of the twenty-first century, that record needs to be remembered and celebrated. Indeed, perhaps all of us could learn much of value from our friends in Mozambique.

Notes

Notes for Chapter 1

1. The interview with Agnès was conducted on behalf of the present book by Gabriel Gabiro, Rwanda correspondent for AP news service. He conducted it in early 2004, in the indigenous language of Rwanda, Kinyarwanda.

2. In 2001, the ICTR judges in one particular chamber were criticized for failing to protect a witness and victim of gang rape from a combative attorney who asked her questions like "What was the size of the penis of the accused when he allegedly raped you?" Video footage of the trial showed that the judges were laughing openly as these questions were asked. The court later apologized for the incident but denied allegations from human rights organizations that the judges had found the questions themselves amusing. Instead, they said, they were laughing at the trivial nature of the questions being put by the attorney.

3. Under the Genocide Convention of 1948 all signatory states—which included, by 1994, nearly all the world's major powers—commit themselves explicitly to intervening to "repress" genocide wherever it occurs, and to "prevent" it where it threatens to occur. Yet, during the Rwandan genocide of 1994, the U.S. government worked actively at the United Nations to *disband* the small UN force that was already in the country. See Samantha Power, *A Problem from Hell: America and the Age of Genocide* (New York: Basic Books, 2002).

4. The United Nations has also been involved in establishing and running a third ad hoc tribunal, the "Special Court for Sierra Leone,"

which the United Nations runs jointly with the Sierra Leonean national government.

5. For the international community as a whole, it is also evidently important to subject the work of the court for former Yugoslavia to a similar evaluation. That task, however, is generally outside the scope of the present inquiry.

6. Often, when writing about the situation of South Africa under apartheid, I find it hard to do so without using the racial classifications that were rigidly imposed on all citizens under the apartheid system. My use of these categories where necessary in the present work in no way implies that I subscribe to the ugly racial theories that underlay them.

7. Some of the apartheid regime's most ferocious acts of physical violence were perpetrated against citizens of neighboring countries, including Angola, Mozambique, and Namibia. Responsibility for those atrocities was briefly addressed in the TRC's report (Volume 2, Chapter 2).

8. See chapter 16 of South Africa's Interim Constitution of April 27, 1994. The full text is available online at http://www.oefre.unibe.ch/law/icl/sf10000_.html.

9. The proper treatment of mortal remains of family members is an important responsibility in cultures inside Africa, as in many other parts of the world.

10. Tutu's thinking on this subject is examined in depth in chapter 7 of Helena Cobban, *The Moral Architecture of World Peace: Nobel Laureates Discuss Our Global Future* (Charlottesville: University Press of Virginia, 2000).

11. The 21,000 or so written testimonies of victims who were never invited to a public victim hearing were compiled to provide a lasting memorial to the violence and suffering experienced by those who wrote them.

12. The official TRC transcript is available online at http://www.doj.gov.za/trc/hrvtrans/hrvel1/calata.htm. (See p. 10.)

13. Contemporary news footage of this scene is included in the 2000 documentary movie *Long Night's Journey into Day*, directed by Deborah Hoffman.

14. Antjie Krog, *Country of My Skull: Guilt, Sorrow, and the Limits of Forgiveness in the New South Africa* (New York: Random House, 1998), p. 57.

15. Primo Levi has written extensively about the large number of people whose actions, in the context of the Holocaust death camps with which he was so intimately acquainted, fell into an ethical "gray zone." See chapter 2 of *The Drowned and the Saved* (New York: Summit Books, 1986), pp. 36–69.

16. Interview with Dr. Zimba, Maputo, Mozambique, August 2001.

17. Carolyn Nordstrom, *A Different Kind of War Story* (Philadelphia: University of Pennsylvania Press, 1997), p. 147.

18. These were almost exactly the words that, in April 2003, I heard used (and then interpreted for me from their own native language) by Priscina, Antonietta Jeremias, and Ana-Paula, three Mozambican women who tended the mass graves of forty-four civil war victims slaughtered near Chiboene, Mozambique.

19. Since I grew up in England in the 1950s and early 1960s, I can attest that not all Western societies have such a deep "buy-in" to this view of the value of talk therapy as seems to prevail in the present-day United States.

20. Alcinda Honwana, "Children of war: Understanding war and war cleansing in Mozambique and Angola," in Simon Chesterman, ed., *Civilians in War* (Boulder: Lynne Rienner, 2001), p. 139.

21. Nordstrom, *A Different Kind of War Story*, pp. 145–146.

22. Two important books by Rwandans that contain significant references to the acts of such courageous Hutus are Antoine Rutayasire, *Faith Under Fire: Testimonies of Christian Bravery* (London: African Enterprise, 1995), and André Sibomana, *Hope for Rwanda*, trans. Carina Tertsakian (London and Sterling, VA: Pluto Press/Dar es Salaam: Mkuki na Nyota Publishers, 1997).

23. Sibomana, *Hope for Rwanda*, pp. 108–109. Scott Peterson has given a similar description of a visit he made to Gitarama in mid-1995. See his *Me Against My Brother: At War in Somalia, Sudan, and Rwanda* (New York and London: Routledge, 2000), p. 318.

24. In the tumultuous events of 1994, around 800,000 of the million Tutsis who had been in the country at the beginning of the year were killed, and around 800,000 Tutsis who had previously lived in exile in neighboring countries returned to Rwanda.

25. For some of the cases kept in the regular court system, the death penalty would still potentially be applicable. The anomalous fact that this was *not* an available punishment in the ICTR—the place where the "biggest fish of all" would still be tried—continued to rankle many Rwandan officials.

26. Martha Minow, "Hope for healing," in Robert I. Rotberg and Dennis Thompson, eds., *Truth v. Justice: The Morality of Truth Commissions* (Princeton and Oxford: Princeton University Press, 2000), p. 253.

27. One clear example of such a factor is the maturity and nature of a country's existing justice system. The emphasis that global rights advocates place on criminal prosecutions is based on an assumption that all countries should either have or aspire to have a fully functioning Western-style legal system. The existence of other kinds of justice systems in societies is almost completely ignored, and their contribution neglected. But such "traditional and informal" justice systems often make a big contribution to the well-being of citizens of countries that have only a few Western-style courts. See, for example, "Penal Reform International," *Access to Justice in*

Sub-Saharan Africa: The Role of Traditional and Informal Justice Systems (London: PRI, 2001).

Notes for Chapter 2

1. The material in this section about Agnès comes from the interview Gabriel Gabiro conducted, in Kinyarwanda, in 2004. He originally wrote up the interview.

2. The complex question of whether the Tutsi-Hutu divide is one of ethnicity, as such, is discussed further below.

3. André Sibomana, *Hope for Rwanda*, trans. Carina Tertsakian (London and Sterling, VA: Pluto Press/Dar es Salaam: Mkuki na Nyota Publishers, 1997).

4. Sibomana, *Hope for Rwanda*, pp. 63–64.

5. Ibid., p. 64.

6. Ibid., pp. 67–68; emphasis added.

7. Ibid., pp. 58–59.

8. Ibid., pp. 68–69.

9. Ibid., p. 74. Sibomana wrote that he tended to believe a theory that the clerics had been killed because the bishop of Kabgayi had been promoting a ceasefire plan that was opposed by the RPF leaders.

10. Ibid., pp. 75–76.

11. Testimony of Jean Bosco Bugingo, quoted in African Rights, *Death, Despair and Defiance*, rev. ed. (London: African Rights, August 1995), p. 998.

12. Ibid., p. 999.

13. The proportion of Muslims grew rapidly after the genocide, as did that of avowed Protestant believers relative to that of Catholics.

14. Making this judgment has potentially vast juridico-political consequences, since "caste" is not one of the types of human groups protected under the 1948 Genocide Convention.

15. Another network of Rwandan refugees was meanwhile reportedly playing an important role in Amin's own security services. See Mahmood Mamdani, *When Victims Become Killers: Colonialism, Nativism, and the Genocide in Rwanda* (Princeton and Oxford: Princeton University Press, 2001), p. 167.

16. The account in these past three paragraphs is based primarily on ibid., pp. 164–182. See also Philip Gourevitch, *We Wish to Inform You That Tomorrow We Will Be Killed with Our Families: Stories from Rwanda* (New York: Farrar, Straus and Giroux, 1998), pp. 212–217; and Colin M. Waugh, *Paul Kagame and Rwanda: Power, Genocide and the Rwandan Patriotic Front* (London and Jefferson, NC: McFarland, 2004).

17. Information in this paragraph is taken mainly from Gérard Prunier, *The Rwanda Crisis: History of a Genocide*, 2nd ed. (New York: Columbia University Press, 1997), pp. 93–97.

18. See Prunier, *The Rwanda Crisis,* pp. 100–107.

19. Entry on "Rwanda" in *Human Rights Watch World Report 1994* (New York: Human Rights Watch, 1994); available online at http://www.hrw.org/reports/1994/WR94/Africa-06.htm#P258_112461.

20. Prunier, *The Rwanda Crisis,* p. 175n33.

21. Information about UNAMIR is available online at http://www.un.org/Depts/dpko/dpko/co_mission/unamirS.htm.

22. Mamdani, *When Victims Become Killers,* p. 191.

23. Taylor, *Sacrifice as Terror,* pp. 133–134. The widespread use of intoxicants, time spent indulging in abusive sexual relations, and frequent contests over the fruits of looting that marked the genocide were probably also associated with a much broader breakdown in the discipline of the government forces.

24. People inside the Clinton administration argued at the time that if there was any attempt by a UN force to save lives in dangerous situations—as had happened in Somalia just the preceding September—then soon enough the US would get sucked in, and another Somali-type debacle could ensue. See Samantha Power, *"A Problem from Hell": America and the Age of Genocide* (New York: Basic Books, 2002), pp. 341–370 passim.

25. When André Sibomana was in Kibuye, that area came under the umbrella of the French-run "safe zone." His evaluation of the role the French played there can be found in Sibomana, *Hope for Rwanda,* pp. 73–74.

26. Prunier, *The Rwanda Crisis,* pp. 312–313.

27. Ibid., p. 299.

28. Ibid., p. 327.

29. Ibid., p. 310.

30. Ibid., p. 322.

31. Ibid.

32. An excellent account of the role of postgenocide guilt in determining the policies Western governments adopted toward Rwanda in the late 1990s is Peter Uvin, "Ethics and the new postconflict agenda: The international community in Rwanda after the genocide," *Third World Quarterly* 22 (2001).

33. The aid organizations had faced almost exactly the same dilemma in the case of the Khmer Rouge's success in organizing inside the Cambodian refugee camps in the 1970s. For an excellent description of these issues as aid workers confronted them in Rwanda, see Ian Martin, "Hard choices after genocide: Human rights and political failures in Rwanda," in Jonathan Moore, ed., *Hard Choices: Moral Dilemmas in Humanitarian Intervention* (Oxford and Lanham, MD: Rowman & Littlefield, 1998). Martin, previously the secretary general of Amnesty International, worked as chief of the UN Human Rights Field Operation in Rwanda after the genocide.

34. They also, as noted in greater detail below, objected to many specifics of the new court's procedure, including the fact that—in line with emerging international norms regarding criminal justice—it did not allow for any death sentences for those convicted of even the most heinous crimes.

35. See http://ictr.org/ENGLISH/cases/Kajelijeli/minutes/2003/011203.pdf.

36. See ICTR Appeals Chamber, *Judgment in the Case of Juvénal Kajelijeli v. The Prosecutor*, May 23, 2005, p. 119; available online at http://65.18.216.88/ENGLISH/cases/Kajelijeli/judgement/appealsjudge230505.doc.

37. Richard J. Goldstone, *For Humanity: Reflections of a War Crimes Investigator* (New Haven: Yale University Press, 2000), p. 21.

38. The prospect that the court would be seated outside Rwanda was one of the Rwandan government's three principal objections to resolution 955. The others were that, in line with the emerging UN norm against the death penalty, the statute specifically ruled out its use, and that the crimes to be investigated and prosecuted would not include those committed prior to 1994 that had helped to prepare the genocide project.

39. See Goldstone, *For Humanity*, pp. 109–115.

40. Goldstone and other court officers were able to help cover their costs by drawing on funds in a special Trust Fund the UN had established to provide extra financial resources to the work of ICTY and ICTR. They also received the free labor of numerous staff people seconded to the court from national governments.

41. See ICTR's first report to the UN General Assembly and Security Council, dated September 24, 1996 (UN document no. A/51/399–S/1996/778), para. 42.

42. Goldstone, *For Humanity*, p. 112.

43. The text of the Nuremberg Principles is available online at http://www.un.org/law/ilc/texts/nurnberg.htm.

44. For further exploration of these issues, see Antonio Cassese, *International Criminal Law* (New York and Oxford: Oxford University Press, 2003), Ch. 20.

45. In May 1998, genocide-era Prime Minister Jean de Dieu Kambanda had pled guilty to the charge of genocide as part of a plea bargain. Akayesu was the first person whose judgment of "guilty" was the result of a contest in the court.

46. The records of the case are available online at http://www.ictr.org/ENGLISH/cases/Bagosora/index.htm.

47. UN Office of Internal Oversight Services, *Report of the Office of Internal Oversight Services on the Investigation into Possible Fee-Splitting Arrangements ... at ICTR and ICTY,* February 1, 2001 (UN document A/55/759), pp. 2, 3. Of course, one person's "frivolous motion" may be another's "essential due-process protection." (In connection with that investigation, ICTR's registrar also terminated the employment of two defense investigators who

were credibly accused of having actually participated in the genocide. One of these investigators, Joseph Nzabirinda, was himself later indicted by the court.)

48. See UN Department of Public Information, "General Assembly adopts 2006–2007 budget of $3.79 billion," December 23, 2005; available online at http://www.un.org/News/Press/docs/2005/ga10442.doc.htm.

49. It is extremely hard to locate and add up the total amount of international funds invested in ICTR (or in ICTY). In addition to the amounts the UN formally allocates to them as part of its regular budgeting process, each of them benefits from funding from a special Trust Fund, as well as from bilateral donations, many of them in-kind donations, from some UN member governments.

50. In 2004, Ngoga was called back to Rwanda to serve as deputy attorney general.

51. For more information from that interview, as well as from interviews with ICTR judges, attorneys, and other participants, and a lot more background information on the court, see Helena Cobban, "Healing Rwanda: Can an international court deliver justice?" in *Boston Review,* December 2003/January 2004; available online at http://bostonreview.net/BR27.2/cobban.html.

52. Gourevitch, *We Wish to Inform You,* pp. 252–253.

53. Sibomana, *Hope for Rwanda,* pp. 110–111; emphasis added.

54. Elizaphan Ntakirutimana was arrested at a family-owned property in Laredo, Texas, in 1996. ICTR requested his extradition at that point, but it took the U.S. courts a further four years to agree to extradite him to Arusha.

55. Mary Kimani, "Conflicting reactions to ICTR sentence in father and son trial," Kigali, February 21, 2003. Distributed by Internews; available online at http://www.internews.org/activities/ICTR_reports/ICTRnews Feb03.html; emphasis added. Hirondelle News Agency has also done some good reporting on reactions inside Rwanda to ICTR's judgments and sentences.

56. Mary Kimani, "Living a death sentence: Rape victims of the Rwanda genocide," Kigali, 1 September 2003. Distributed by Internews; available online at http://www.internews.org/activities/ICTR_reports/ICTRnews Sep03.html.

57. Nyiramasuhuko's trial of first instance opened in June 2001. It continued at least until March 2005. For the case minutes, see http://www.ictr.org/ENGLISH/cases/Nyira/minutes/index.htm.

58. Mary Kimani, "When justice takes too long," Kigali, 1 September 2003. Distributed by Internews; available online at http://www.internews.org/activities/ICTR_reports/ICTRnewsSep03.html.

59. The full table of results from this survey can be found in Eric Stover and Harvey M. Weinstein, eds., *My Neighbor, My Enemy: Justice and*

Community in the Aftermath of Mass Atrocity (Cambridge and New York: Cambridge University Press, 2004), p. 214.

60. See Fondation Hirondelle, "Thousands demonstrate against UN tribunal," Kigali, February 29, 2004; available online at http://www.hirondelle.org/hirondelle.nsf/0/48946dbe58a37270c125680100703134?OpenDocument.

61. Rutayisire's memoirs of and reflections upon the genocide period can be found in Antoine Rutayasire, *Faith Under Fire: Testimonies of Christian Bravery* (London: African Enterprise, 1995).

62. This man was speaking to me in an informal setting, not for attribution.

63. Eric Stover and Harvey M. Weinstein, eds., *My Neighbor, My Enemy*, p. 214.

64. Serushago was one of only two or three of the court's indictees who belong to Rwanda's minority Muslim population. The rest were (at least nominally) Christians—and four, including an Anglican bishop, were men of the cloth.

65. This fact was also duly noted by the court. See paragraph 51 of the official record of his presentencing hearing, which is available online at http://www.ictr.org/ENGLISH/cases/Kambanda/judgement/kambanda.html.

66. Carol Off, *The Lion, the Fox and the Eagle: A Story of Generals and Justice in Rwanda and Yugoslavia* (Toronto: Random House Canada, 2000), pp. 244–245.

67. Sibomana, *Hope for Rwanda*, pp. 109–110. Scott Peterson, too, has given a vivid description of a visit he made to Gitarama in mid-1995; see his *Me Against My Brother: At War in Somalia, Sudan, and Rwanda* (New York and London: Routledge, 2000), p. 318. By the time Philip Gourevitch visited in mid-1996, conditions had gotten a little better, but apparently not much; see Gourevitch, *We Wish to Inform You*, pp. 246–248.

68. Gourevitch, *We Wish to Inform You*, p. 189.

69. *Human Rights Watch World Report, 1996* (New York: Human Rights Watch, 1966), p. 42.

70. See, for example, the report to the UN Security Council, *Final Report of the Panel of Experts on the Illegal Exploitation of Natural Resources and Other Forms of Wealth of DR Congo*, UN document S/2002/1146 of 16 October 2002; available online at http://www.natural-resources.org/minerals/law/docs/pdf/N0262179.pdf.

71. Kabila later fell out with Kagame. He was assassinated in 2001, after which his son, Joseph Kabila, took over in Kinshasa. Joseph Kabila's relationship with Kagame was also often badly strained.

72. "Rwandese-controlled eastern DRC: Devastating human toll," Amnesty International news release and accompanying report, June 19, 2001; available online at http://web.amnesty.org/library/Index/ENGAFR62015 2001?open&of=ENG-COD.

73. Many other returning Hutus were sent by the government to participate in forced "re-education" camps.

74. "Rwanda: Ending the silence," Amnesty International report of September 25, 1997 (AI index # AFR 47/032/1997). The report noted the huge role that Western (particularly American) military aid had played in allowing the Rwandan government to pursue its campaigns against its opponents, and recommended that "[g]overnments considering transfers of military, security and police equipment or training to Rwanda should insist on independently verifiable guarantees that human rights violations and breaches of international humanitarian law have ceased and that the equipment will not be used against unarmed civilians, before agreeing to such transfers."

75. This categorization notably adds property crimes to those defined in the 1948 Genocide Convention.

76. The full text of the law is available online at http://www.prevent genocide.org/law/domestic/rwanda.htm.

77. Off, *The Lion, the Fox and the Eagle,* p. 333.

78. "Rwanda: First defendants faced unfair trials," Amnesty International report of 14 January 1997 (AI index # AFR 47/003/1997). This report also restated Amnesty's long-standing opposition to the death penalty, noting that when trials were conducted with such great lack of fairness, the irrevocability of the death sentence was of particular concern.

79. "Rwanda: Major step back for human rights as Rwanda stages 22 public executions," Amnesty International report of April 24, 1998 (AI index # AFR/47/14/1998). Also consult "Rwandan execution" on Canadian Broadcasting Corporation's *As It Happens,* April 24, 1998; available online at www.cbc.ca/insite/AS_IT_HAPPENS_TORONTO/1998/4/24.html.

80. Interview with Augustin Nkusi, counselor at the Supreme Court of Rwanda, Kigali, May 2002. The interview was conducted in French.

81. Ibid.

82. "Perceptions about the gacaca law in Rwanda: Evidence from a multi-method study," in National University of Rwanda, Centre for Conflict Management, *Les Juridictions Gacaca et les Processus de Réconciliation Nationale* (Kigali: Editions de l'Université National du Rwanda), pp. 104, 119, 118, 120, 115.

83. Amnesty International, "Rwanda: The troubled course of justice," April 26, 2000; available online at http://web.amnesty.org/ai.nst/print/AFR470152000?OpenDocument [March 8, 2002]. The report fails to indicate how, with the resources available, Rwanda could be expected to provide the elements of "fair trials" that the report specified, such as legal representation for all defendants, and so on.

84. Gahima, quoted in International Crisis Group, *Justice Delayed,* p. 36.

85. For this reason, officials of the U.S. government went to extraordinary circumlocutory lengths to avoid saying that what was happening was genocide. See Power, *"A Problem from Hell,"* Ch. 10.

86. Chapter 2 of Primo Levi's *The Drowned and the Saved* deals precisely with what Levi called "the gray zone" of such forms of action.

87. After leaving Rwandan government service in 2004 Gahima developed even further his theory that "mass violence" is sufficiently different from the violence of normal criminal events in peaceful societies that the tools of criminal prosecution may be inadequate to deal with it.

88. Christopher C. Taylor, "Kings and chaos in Rwanda: On the order of disorder," *Anthropos* 98 (Sankt Augustin, Germany) (2003): 41.

89. Filip Reyntjens, "Le *gacaca* ou la justice du gazon au Rwanda," *Politique Africaine* 40 (1990): 31–41. The author noted that the case of banana beer would cost the defendant 300 francs—far more than the sum originally at issue.

90. That fact had made the centralized organization of the genocide much easier than it would have been in less well-organized societies.

91. Participation in the elections was estimated by organizers at more than 90 percent. For a good eye-witness description of an election meeting, see Julia Crawford, "Women take centre stage in election of 'people's judges,'" October 5, 2001, Foundation Hirondelle; available online at www.hirondelle.org. The number of cells in the country has been given as 11,000, but in June 2004 it was reported as 9,010.

92. Lunch conversation with Gérald Gahima, Kigali, May 2002.

93. *Research on the Gacaca—PRI, Report V* (London: Penal Reform International, September 2003), p. 4. The report is available online at http://www.penalreform.org/download/Gacaca/september2003.pdf.

94. Ibid., pp. 36, 40.

95. Gabriel Gabiro, "Mysterious murders threaten to derail gacaca courts," Fondation Hirondelle from Kaduha, Rwanda, June 4, 2004.

96. "President Kagame launches *gacaca* tribunals in Rwanda," Fondation Hirondelle from Arusha, June 24, 2004.

97. Information from "Rwanda asks for judicial probe on controversial 'genocide ideology' report," Fondation Hirondelle from Kigali, September 21, 2004.

98. "Rwanda: Human rights organization forced to close down," Amnesty International public statement, January 10, 2005; available online at http://web.amnesty.org/library/Index/ENGAFR470012005?open&of=ENG-2F2.

99. "30 found guilty, one acquitted on first day of *gacaca*," Fondation Hirondelle from Arusha, March 14, 2005.

100. "Gacaca goes for the big fish: Views in the Rwandan press," Fondation Hirondelle from Kigali, March 29, 2005. Gatsinzi was still at his job some months later.

101. This figure was reported in "Six hundred flee to Burundi over gacaca," Fondation Hirondelle from Kigali, April 19, 2005. The 600 figure was that provided by a Rwandan government official. Other reports put the total much higher than 2,000. The government official also acknowledged

that Rwandan citizens had fled to other countries such as Uganda and DRC, as well as Burundi.

102. "Stunned by growing numbers of genocide suspects, Rwanda revisits categorization," Fondation Hirondelle from Kigali, October 7, 2005.

103. Information from Amnesty International, "Rwanda" Number of Prisoners of Conscience on the Rise," June 7, 2002 (AI Index # AFR 47/002/2002). Bizimungu and nineteen other proponents of nonviolent political change inside Rwanda had been named by Amnesty as "prisoners of conscience." By chance, on the day I visited Kigali Central prison in May 2002, Bizimungu was being transferred there. He was wearing the same distinctive pink outfit that all the inmates wore and looked confused and slightly traumatized.

104. Available online at http://www.electionworld.org/rwanda.htm; accessed July 12, 2004.

105. A group of researchers writing in Eric Stover and Harvey M. Weinberg's book *My Neighbor, My Enemy* noted the difficulties caused in Rwanda by the fact that this restriction meant that no one was able to construct a meaningful curriculum for teaching the nation's history. (In particular, see Chapter 12, by Sarah Warshauer Freedman et al., titled "Confronting the past in Rwanda's schools.")

106. An intriguing account of the content of the national history courses taught at NURC solidarity camps in 2003 can be found in *Research on the Gacaca—PRI, Report VI: The Reintegration of Released Prisoners* (London: Penal Reform International, May 2004).

107. *Research on the Gacaca—PRI, Report V*, pp. 55–57 passim.

108. See Emily Wax, "Islam attracting many survivors of Rwanda genocide," *Washington Post*, September 23, 2002, p. A10.

109. See "Perceptions about the gacaca law in Rwanda: Evidence from a multi-method study," p. 102. The report further notes that "the proportion of Moslems varied conspicuously by prefecture. Whereas more than one-fifth (22 percent) of the respondents from Kigali Ville were Moslems, the other prefectures ... had few or no Moslem respondents."

110. He has also compiled a moving collection of short testimonies of genocide survivors who describe how their faith helped them to survive the horrors of the genocide. Included in the compilation are testimonies from himself and from Michel Kayetaba. See Rutayasire, *Faith Under Fire*.

Notes for Chapter 3

1. Eugene de Kock, *A Long Night's Damage: Working for the Apartheid State* (Saxonwold, South Africa: Contra Press, 1998), pp. 43–145 passim. De Kock is also the major subject of Pumla Gobodo-Madikizela, *A Human Being Died That Night: A South African Story of Forgiveness* (Boston and New York: Houghton Mifflin, 2003).

2. De Kock added, "According to testimony given to the Truth Commission by retired Police Commissioner Johan van der Merwe on 9 May 1997, State President PW Botha personally ordered the bombing of Khotso House."(p. 145).

3. Afrikaans is a Creole of Dutch. South Africans of Dutch origin call themselves Afrikaners.

4. These and many other legislative landmarks of the move to apartheid are listed in *Truth and Reconciliation Commission of South Africa Report*, Vol. 3 (Cape Town: TRC and Department of Justice, 1998), Ch. 13; available online at http://www.news24.com/Content_Display/TRC_Report/1chap13. htm. One of the central aspects of the apartheid system was its rigid categorization of people into strict racial categories, and it is hard to discuss the violence of that era without also using those categories. My use of them in a primarily historical context in the present work in no way implies that I subscribe to the ugly racial theories that underlie them.

5. UN General Assembly resolution 3068 (XXVIII), of November 30, 1973. The text is available online at http://www.unhchr.ch/html/menu3/ b/11.htm.

6. The text of the Freedom Charter can be found at http://www.anc. org.za/ancdocs/history/charter.html.

7. Figures taken from Chart E2.1–1 in *Truth and Reconciliation Commission of South Africa Report*, Vol. 3, Ch. 1, p. 9. The numerical data used by the TRC were nearly all taken from the formal "victim statements" submitted to it. They certainly represent an underestimation of the total numbers of violations since many eligible victims/survivors of apartheid-era violence did not submit statements. (Hugo van der Merwe of the Center for the Study of Violence and Reconciliation noted that the families of only around 20 percent of victims of one form of gross rights violation submitted statements to the TRC.) The TRC's data do, however, indicate broad trends over time.

8. Laloo Chiba, testimony at TRC Human Rights Violations Hearing, Johannesburg, July 24, 1996; available online at http://www.doj.gov. za/trc/hrvtrans/soweto/chiba.htm.

9. *Truth and Reconciliation Commission of South Africa Report*, Vol. 2, Ch. 3, p. 235. Amnesty applicants other than Coetzee gave different versions of the details of what had happened.

10. One particularly gruesome case described in the *TRC Report* was that of Jackson Maake, Andrew Makupe, and Harold Sefolo. See *Truth and Reconciliation Commission of South Africa Report*, Vol. 2, Ch. 3, p. 239.

11. *Truth and Reconciliation Commission of South Africa Report*, Vol. 3, Ch. 3, paras. 263, 277, 288.

12. The British Empire had, indeed, invented the concept of "concentration camps" as a means of controlling Afrikaners during the Anglo-Boer Wars at the turn of the twentieth century.

13. Interview with Fanie du Toit, Cape Town, May 2003. A good account of the process of pronegotiation convincement within the Afrikaner community can be found in Hermann Giliomee, "*Broedertwis:* Intra-Afrikaner conflicts in the transition from apartheid, 1969–1991," in Norman Etherington, ed., *Peace Politics and Violence in the New South Africa* (London, Melbourne, Munich, and New York: Hans Zell, 1992).

14. Nelson Mandela, *Long Walk to Freedom* (New York: Little, Brown, 1994), p. 480.

15. Articles 14–16 of the Harare declaration, which is available online at http://www.anc.org.za/ancdocs/history/transition/harare.html.

16. See F.W. De Klerk, *The Last Trek—A New Beginning* (New York: St. Martin's Press, 1998), pp. 157–158; and Mandela, *Long Walk to Freedom,* p. 484.

17. De Klerk, *The Last Trek,* p. 163.

18. Slovo was a leading figure in the South African Communist Party, which was a constituent part of the ANC. He had been the first White member of the ANC's National Executive Council. His wife, the scholar and writer Ruth First, was killed by a letter bomb in Mozambique, in 1982.

19. Richard Spitz, with Matthew Chaskalson, *The Politics of Transition: A Hidden History of South Africa's Negotiated Settlement* (Oxford: Hart Publishing, 2000), p. 31.

20. De Klerk had taken his cabinet to exactly the same place for a strategic planning retreat, shortly before his first meeting with Mandela in December 1989.

21. Cited in Richard Spitz, with Matthew Chaskalson, *The Politics of Transition,* p. 37. Most of the information from the preceding two paragraphs and the two paragraphs that follow comes from this excellent work.

22. Paul Taylor, "South Africans agree to consider white state," *Washington Post,* April 24, 1994, p. A21. Viljoen did not specify what he meant by "substantial support," but said he hoped the Freedom Front could win 700,000 votes. It ended up winning just under 425,000 votes.

23. Princeton Lyman, *Partner to History: the U.S. Role in South Africa's Transition to Democracy* (Washington, DC: U.S. Institute of Peace Press, 2002), p. 214.

24. Chapter 15 of the Interim Constitution of April 27, 1994; available online at http://www.oefre.unibe.ch/law/icl/sf10000_.html.

25. *Washington Post* reporting from various editions, April 25–28, 1994. These reports disclose that a certain degree of violence upset the voting plans—including a car bomb that exploded near two ANC buildings in Johannesburg on April 24, killing nine. But still, the voting went ahead.

26. Text available in *Washington Post,* May 3, 2004, p. A18.

27. Paul Taylor, "S. African election declared free, fair," *Washington Post,* May 7, 1994, p. A01.

28. Peter Batchelor, Jacklyn Cock, and Penny Mackenzie, *Conversion in South Africa in the 1980s: Defence downsizing and human development*

challenges (Bonn, Germany: Bonn International Center for Conversion, n.d.), p. 43; available online at http://www.bicc.de/publications/briefs/brief18/brief18.pdf.

29. For more details of the campaign see James A. Higgs, "Creating the South African National Defence Force," *Joint Force Quarterly*, Summer 2000, pp. 50, 48; available online at http://www.dtic.mil/doctrine/jel/jfq_pubs/1025.pdf.

30. The texts of the reports of two of these commissions can be found on the ANC website at http://www.anc.org.za/ancdocs/misc/.

31. ANC National Executive Committee document of August 1993, cited in Alex Boraine, *A Country Unmasked: Inside South Africa's Truth and Reconciliation Commission* (Oxford: Oxford University Press, 2000), p. 12.

32. Article 3 of the Promotion of National Unity and Reconciliation Act, 1995. The "start" date for the TRC's purview was defined to allow inclusion of the Sharpeville Massacre. Its cutoff date was later specified as May 10, 1994, which allowed the TRC to investigate violations committed during the election period and up to the inauguration of the first democratic parliament and the first democratic president.

33. A good account of this incident can be found online at http://observer.guardian.co.uk/2003rugbyworldcup/story/0,13946,1054749,00.html.

34. Boraine, *A Country Unmasked*, p. 82.

35. The Amnesty Committee's numbers were brought up to eleven members in January 1997, and to nineteen members in February 1998. The additional members were all lawyers, too.

36. *Truth and Reconciliation Commission of South Africa Report*, Vol. 1, Ch. 11, pp. 356–358.

37. Information from *Truth and Reconciliation Commission of South Africa Report*, Vol. 4, Ch. 1; available online at http://www.news24.com/Content_Display/TRC_Report/4chap1.htm.

38. That prosecution succeeded, and in August 1998 he was sentenced to a fine of 10,000 Rand or twelve months' imprisonment. However, he subsequently won the case on appeal. For details, see Boraine, *A Country Unmasked*, pp. 198–217.

39. Quoted in Antjie Krog, *Country of My Skull: Guilt, Sorrow, and the Limits of Forgiveness in the New South Africa* (New York: Times Books, 1998), p. 339.

40. Ibid., p. 60.

41. Ibid.

42. More demographic details about the people who presented statements can be found in *Truth and Reconciliation Commission of South Africa Report*, Vol. 1, Ch. 6, Appendix 2. More information about the form of the victim statements is in Richard Wilson, *The Politics of Truth and Reconciliation in South Africa: Legitimizing the Post-Apartheid State* (Cambridge and New York: Cambridge University Press, 2001), pp. 44–48.

43. *Truth and Reconciliation Commission of South Africa Report*, Vol. 5, Ch. 6, p. 212.

44. *Truth and Reconciliation Commission of South Africa Report*, Vol. 5, Ch. 6, paras. 136–138.

45. For details, see Boraine, *A Country Unmasked*, pp. 305–316.

46. Truth and Reconciliation Commission of South Africa Report, Vol. 5, Ch. 5, pp. 175–6.

47. *Truth and Reconciliation Commission of South Africa Report*, Vol. 5, Ch. 5, pp. 184–7.

48. Figure RR-1 in *Truth and Reconciliation Commission of South Africa Report*, Vol. 5, Ch. 5, p. 179. On the chart itself, the values are described as those for the deponents' "[e]xpectations" of the TRC. In the accompanying text, they are described as relating to "requests" from the TRC.

49. Information from Matome Sebelebele, "Reparations: Grants still unclaimed," November 4, 2004; available online at http://www.southafrica. info/public_services/citizens/reparations-outstanding.htm, January 2006.

50. *Truth and Reconciliation Commission of South Africa Report*, Vol. 1, Ch. 10, p. 276.

51. Counted from *Truth and Reconciliation Commission of South Africa Report*, Vol. 5, Ch. 3, pp. 119–123.

52. *Truth and Reconciliation Commission of South Africa Report*, Vol. 6, sect. 1, Ch. 3, p. 49.

53. *Truth and Reconciliation Commission of South Africa Report*, Vol. 6, p. 750.

54. Transcript of Benzien amnesty application, available online at http://www.doj.gov.za/trc/amntrans/capetown/capetown_benzien.htm.

55. *Truth and Reconciliation Commission of South Africa Report*, Vol. 7, pp. 1, 2.

56. Ntsebeza's own account of these incidents can be found in Terry Bell, with Dumisa Buhle Ntsebeza, *Unfinished Business: South Africa, Apartheid and Truth* (London and New York: Verso, 2003), pp. 319–343. Judge Richard Goldstone, now returned from his work at ICTR and ICTY, was named to conduct an investigation into who had organized the smear but concluded that the evidence "did not sufficiently establish the identity of any person or persons who might have conspired with [the accuser]" (p. 343.)

57. The text of the foreword to Volume 6 is available at http://www. doj.gov.za/trc/report/finalreport/vol6_amnesty_foreword.pdf.

58. Frederik van Zyl Slabbert was a prominent, antiapartheid politician who was head of the opposition party in Parliament from 1977 through 1986.

59. The entire text of the poem can be found at Krog, *Country of My Skull*, pp. 364–365; available online at http://www.doj.gov.za/trc/report/ finalreport/victims_main_vol7.pdf, p. 2.

60. Krog, *Country of My Skull*, p. 15; emphasis added. On the subject of civil servants, see p. 16.

61. Ibid., p. 19. Later on, the SABC assigned more Black journalists to the Commission. On pp. 222–223, Krog gives some interesting snapshots of these colleagues' feelings about their work. Basically, they said that the "revelations" made at the TRC were nothing new to them, while the pain they felt at having all that information aired again, in public, was often huge.

62. Ibid., pp. 194–195 passim.

63. Ibid., pp. 212–213. Krog also presents the interesting responses of Black clinical psychologist Nomfundo Walaza, to whom she had described these utterances.

64. Hermann Giliomee, *The Afrikaners: Biography of a People* (Cape Town: Tafelberg Publishers, and Charlottesville, VA: University of Virginia Press, 2003), p. 648; emphasis added.

65. Giliomee, *The Afrikaners,* pp. 648–655 passim. He mentioned only in passing the finding the IJR poll had made, that "77" percent (actually, 76 percent) of South African Blacks thought the TRC had done a generally good job.

66. Krog, *Country of My Skull,* pp. 216–217. Kübler-Ross's observations led her to identify a number of stages of such grieving: denial, anger, bargaining, depression, and finally acceptance.

67. Quoted in Antjie Krog, "South Africa: The Truth Commission: Unto the third or fourth generation," *Mail and Guardian* (Johannesburg), June 13, 1997; available online at http://www.bard.edu/hrp/krog4.htm.

68. Krog, *Country of My Skull,* pp. 364–365; available online at http://www.doj.gov.za/trc/report/finalreport/victims_main_vol7.pdf, p. 2.

69. AP news story from Johannesburg, "Companies sued over apartheid," November 12, 2002. Archived at http://www.preventgenocide.org/prevent/news-monitor/2002nov.htm.

70. *Truth and Reconciliation Commission of South Africa Report,* Vol. 4, Ch. 2, para. 161; available online at http://www.news24.com/Content_Display/TRC_Report/4chap2.htm.

71. *Truth and Reconciliation Commission of South Africa Report,* Vol. 5, Ch. 8, para. 39 (p. 319).

72. Letlapa Mphalele, "The case for a general amnesty," in Charles Villa-Vilencio and Erik Doxtader, *The Provocations of Amnesty: Memory, Justice and Impunity* (Trenton, NJ, and Asamara, Eritrea: Africa World Press, 2003), pp. 11–12.

73. Dumisa Ntsebeza, "The legacy of the TRC," in Villa-Vilencio and Doxtader, *The Provocations of Amnesty,* p. 25.

74. Zola Sonkosi, "Amnesty from an African point of view," in Villa-Vilencio and Doxtader, *The Provocations of Amnesty,* pp. 156–157. The similarities between the procedure he described and Filip Reyntjens' description of traditional *gacaca* in Rwanda seem evident.

75. Ibid., pp. 163–164.

76. Piers Pigou, "The murder of Sicelo Dlomo," in Deborah Posel and Graeme Simpson, eds., *Commissioning the Past: Understanding South Africa's Truth and Reconciliation Commission* (Johannesburg: Witwatersrand University Press, 2002), p. 97.

77. Pigou, "The murder of Sicelo Dlomo," pp. 105–114 passim. One of these amnesty applicants was now a captain in the SANDF. All four won their amnesties.

78. *Truth and Reconciliation Commission of South Africa Report*, Vol. 5, Ch. 9, para. 63 (p. 392). At that time, Ismail was head of policy and planning in the government's Defense Secretariat.

79. *Truth and Reconciliation Commission of South Africa Report*, Vol. 5, Ch. 9, para. 46 (p. 379).

80. *Truth and Reconciliation Commission of South Africa Report*, Vol. 5, Ch. 9, para. 101 (p. 403).

81. Transcript of HRVC hearing of 18 November, 1996, in East London; available online at http://www.doj.gov.za/trc/hrvtrans/bisho2/meyer.htm.

82. K. Lombard, *Opportunities and Obstacles: The State of Reconciliation: Report of the Second Round of the SA Reconciliation Barometer Survey* (Rondebosch, South Africa: Institute for Justice and Reconciliation, May 2004), p. 25.

83. Rupert Taylor, "Justice denied: Political violence in KwaZulu-Natal after 1994," *African Affairs* 101 (2002): 473–508.

84. Lombard, *Opportunities and Obstacles*, p. 35. Agreeing with the more personal statement "I am trying to forgive those who hurt me during apartheid" were 65.1 percent of Blacks and 22.4 percent of Whites (p. 36). It is possible that many Whites considered they had little or nothing to forgive.

85. Lombard, *Opportunities and Obstacles*, pp. 39, 29. The percentage of Whites expressing support for the latter statement had climbed by nearly ten percentage points between April and November 2003.

86. United Nations Development Program, *South Africa Human Development Report 2003* (Cape Town: Oxford University Press, 2003), p. 58.

87. United Nations Development Program, *Human Development Report 2005* (New York and Oxford: Oxford University Press, 2005), p. 260.

88. United Nations Development Program, *Human Development Report 2005*, p. 286.

89. Ibid., p. 248.

90. Actually, this was not so. Many of those who admitted to having committed gross rights violations in the apartheid years and won amnesties from the TRC were—and continued to be—employed by the government or are even members of the government.

91. Interview with Richard Goldstone, Johannesburg, August 2001. IJR's November 2003 opinion poll found that 58.6 percent of White South Africans—and 85.6 percent of Blacks—agreed with the statement that "South Africa has great income differences today because in the past Blacks

were not given the same education opportunities as Whites" (Lombard, *Opportunities and Obstacles*, p. 34). It seems likely that the degree of White "understanding" of the realities of Black life would have been quite a lot lower without the "re-educative" effects of the TRC.

92. Interview with Albie Sachs, Cape Town, May 2003. Sachs has written his own very poignant little TRC-related story; see his *Post-Apartheid South Africa: Truth, Reconciliation and Justice* (New Delhi: Institute of Social Sciences, 1999), pp. 18–20, 45.

93. Dumisa Ntsebeza, "A lot more to live for," in Wilmot James and Linda van de Vijver, eds., *After the TRC: Reflections on Truth and Reconciliation in South Africa* (Athens, OH: Ohio University Press/Cape Town: David Philip Publishers, 2000), pp. 102–105 passim.

Notes for Chapter 4

1. Alex Vines, *Renamo: Terrorism in Mozambique* (London: James Currey/Bloomington: Indiana University Press: 1991), p. 8. Vines also notes here that only 5 percent of the people in the new nation were literate—and that figure reflects a measurement of the literacy rate amongst the Portuguese settlers as well as the indigenes. Nearly all the Portuguese left the country at the time of independence. Many headed to South Africa.

2. "Africa Watch," in *Conspicuous Destruction: War, Famine and the Reform Process in Mozambique* (New York: Human Rights Watch, 1992), pp. 2–3. This report makes scant mention of landmines, the large number of which left in areas around Mozambique would make the rebuilding after October 1992 much, much harder.

3. *Conspicuous Destruction*, p. 48. "Matsanga" was an informal term used to describe Renamo fighters.

4. Ibid., p. 65.

5. James Brooke, "Visiting State Department Official Condemns ... ," *New York Times*, April 27, 1988; as cited in *Conspicuous Destruction*, p. 192.

6. Marcelino Liphola, "The use of Mozambican languages in the elections," in Brazão Mazula, ed., *Mozambique: Elections, Democracy, and Development* (Maputo, Mozambique: n.p., 1996), p. 268.

7. The regional variations in support for the two parties that were revealed during the postconflict elections of 1994 can be seen in the maps presented in Mazula, *Mozambique*, pp. 471–475.

8. Anders Nilsson, *Peace in Our Time: Towards a Holistic Understanding of World Society Conflicts* (Göteborg, Sweden: PADRIGU, 1999), p. 133.

9. Nilsson, *Peace in Our Time*, p. 122; emphasis added. See also the interviews on pp. 123–124.

10. Later, while defense minister, Dai became known as a practitioner and advocate of yogic flying.

11. Sengulane has written a memoir of his contribution to the peace-making. Its title is *Vitória sem Vencidos* ("Victory Without Losers"). That title was, he said, his personal slogan throughout his peacemaking efforts.

12. In this period, Mozambique had provided an important safe haven for many leaders of South Africa's ANC. But as Albie Sachs, Ruth First, and many others discovered, Maputo was still very vulnerable to the activities of South African hit squads.

13. Mazula quoted in Priscilla Hayner, *Unspeakable Truths: Confronting State Terror and Atrocity* (New York and London: Routledge, 2001), pp. 191–192.

14. Matteo Zuppi, "The Santo Egidio Community and the General Peace Agreement," in Mazula, *Mozambique,* p. 114; emphasis added. Another good account of Sant' Egidio's role in this negotiation can be found at Andrea Bartoli, "Providing space for change in Mozambique," in Judy Zimmerman Herr and Robert Herr, eds., *Transforming Violence: Linking Local and Global Peacemaking* (Scottdale, PA/Waterloo, ON: Herald Press, 1998. Bartoli has noted that the fall of the Soviet bloc coupled with the changes getting under way in South Africa made possible an equilibrium in Mozambique that previously would have been unthinkable (p. 198).

15. The text of the GPA can be found in Stephen Chan and Moisés Venâncio, eds., *War and Peace in Mozambique* (New York: St. Martin's Press/Basingstoke, UK: Macmillan, 1998); emphasis added. The quoted passage is on p. 148.

16. Basic information about UNOMOZ can be found online at http://www.un.org/Depts/dpko/dpko/co_mission/onumoz.htm.

17. Iraê Baptista Lundin et al., "'Reducing costs through an expensive exercise': The impact of demobilization in Mozambique," in Kees Kingma, ed., *Demobilization in Sub-Saharan Africa: The Development and Security Impacts* (New York: St. Martin's Press/Basingstoke, UK: Macmillan, 2000), pp. 182–183. The reason for the discrepancy between the figure given here for women soldiers demobilized and that cited by Jacinta Jorge is not clear.

18. Cited in ibid., p. 186.

19. Ibid., pp. 189–190.

20. Ibid., p. 208.

21. Richard Synge, *Mozambique: UN Peacekeeping in Action 1992–94* (Washington, DC: U.S. Institute of Peace Press, 1997), p. 118.

22. Ibid., p. 122.

23. Quoted in Hayner, *Unspeakable Truths,* pp. 189–190.

24. Synge, *Mozambique,* p. 136.

25. Ibid., p. 140. A full analysis of the behavior of the Mozambican voters in the 1994 elections can be found in Luis de Brito, "Voting behaviour in Mozambique's first multiparty elections," in Mazula, *Mozambique,* pp. 455–481.

26. These figures are taken from various tables in *Human Development Report 1995* (New York: UN Development Program, 1995), pp. 161–183.

27. Brazão Mazula, "The Mozambican elections: A path of peace and democracy," in Mazula, *Mozambique*, p. 69.

28. This understanding of the nature of violence seems to be widely shared in many indigenous cultures both within and far beyond Africa.

29. Carolyn Nordstrom, *A Different Kind of War Story* (Philadelphia: University of Pennsylvania Press, 1997), pp. 142–143; emphasis added.

30. Honwana, "Children of war," pp. 137–138.

31. Carolyn Nordstrom has written that "a very nuanced and widely shared set of practices and cultural responses were transmitted from person to person, from province to province around the country along with the war." (See *A Different Kind of War Story*, p. 147.)

32. In one of its few references to the enactment of any kind of traditional healing process in South Africa, the TRC's report contains testimony from a youth group in East London that describes a very similar kind of ritual being undertaken there: "We'd slaughter a goat and cleanse ourselves with the blood that is shed. In a symbolic sense we'd cleanse ourselves of the wrong deeds, even if they were justifiable." (See *Truth and Reconciliation Commission of South Africa Report*, Vol. 5, Ch. 9, para. 52 [p. 383].) The person making this submission to the TRC claimed, notably, that the ritual was conducted in the context of an activity undertaken by the "Inter-Church Youth."

33. *Human Development Report 2003* (New York: UN Development Program, 2003), p. 261.

34. The Carter Center, "Postelection statement on Mozambique elections, Jan. 26, 2005"; available online at http://www.cartercenter.org/doc1999.htm.

35. Swisspeace/Swiss Agency for Development and Cooperation, *Mozambique: Semi-annual Risk Assessment, January 2005–June 2005*, pp. 3, 4; available online at http://www.swisspeace.org/uploads/FAST/updates/MOZ%20Update%201_2005%20final.pdf.

36. *Human Development Report 2005*, p. 266.

37. Ibid., p. 261.

38. Calculated from the figures for Mozambique in *The Military Balance 1993–1994* (London: International Institute for Strategic Studies, 1993), p. 212, and *The Military Balance 2005–2006* (London: International Institute for Strategic Studies, 2005), p. 389.

39. My discussion with Inglês, like all the others I had in Maputo in August 2001, was set up, facilitated, and interpreted by Francisco Assis, a staff member of the social justice organization JustaPaz.

40. Zita told me that Frelimo founder Eduardo Mondlane had been a student here in the 1930s.

41. Wanela, too, like many Mozambicans I talked with, warned that the return of Portuguese business interests to the country, which seemed to be under way, might be very bad for him and his countrymen.

42. Dos Santos also pointed out that he likes to use the Portuguese people's language in his own poetry.

43. Some historians of Mozambique have judged that resentment against those postindependence re-education camps had helped incubate Renamo, and that at the time of the peace with Renamo, Frelimo's top leaders had made an intentional decision not to repeat that error. The long-term effects of the re-education camps run by the RPF in Rwanda remain to be seen.

44. Mondlane was sent to Oberlin College at age 31—"to learn the witchcraft of white men," as his mother reportedly put it—and he graduated in the class of 1953. He founded Frelimo in 1962 and in 1969 was assassinated by the Portuguese—who sent him a bomb disguised as a book.

45. He would give no further details of what this process involved.

46. Mungoi also noted at this point in our conversation that he and other Mozambicans sometimes found it hard to remember *which side* one of their current acquaintances had fought on during the civil war—or even whether they had never known that information.

Notes for Chapter 5

1. *Research on the Gacaca—PRI, Report V* (London: Penal Reform International, September 2003), p. 68. The report is available online at http://www.penalreform.org/download/Gacaca/september2003.pdf.

2. This total has been summed from the separate "Expenditure" line items given in each of the annual budgets presented in vols. 1 and 6 of the *Truth and Reconciliation Commission of South Africa Report.*

3. Analysis by René Lemarchand in Swisspeace, *FAST Early Warning System Report for Rwanda, Sept.–Nov. 2004,* available online at http://www.swisspeace.org/uploads/FAST/updates/Rwanda%20Update%204_2004%20final.pdf, pp. 3, 5.

4. Ibid., p. 6.

5. K. Lombard, *Opportunities and Obstacles: The State of Reconciliation: Report of the Second Round of the SA Reconciliation Barometer Survey* (Rondebosch, South Africa: Institute for Justice and Reconciliation, May 2004), pp. 39, 29. The percentage of Whites expressing support for the latter statement had climbed by nearly ten percentage points between April and November 2003.

6. James L. Gibson and Helen Macdonald, *Truth—Yes, Reconciliation—Maybe: South Africans Judge the Truth and Reconciliation Process* (Rondebosch, South Africa: Institute for Justice and Reconciliation, 2001), p. 19.

7. The figures for "approve" and "strongly approve" were aggregated from Table 10.4 (line 1) and Table 10.5 (line 1) in Timothy Longman et al., "Connecting justice to human experience: Attitudes toward accountability and reconciliation in Rwanda," in Eric Stover and Harvey M. Weinstein,

eds., *My Neighbor, My Enemy: Justice and Community in the Aftermath of Mass Atrocity* (Cambridge and New York: Cambridge University Press, 2004), pp. 214 and 216.

Notes for Chapter 6

1. Diane F. Orentlicher, "Settling Accounts: The Duty to Prosecute Human Rights Violations of a Prior Regime," *Yale Law Journal* 100 (1991), pp. 2537–2614.

2. The mastermind of the assassination plot, Anibal dos Santos Junior, escaped from a Mozambican prison but was rearrested, retried, and, in January 2006, sentenced to thirty years in prison. See http://allafrica.com/stories/200601200331.html.

3. One group of unhappy Afrikaners migrated internally, by establishing a tiny, intentionally segregated community in Orania, in the Northern Cape. But by 2004, that project had only 500–600 residents and was described as "fading away." See "10 years on, Orania fades away," in *News24.com,* April 22, 2004; available online at http://www.news24.com/News24/South_Africa/Decade_of_Freedom/0,,2-7-1598_1515558,00.html.

4. "South Africa," in *Human Rights Watch World Report 2005*; available online at http://hrw.org/english/docs/2005/01/13/safric9886.htm. The report judged that "[w]hile it is encouraging that the reporting mechanism is in place, the increasing number of deaths, particularly in police custody, is worrying."

5. The general fearfulness inside Rwanda was most likely also fueled in part by the sense, among many Rwandans, that their tiny country is very vulnerable to violent influences from its neighbors, particularly the massive and violence-wracked DRC. But the Rwandan government seemed trapped in a classic "security dilemma" with respect to the DRC: The escalatory actions that it repeatedly undertook there with the stated aim of increasing Rwanda's security only ended up, time and again, increasing the overall insecurity of the entire region, including their own country.

6. "Rwanda," in *Human Rights Watch World Report 2005*; available online at http://hrw.org/english/docs/2005/01/13/rwanda9860.htm.

7. It is also true that, in a number of cases, amnesty-reliant peace agreements have failed, and that the countries concerned have been plunged back into conflict, lawlessness, and the commission of atrocities. But the failure in those cases represented a failure of peacemaking diplomacy at a broad, political level rather than being related to the offers of amnesties per se.

8. A prime example of such a discussion is the collection of essays in the volume edited by Robert I. Rotberg and Dennis Thompson: *Truth v. Justice : The Morality of Truth Commissions* (Princeton and Oxford: Princeton University Press, 2000).

9. Bradley F. Smith, *The Road to Nuremberg* (New York: Basic Books, 1981), pp. 54–55.

10. Bradley F. Smith, *Reaching Judgment at Nuremberg* (New York: Basic Books, 1977), pp. 305–306. Smith also wrote here: "By being normally unpredictable and biased, the Nuremberg bench graphically demonstrated that such war crimes tribunals have little of value to offer in dealing with transitions from war to peace."

11. Indeed, in 1945, the three European Allies were all arguing for policies toward Germany that were considerably more punitive than those that Roosevelt, and Truman, had chosen to pursue. It is lucky for all of us that, in most of occupied Germany, Stimson's strategic wisdom prevailed.

12. In early April 2005, two dozen community leaders from northern Uganda visited the ICC's headquarters in The Hague to urge the chief prosecutor to hold off on the issuing of indictments regarding events in their region. They expressed a strong preference for peace negotiations and the use of methods of traditional healing to reintegrate their war-shattered communities. But the prosecutor issued indictments and international arrest warrants, anyway. See Helena Cobban, "The ICC and Uganda, contd.," on the Transitional Justice Forum Weblog, November 4, 2005, at http://tj-forum.org/archives/001552.html.

13. I realize that the ideal would be for all the world's rich countries to live up to their commitments and actually increase the proportion of their GDP that they devote to international development aid to the promised 0.7 percent. But especially egregious is the fact that, even while most rich countries remain very far from meeting that goal, much international aid is diverted to sustaining a court system whose primary financial beneficiaries have been highly paid international lawyers rather than the people in the impoverished and war-torn communities themselves.

14. National University of Rwanda, Centre for Conflict Management, *Les Juridictions Gacaca et les Processus de Réconciliation Nationale* (Kigali: Editions de l'Université National du Rwanda), p. 106. Since some respondents described more than one of the eight suggested problems as "major," the figures for all eight items totaled 152.5 percent rather than 100 percent.

15. Eric Stover and Harvey M. Weinstein, eds., *My Neighbor, My Enemy: Justice and Community in the Aftermath of Mass Atrocity* (Cambridge and New York: Cambridge University Press, 2004), p. 325.

16. The aim of the Truman administration in launching the Marshall Plan was not totally irenic, since the broader goal being pursued there was to buttress West Germany as a Cold War bulwark against the Soviet Union. Within West Germany, however, the general effect of the Marshall Plan and the European Coal and Steel Community (ECSC) (as well as of the subsequent consideration of all the disturbing facts

that the Nuremberg Trials had put into the public record) was to turn new generations of West Germans increasingly against any fascination with militarism—an outcome we should all surely applaud.

17. Tim Judah, "The Fog of Justice," *New York Review of Books* 51, no. 1 (January 15, 2004). Judah also expressed his own judgment here: "I don't believe that the Hague Tribunal is the only, or even a major, reason for the collapse of the reformist government that led Serbia since 2000, but *it has contributed to it*" (emphasis added).

18. See Figure 9.7 in Stover and Weinstein, *My Neighbor, My Enemy,* p. 194. This figure presents "acceptance" of the court on a scale of 1 through 5, with 5 being "absolute acceptance" and 1 being "absolute nonacceptance." The midpoint of the scale is therefore 3.

19. Stover and Weinstein, *My Neighbor, My Enemy,* p. 323.

20. One defendant, Hermann Goering, "cheated" the hangman by swallowing a suicide pill the night before the scheduled group execution. For discussion of the inhumane manner of these executions, see Rebecca West, *A Train of Powder: Six Reports on the Problem of Guilt and Punishment in Our Time* (Chicago: Ivan R. Dee, 1955), p. 72.

21. Alternatively, punishment of perpetrators may simply help make people elsewhere in the international community feel better about themselves.

22. At the hearings held by East Timor's Commission for Reception, Truth, and Reconciliation (CAVR), amnesty applicants were required, in addition to telling all they knew about the perpetration of politically related atrocities, to undertake a "Community Reconciliation Act," which in most cases was described as "Apologise, bound not to repeat." See, for example, the section on "Community Reconciliation" in *CAVR Update, Dec. 03–Jan 04,* which is available online at http://www.easttimor-reconciliation. org/cavrUpdate-Dec03Jan04–en.html.

23. Primo Levi, *The Drowned and the Saved* (New York: Summit Books, 1986), pp. 43–44.

24. In Hannah Arendt's 1946 correspondence with her mentor and friend Karl Jaspers, she expressed some of the same sentiments regarding the moral climate in Germany during the Nazi atrocities. See, for example, her letter to him of August 17, 1946, in Hannah Arendt and Karl Jaspers, *Hannah Arendt Karl Jaspers: Correspondence, 1926–1969* (New York: Harcourt Brace Jovanovich, 1992), p. 54.

25. Rama Mani, *Beyond Retribution: Seeking Justice in the Shadows of War* (Cambridge, UK: Polity Press/Malden, MA: Blackwell Publishers, 2002), p. 123.

26. Pumla Gobodo-Madikizela, *A Human Being Died That Night: A South African Story of Forgiveness* (New York: Houghton Mifflin, 2003), p. 130.

27. Ibid., p. 128.

28. Ibid., pp. 14–15.

29. This point was underlined in a number of interviews with experts on modern German history that took place during my research project, including one conducted in Potsdam on May 28, 2002, by research associate Sarah McKim with German historian Konrad Jarausch.

30. Alcinda Honwana, "Children of war: Understanding war and war cleansing in Mozambique and Angola," in Simon Chesterman, ed., *Civilians in War* (Boulder, CO: Lynne Rienner, 2001), p. 139.

31. Alcinda Honwana, "Sealing the past, facing the future," in Jeremy Armon, Dylan Hendrickson, and Alex Vines, eds., *The Mozambique Peace Process in Perspective* (London: Conciliation Resources, 1998); available online at http://www.c-r.org/accord/moz/accord3/index.shtml.

32. João Paulo Borges Coelho, "'Purification' versus 'reconciliation' amongst ex-combatants," epilogue to Honwana, "Sealing the past, facing the future."

33. Priscilla Hayner, *Unspeakable Truths: Confronting State Terror and Atrocity* (New York and London: Routledge, 2001), p. 185. The section of this book that deals with Mozambique (pp. 186–195) is also worth reading in its entirety.

34. The charge sheet at ICTY has not been as one-sided as that at ICTR; but even so, the fact that many members of society have been forced to endlessly remember, consider, and describe the harms of the conflict years has kept the hurts and sensitivities of those years much more alive in people's consciousness than they might otherwise have been.

35. Isabel Fonseca, *Bury Me Standing: The Gypsies and Their Journey* (New York: Alfred A. Knopf, 1995), p. 243.

36. Andrew Rigby, *Justice and Reconciliation: After the Violence* (Boulder, CO: Lynne Rienner, 2001), p. 54.

37. My thanks go to Martha Minow for talking through some of this issue of changes in attitudes over time with me during a conversation in April 2001.

38. One compendium that identifies and describes the workings, philosophies, and status of a number of still-existing non-Western justice systems around the world is Penal Reform International, *Access to Justice in Sub-Saharan Africa: The Role of Traditional and Informal Justice Systems* (London: Penal Reform International, 2001).

39. These comments are also relevant to the position of US occupation authorities in post-2003 Iraq.

40. See Mani, *Beyond Retribution,* pp. 38–46 and Ch. 5.

41. Roland Paris, *At War's End: Building Peace After Civil Conflict* (Cambridge, UK/New York: Cambridge University Press, 2004), p. 188.

Name Index

Agnès, genocide survivor, Rwanda, 12, 17, 46, 235, 242, 246n1; interview with, 243n1; testimony of, 1, 2, 3, 25–27

Ajello, Aldo, UN Special Representative for Mozambique peacemaking, 155

Akayesu, Jean-Paul, ICTR defendant, 48, 248n45

Amin, Idi, former president of Uganda, 34, 246n15

Arendt, Hannah, German-American philosopher, 266n24

Assis, Francisco, researcher, Mozambique, 262n39

Assuate, Paul, excombatant, Mozambique, 175

Bagosora, Théoneste, ICTR defendant, 47, 49

Bakuramutsa, Manzi, former ambassador to the United Nations, Rwanda, 7

Baptista Lundin, Iraê, sociologist, Mozambique, on demobilization, 151, 152

Benzien, Jeffrey, amnesty applicant, South Africa, 110–111, 112

Biddle, Francis, U.S. judge at Nuremberg trial, 206

Biko, Nkosinathi, son of Steve Biko, 125

Biko, Steve, Black power activist, South Africa, 86, 109, 110, 125

Bizimungu, Pasteur, former prime minister of Rwanda, 37, 74, 75, 253n103

Bizos, George, antiapartheid lawyer, South Africa, 110

Boraine, Alex, vice chair of TRC, South Africa, 96, 97, 101

Botha, P. W., former president of South Africa, 82, 90, 102, 105, 123; Khotso House and, 254n2; subpoenas for, 103

Brandt, Willy, former chancellor of West Germany, apology by, 171

Breytenbach, Breyten, Afrikaans language poet, South Africa, White power and, 89

Bugingo, Jean Bosco, confessed genocide participant, Rwanda, 32, 66

Cabaço, José Luis, former government minister, Mozambique, on 1994 election, 154

Subject Index

AC. *See* Amnesty Committee

Accountability, 22, 41, 66, 216–221, 225; amnesty and, 141, 217; criminal-justice form of, 16; *gacaca* courts and, 71; human rights movement and, 213; individual, 166, 188–189, 216, 217, 218, 219, 228; notion of, 211–216; reconciliation and, 79; religion and, 234; unsatisfactory, 214

"Accusation-confession" paradigm, 223, 224

Accusation-(optional)-confession-punishment (ACP) paradigm, 224

Ademimo, 169

Ad hoc tribunals, 24, 215, 243–244n4; acceptance of, 211; creation of, 5; Nuremberg principles and, 48

Affetados/affetadas, 220, 237–238

Affirmative action, 134, 201

African National Congress (ANC), 80, 83, 90, 94, 95, 172; amnesty and, 96, 97; black community and, 91; challenge for, 89, 91; founding of, 85; Inkatha and, 87, 91, 184; Mozambique and, 176, 261n12; negotiations with, 88; NP and, 92, 154; PAC and, 91; peace accord with, 237; representation of, 130;

rights violations and, 96–97, 106; TRC and, 98, 106, 172; victims of, 11; vote for, 95, 131 (table)

Africa Watch, 142

Afrikaners, 89, 91, 221, 254nn3, 12; colonial project of, 233; confronting, 116; HRVC hearings and, 113; Orania and, 264n3; Protestant Christianity and, 233; remorse and, 120–121, 122; TRC and, 117–122; victimization of, 88

Air Force Headquarters, ANC attack on, 129

Amnesty, 94, 124, 130, 148, 241; accountability and, 141, 217; applications for, 96, 112, 112 (table), 192; blanket, 4–5, 16, 125, 150, 162, 188; *gacaca* courts and, 71; granting, 5, 97, 199; offers of, 194–195, 207; peacemaking and, 24, 240; political transformation and, 242; promise of, 8–9; remorse and, 126; truth-telling and, 4, 141, 216; types of, 4–5

Amnesty Committee (AC), 101, 189, 256n35; amnesty applicants/accountability and, 217; perpetrators and, 129; truth-telling and, 216; work of, 99–100, 108, 109–112, 118, 126–127

Subject Index

Subject Index

Solidarity camps (*ingando*), 75
South African Broadcasting
  Corporation (SABC), 102, 103, 118;
  Black journalists and, 258n61
South African Communist Party,
  255n18
South African Constitutional Court,
  109
South African Council of Churches, 83
South African Defense Force (SADF),
  95, 96
South African Human Development
  Report (UN), 132
South African National Assembly, 94
South African National Defense Force
  (SANDF), 95
South African Police (SAP), 82, 95
South African Senate, 94
Soweto Uprising (1976), 86, 185
Special Forces (Renamo), 146, 159,
  170, 242
Stakeholders, 126, 205; satisfaction of,
  194, 195; TRC and, 114–117
Structural adjustment, 99, 163
Structural Adjustment Program (SAP),
  110, 167
Subnational community, survival of,
  232
Survivors, 13, 17, 21, 23, 103, 219,
  220; groups of, 56; as judges, 70;
  rituals and, 238; treatment of, 51,
  54, 56, 57; views of, 231. *See also*
  Victims

Testimonies, 25–30
Torture, 7, 87, 103, 214
Total Onslaught, 83
Total Strategy, 83, 85, 86, 90
Transformation, 204; cultural, 227;
  political, 134, 242
Transition, 92–93, 95, 189, 200, 235,
  237; rituals and, 236
Transitional Executive Council (TEC),
  93
Trauma, 42; counseling, 78;
  reeruption of, 224, 232, 237
TRC. *See* Truth and Reconciliation
  Commission

TRC Special Report, 102
Treaty of Berlin (1885), 33
Treaty of Versailles (1919),
  punitiveness of, 205
Truth, 24; justice and, 203;
  reconciliation and, 110
Truth-acknowledgment, 172, 212
Truth and Reconciliation
  Commission (TRC), 17, 82, 166,
  235; accountability and, 215–216;
  Afrikaners and, 117–122; amnesty
  and, 101, 124, 189, 259n90; ANC
  and, 98, 106, 172; approval ratings
  for, 116 (table), 117 (table); Blacks
  and, 116, 117, 118, 122–126;
  challenges for, 203; change and,
  98–101; Coloureds and, 122–126;
  committees of, 99–100; criticism of,
  80, 119; establishment of, 4, 8, 96,
  98; forgiveness and, 129; and *gacaca*
  courts compared, 21; gross human
  rights abuses and, 97, 102; healing
  and, 127, 133; legacy of, 124–125;
  NP and, 118, 120; Nuremberg Trials
  and, 206; recommendations by, 108–
  109; reconciliation and, 116, 121,
  128–130, 133–134; re-education and,
  223, 260n91; reparations and, 108,
  125; report on killings, 88 (table);
  reproach and, 222–223; success for,
  130; truth-establishment and, 230;
  victims and, 9–10, 11; work of, 10,
  97, 98–114, 115–116, 118, 119, 121,
  122, 123, 134, 194, 217, 228
Truth and Reconciliation Commission
  of South Africa Report (TRC), 102,
  104–109, 112, 123, 128; Krog poetry
  in, 118, 122
Truth commissions, considering, 161,
  162, 254n2
Truth-establishment, 16, 230
Truth-seeking, reconciliation and, 128
Truth-telling, 172; amnesty and, 4,
  141, 216; attitudes toward, 225–226;
  processes of, 16; sentences and, 21
Tutsi Power, 36
Tutsis, abduction of, 29; condition
  of, 38; death of, 25; diaspora of,

283